The Frontier Camp Meeting

The
Frontier Camp Meeting

RELIGION'S HARVEST TIME

CHARLES A. JOHNSON

WITH A NEW INTRODUCTION BY FERENC M. SZASZ

"We must attend to camp-meetings,
They make our harvest times...."
— Bishop Francis Asbury, 1809

SOUTHERN METHODIST UNIVERSITY PRESS

1955 • 1985

To Marian

Contents

Illustrations

Introduction

On DECEMBER 24,
1784, a group of about sixty Methodist preachers gathered in a
small chapel on Lovely Lane in Baltimore. There, in a ten-day
session, they formally established the Methodist Episcopal Church
in America. The beginning was decidedly inauspicious. A society
of eighty-one preachers and about 15,000 members could hardly
be expected to flourish in an ecclesiastical world dominated by the
powerful Congregationalists, Episcopalians, and Presbyterians.[1]

Surprisingly, however, Methodist theology, organization, and
institutions meshed perfectly with the religious needs of the new
American republic. The rise in membership proved startling. From
65,000 in 1800, Methodism grew to 274,000 in 1820 and over
1.25 million in 1850, when it became the largest Protestant church
in the nation. Today, two hundred years after that first Christmas
Conference, Methodism claims over twelve and a half million
adherents. It currently ranks third among all American denominations. Only the Roman Catholics and the Baptists claim larger
membership.[2]

In addition to their rapid statistical growth, the Methodists also
rose steadily in social class. The majority of the early converts
came from humble backgrounds and were primarily artisans and
small farmers. But over the course of the nineteenth century, many
Methodists moved steadily up the social scale. By the early twentieth century, President Theodore Roosevelt could state that he
enjoyed addressing a Methodist audience because they reflected
the great middle class and thus were typical of most Americans.

Given this success story, it is highly appropriate that Southern

Methodist University Press has decided to reissue Charles A. Johnson's *The Frontier Camp Meeting* as part of the 1984 Methodist bicentennial. Johnson's discussion of the key roles played by the camp meeting and the frontier circuit rider helps explain Methodism's early triumphs. First published in 1955, *The Frontier Camp Meeting* still remains the most thorough account of the subject.[3]

Charles A. Johnson studied with William Warren Sweet, perhaps the foremost Methodist historian of the century. Sweet's influence is felt throughout the book. It is especially evident in Johnson's extensive use of original sources, his narrative style, and his sympathetic approach to faith on the frontier. The ante-bellum religious world evokes many images—romantic circuit riders, ignorant stump speakers, people caught by the jerks, shakes, and shouts of the early revivals, and widespread expectation of the imminent Second Coming of Christ.[4] Johnson does yeoman service in grounding these stories in historical reality.

Perhaps no aspect of frontier religion has spread more tales than that of the camp meeting: thousands of people listening simultaneously to a myriad of sermons. Stout men keeling over "as if felled by cannon shot," while other followers danced, rolled, barked, shouted, or thrashed about with the jerks. European visitors to America were astounded. Foreign travelers would no more miss a camp meeting than they would neglect Niagara Falls or a visit to a slave plantation. Given this publicity, later camp meetings often attracted as many of the curious as the faithful.

But Johnson demonstrates that such unbridled emotions characterized only the earliest camp meetings. He stresses the fact that the camp meetings changed considerably over time. By the mid-1820's, the excessive emotionalism of the early gatherings had moderated considerably. The Methodist leaders began to plan their meetings carefully, and surviving lists of rules and regulations show that the typical camp meeting day was tightly structured. Oftentimes guards patrolled the area to make sure that the rules were enforced. As the rough-hewn days of the frontier faded, the camp meetings became respectable.

Johnson notes that these large gatherings offered an excellent opportunity for companionship, and this social aspect always formed an integral part of their success. Political discussions, business deals, courtships, and simple gossip became intertwined with talk of justification and sanctification. Such camaraderie proved especially important for the frontier women. While the men might join together for political debate or voting, the women had no such outlet. Religious gatherings alone provided them the opportunity to come together in large numbers.

The southern camp meetings also developed an interesting compromise on the matter of race. As historian Donald G. Mathews has shown, the world of ante-bellum religion (alone of all the southern institutions) included a place for both blacks and whites.[5] Slaves were excluded from the realms of politics, economic gain, and society, but they often shared a common evangelical heritage. Slave owners brought their slaves to the camp meetings, and free blacks often attended as well. Gradually, the slaves established their own services—usually with a black preacher—on part of the meeting grounds. In some cases the slave area was separated by a partition made of wooden planks. On the last day of the meeting (symbolically enough) the plank barrier was torn down, and the two groups joined for common hymns and a "marching ceremony."

Johnson also stresses the importance of music to the camp meeting experience. Singing had always formed an integral part of English Methodism under John and Charles Wesley. It was only natural that this tradition would continue in the new world. The Methodist hymnals were so arranged that men and women could learn Christianity as they sang. Often the hymns condensed complex theological ideas into easily memorized verses. Many of the people on the frontier were illiterate. Thus, a powerful hymn proved far more effective in teaching Christianity than a learned theological treatise.

When hymn books were scarce, as they often were, the leaders would "line out" the song—they would shout out a line or two, and the congregation would follow suit. Almost everyone joined in the singing, and many accompanied the tunes with clapping and stomping. This was especially true for the easily memorized choruses:

> Shout, shout, we're gaining ground,
> Halle, hallelujah!

We'll shout old Satan's kingdom down,
O glory hallelujah!

Or: I'm bound for the promised land,
I'm bound for the promised land,
Oh, who will come and go with me?
I'm bound for the promised land.

Perhaps the emotionalism of the earliest camp meetings gradually became channeled into these rousing hymns.

Side by side with the music and the camp meetings came the Methodist circuit riders. Johnson does much to set the record straight for these early itinerants. While the circuit riders often lacked formal education, they were seldom the ignorant exhorters pictured by their enemies. Many utilized the long hours on horseback to study the Bible, the Methodist *Discipline*, the hymnals, and the writings of John Wesley. In addition, they often distributed literature for the publishing arm of the denomination, the Methodist Book Concern (founded 1789).[6] The autobiographies of circuit riders Peter Cartwright and James B. Finley—now considered classics of their genre—are filled with the practical wisdom of the ante-bellum era.

Following their bishop's orders, these circuit riders crisscrossed the trans-Appalachian frontier amid the most primitive conditions. There were few roads, fewer bridges, and no hotels or restaurants. In addition, they were hard pressed to survive on a yearly stipend of sixty-four dollars. Not surprisingly, most itinerants were single. Whenever a circuit rider married, he invariably had to locate somewhere. Celibacy, poverty, and obedience were their daily fare. In this respect, the followers of John Wesley may, perhaps, have resembled the followers of Ignatius Loyola. Despite diverse beliefs, they shared a common challenge.

The Methodist circuit riders' success on the frontier can be traced to many factors, but perhaps the most important was the open, democratic nature of their Gospel message. Methodism emphasized that all people were equal in the sight of God. Through Jesus Christ, God had given His grace to all mankind. A person had only to exert his own free will and accept this divine offer. An honest human effort would likely be rewarded by an experience of grace, a sign that God had cleansed the individual's sins away. From then on, the convert would lead a new life, striving for holiness on both a personal and social level. Not only did the circuit riders present a very democratic Gospel, they carried this Gospel all across the land. As one settler grumbled:

> I quit Virginia to get out of the way of [the Methodist ministers], and went to a new settlement in Georgia, where I thought that I should be quite beyond their reach, but they got my wife and daughter into the church. Then in the late purchase—Choctaw Corner—I found a piece of good land and was sure that I would have some peace of the preachers; but here is one of them before my wagon is unloaded.

The early Methodist preachers had little personal experience with colleges. Nonetheless, in 1785 they founded a denominational college, Cokesbury, in Abingdon, Maryland. Two bad fires and increasing financial difficulties, however, brought the brief experiment to an end. Bishop Francis Asbury may have interpreted this as a sign from Providence that the Methodists should avoid colleges and concentrate on establishing lower-level schools.

Thus it was not until over a decade after Asbury's death in 1816 that the church began planting colleges in earnest. Before the Civil War, the Methodists established about thirty colleges, including Emory (1836), Indiana Asbury [Depauw] (1837), Trinity [Duke] (1838), Boston (1839), Ohio Wesleyan (1842), and Northwestern (1851). After the war, they added Syracuse (1870), Vanderbilt (1875), University of Southern California (1880), American University (1893), and Southern Methodist (1911). Today about seventy-five colleges maintain a close relationship with American Methodism.

The determined Methodist circuit riders were so integral to the frontier religious world that a body of folklore developed around them.[7] Numerous stories of remarkable deliverances from all types of danger, of the sudden conversion of scoffers and skeptics, and special acts of divine providence made the rounds of the pre–Civil War world. So, too, did religious humor. One stump preacher attacked those who played "marvels," for the scriptures said "marvel not." Methodist circuit riders came by so often for a Sunday dinner of fried chicken that all self-respecting chickens ran in terror when such a visitor rode into the yard. Few could improve on evangelist Lorenzo Dow's parody of Calvinism:

You can and you can't; you
will and you won't; you shall and
you shan't; you'll be damned if you
do, and you'll be damned if you don't.

By the latter part of the nineteenth century, both the camp meeting and the circuit rider had changed considerably. The spontaneous camp meeting had gradually evolved into the permanent structures of a denominational campground. Virtually every state today contains several examples. Most of the Methodist circuit riders had settled into permanent positions. Only when Christianity moved across the Mississippi did the circuit riders mount up again. The vast spaces and scattered populations of the Great Plains and Rocky Mountains were such that almost every denomination borrowed the itinerant system to follow their parishioners— a trek which ended only with the advent of the automobile in the 1920's.

In the 1960's, Bishop G. Bromley Oxnam quipped that when life is discovered on another planet, the Methodist church will be ready to send out its "rocket riders." Who would be surprised if the first institution they established was an intergalactic camp meeting? After all, as Charles Johnson points out, that's how American Methodism really began.

FERENC M. SZASZ

University of New Mexico
April 1985

NOTES

1. Three good histories of the church are: William Warren Sweet, *Methodism in American History* (New York and Nashville, 1953); Emory S. Bucke, ed., *The History of American Methodism.* 3 vols. (New York and Nashville, 1964); and Frederick A. Norwood, *The Story of American Methodism: A History of the United Methodists and Their Relations* (New York and Nashville, 1974). See also Sweet's valuable collection of documents in *Religion on the American Frontier, 1783-1840: The Methodists,* Vol. IV (Chicago, 1946) and the various articles in *Methodist History.*

2. The figures are from Edwin Scott Gaustad, *Historical Atlas of Religion in America* (New York, 1962; 1976), 75-82.

3. Along with Johnson's study, two other books from the 1950's have become classics for the world of ante-bellum religion: Whitney R. Cross, *Burned Over District: The Social and Intellectual History of Enthusiastic Religion in Western New York, 1800–1850* (Ithaca, 1950), and Timothy

L. Smith, *Revivalism and Social Reform: American Protestantism on the Eve of the Civil War* (New York, 1957; 1965).

4. There has been a good deal of scholarly attention given to the antebellum religious world. John R. Bodo, *The Protestant Clergy and Public Issues, 1812–1848* (Princeton, 1954); Charles C. Cole, Jr., *The Social Ideas of the Northern Evangelists, 1820–1860* (New York, 1954); Charles I. Foster, *An Errand of Mercy: The Evangelical United Front, 1790–1837* (Chapel Hill, 1960); and Clifford S. Griffin, *Their Brothers' Keepers: Moral Stewardship in the United States, 1800–1865* (New Brunswick, 1960), all treat the "benevolent empire" of the evangelical clergy and their interdenominational reform societies. Lois W. Banner, "Religious Benevolence as Social Control: A Critique of an Interpretation," *Journal of American History* LX (June 1973), is very critical of their major premises, however. In *Religion and the Rise of the American City: The New York City Mission Movement, 1812–1870* (Ithaca, 1971), Carroll Smith Rosenberg shows how the influence of frontier evangelism spread east to the city. John B. Boles argues in *The Great Revival, 1787–1805: The Origins of the Southern Evangelical Mind* (Lexington, 1972) that the southern religious outlook was permanently forged during those years. Ann Douglas, in *The Feminization of American Culture* (New York, 1977), offers the provocative thesis that an alliance between the American clergy and the women helped "feminize" religion and culture in the middle nineteenth century.

William G. McLoughlin offers an excellent overview of revivalism in *Modern Revivalism: Charles Grandison Finney to Billy Graham* (New York, 1959). In *Revivals, Awakenings, and Reform: An Essay on Religion and Social Change in America, 1607–1977* (Chicago, 1978), McLoughlin suggests that each generation must have an "awakening" to help redefine its social goals and norms. Paul E. Johnson, *A Shopkeeper's Millennium: Society and Revivals in Rochester, New York, 1815–1837* (New York, 1978), uses cliometrics to analyze the impact of Charles G. Finney's revivalism on the city of Rochester. For Adventism see Edwin S. Gaustad, ed., *The Rise of Adventism* (New York, 1974). The larger implications are treated in Ernest L. Tuverson, *Redeemer Nation: The Idea of America's Millennial Role* (Chicago, 1968). A good, brief history of the Latter-day Saints is Klaus J. Hansen, *Mormonism and the American Experience* (Chicago, 1981). The numerous essays by Sidney E. Mead, as found in *The Lively Experiment: The Shaping of Christianity in America* (New York, 1963), and *The Nation with the Soul of a Church* (New York, 1975) are always insightful.

5. Donald G. Mathews, *Religion in the Old South* (Chicago, 1977). See also Mathews, *Slavery and Methodism: A Chapter in American Morality, 1780–1845* (Princeton, 1965).

6. For the importance of these religious periodicals, see Wesley Norton, *Religious Newspapers in the Old Northwest to 1861: A History, Bibliography and Record of Opinion* (Athens, Ohio, 1977).

7. An excellent account is Donald E. Byrne, Jr., *No Foot of Land: Folklore of American Methodist Itinerants* (Metuchen, N.J., 1975).

Preface

AMONG ALL OF the weapons forged by the West in its struggle against lawlessness and immorality, few were more successful than the frontier camp meeting. This socioreligious institution helped tame backwoods America. Although the woodland revival was an integral part of pioneer culture, its place in our history has never been clearly established. The stereotype is well known, but the camp meeting itself is little known. In fact, no book or comprehensive article has ever been written on the subject. This study was undertaken to dispel the misconceptions which have long shrouded the western camp meeting.

The scope of the book is limited to the trans-Allegheny West in the first four decades of the nineteenth century. It was on that mobile frontier that the camp meeting was created and experienced its institutional growth, flowering, and decline. How this Kentucky Revival weapon, of Presbyterian origin, became largely the property of the church of John Wesley, utilized by the circuit rider to extend Methodist influence to the remotest edges of settlement, is treated in detail. The four-day encampment's freshening role in the social life of the lonesome pioneer, its singular success in converting sinners and raising community morals (if only temporarily), the impact of its "merry airs" upon American folk music, and its little-known contributions to the humanitarian reform urge of that day are other focal points of the work.

An effort is made here to re-create "Camp Meetin' Time," to portray the ever evolving revival institution against the backdrop of the raw backwoods society that originated and enthusiastically supported it. The magnetic camp leader was the saddlebag preacher, a rough, tough man of the gospel who has been scoffed at by many twentieth-century scholars. In this book he tells his own camp meeting story.

To draw parallels between the crude pioneer revival and the exponents of "Old-Time Religion" in this atomic age of fear is a fascinating but often dangerously misleading pastime. To gain understanding of the true nature of the pioneer revival one must journey once again in spirit with those men and women in homespun along the wagon trails that lead to the forest glade and the old campground.

My debt to two scholars is so great as almost to preclude description. Professor William W. Sweet awakened my interest in the historical field of frontier Christianity, made his library available, and read the entire manuscript, offering friendly guidance in a subject in which he is an acknowledged authority. To Professor Ray A. Billington of Northwestern University, friend and former graduate school adviser, I am indebted for his contagious enthusiasm for frontier history, for his continuous encouragement, and for his incisive appraisals of this work through its many stages. The technical aid of Robert G. McCutchan, musical scholar and editor of *The Methodist Hymnal,* is gratefully acknowledged. I also wish to express my appreciation for the co-operation of Edward Beach, Head Librarian of Garrett Biblical Institute; he supervises a repository that contains one of the best collections of primary materials on western Christianity.

Among those who read portions of the manuscript and made specific suggestions of value were Professor Wesley M. Gewehr and Frank Adams of the University of Maryland, and Professor Paul Erwin of Miami University. My most sincere thanks go to my colleague and friend, Professor Herbert A. Crosman of the University of Maryland. While overseas with me in Germany he meticulously read the entire manuscript, offering many valuable suggestions on style and organization. My wife's role in this book has been virtually that of joint author, and she also performed uncomplainingly the arduous roles of typist and editor.

CHARLES A. JOHNSON

Baltimore, Maryland
January 4, 1955

The Frontier Camp Meeting

Prologue

There are probably more wrangles by day and debauches by night within one mile of a camp [meeting] of the usual size, than occurred in the whole nation of Israel at seven feasts of the tabernacles; or than happened at all the other big meetings of a commonwealth as large as Scotland or Massachusetts.[1]
— Alexander Campbell, 1843

CHURCH HISTORY has long been a controversial field of study; the camp meeting story is no exception. Ever since the appearance of the outdoor revival in 1800 it has been a storm center of clashing opinion. Because of the noise and disorder which were so prominent a feature of its services, and because of its deliberate use of emotional excitement, the camp meeting was greeted from the very beginning with virulent condemnation by some laymen and historians. It has received a measure of tempered praise from others, and not a little extravagant eulogy from its own partisans, particularly from churchmen of the Methodist persuasion. In its heyday the camp meeting produced a sharp impact on the minds of everyone, for that was an era of intense and bitter denominational rivalry. Church members and church chroniclers were divided on this issue into opposing and sometimes acrimonious factions.

Out of all of the disputation scarcely a single dispassionate attempt at appraisal has appeared. To some the pioneer camp meeting was a "holy fair," a "religious orgy," a "system of fanaticism and confusion"; to others it was an institution "originated by divine Providence."[2]

3

One observer concluded that it "found its natural habitat on the frontier and ran riot in every extreme of emotion and primitive abandon," while to another the backwoods revival was "the only practical solution of the problem of carrying the Gospel to the cabin population of a sparsely settled border."[3] Decades after its demise, the frontier camp meeting was blamed for having "introduced a strong flavor of intolerance into the lives of the plain people of the South." Even less charitable opinions have been voiced. It was characterized by one analyst as "an emotional outbreak which was even more psychopathic than the witchcraft mania in early New England."[4] While admitting that the camp meeting grew out of necessity, another critic declared that the institution "was prolonged until its usefulness had not only departed, but became a stench, a byword, a demoralizing power and a blighting curse."[5]

Contemporaries introduced the legend that the camp meeting was nothing but one long orgy of excitement. Their distorted and florid portrayals, often colored by strong bias, were rendered plausible by the fact that there really was much that was absurd and irreligious to be reported. And report the bizarre features they did, employing for the most part the same flaming language which pro- and antislavery zealots loved to use. The camp meeting made excellent copy for the casual traveler-writer who enlarged upon the spectacular and ludicrous in backwoods religion to amuse his readers. Hostile church chroniclers with denominational animus and faulty historical techniques, especially in the weighing of evidence, inveighed against it. The fact that after 1805 the Methodists were almost the only denomination to utilize this evangelical method, and the fact that their sponsorship of it met with phenomenal success, contributed not a little to the bias with which non-Methodist church writers treated the camp meeting.

The fiction writers of the nineteenth century contributed their share to this general vituperation. Written in the "tall tale" or "local color" tradition of humor, laugh-provoking caricatures of the camp meeting were a fertile source of misinformation. Famous western characters mercilessly ridiculed backwoods evangelism in comic speech forms.[6] These stories were a burlesque of frontier life and character as seen by uncomprehending outsiders. The emotionalism of the religious service in the forest glen and the cunning of the frontiersmen were blended into high-spirited, sidesplitting humor.

Secular historians have also frequently presented poorly balanced pictures of the frontier revival. Instead of viewing it as but one of many techniques that the church of John Wesley devised to keep in touch with a people on the move, these scholars all too often consider it the sum total of Methodism in the West. They have frequently neglected to give adequate attention to the routine labors of the circuit rider who spread the gospel through the cabin meeting, the weekly Bible class, and the two-day meeting. Patent distortions in nineteenth-century accounts are repeated in many present-day studies of western society. Reputable historical scholars have been inclined to overemphasize the spectacular and the unusual in the backwoods revival. In magnifying the purely religious, they have also largely ignored the social significance of the camp meeting. Many writers, themselves products of an urban culture, are repelled by the turbulence of the revival and forget that this socioreligious institution flourished on the American frontier side by side with the militia muster, with the cabin raising and the political barbecue.

More important, most historians have failed to utilize materials that are indispensable to an adequate understanding of the frontier revival. They have accepted part of the camp meeting story as representative of the whole. This carelessness has led to such errors as the failure to distinguish between the camp meeting's boisterous youth and its subsequent sober maturity. The first frenzied gatherings of the Great Revival of 1800 and those held when that religious device had crystallized into a frontier institution were distinctly different.

Modern popularizers have contributed more than their share to the caricature. Certainly their books have reached a wider audience than those of the scholars. The popular writers' chief interest has been not to evaluate but to dramatize. Often these writers too have drawn their information in overwhelming measure, and sometimes solely, from the well of the Great Revival (1800-1805).[7]

Finally, the paucity of factual data has undoubtedly produced a picture out of focus. Actually, no book or even comprehensive article has ever been written on the subject of the frontier camp meeting. The usual historical sources offer but fleeting glimpses.[8] Although the Methodist Episcopal Church had adopted the revival weapon as its own by 1805, its records are largely silent. This strange omission is explained by the fact that the camp meeting was never an official institution of that denomination but only an "extra occasion in the economy of Methodism."[9] If Bishop Francis Asbury's proposal of 1812 for a history through letter reports had been adopted, the story of the frontier revival would have been much more accurate and complete. The father of American Methodism urged his presiding elders to give "the general number of annual

Camp-Meetings in the District, numbers attending, souls professing converting grace, days of continuance."[10] Instead, memoranda frequently continued to be as vague as that concerning an Illinois encampment of 1807: "This was a great day. The work became general, the place was awful, and many souls were born of God."[11] The task, then, becomes one of piecing together many scattered fragments to make a composite picture of the camp meeting.

Behind the legend is the living figure of the frontier revival. The institution is properly understood only when viewed against the backdrop of the raw backwoods communities that created and enthusiastically supported it. This study is an attempt to capture the essence of the camp meeting; to place it in proper perspective—as but one of the many effective weapons of American Methodism, as a natural product of a frontier environment, and as one of the most important social institutions in the trans-Allegheny West in the first half of the nineteenth century.

I

The Frontier's Religious Challenge

*The frontier was crude, turbulent, and
godless. Evangelical Protestantism,
more than any other single force,
tamed it.*[1]
     — Ralph H. Gabriel, 1940

R EMOTE FROM
the influence of church, school, and organized society,
the primitive societies which followed each other in
waves across the trans-Allegheny West were often cul-
turally and spiritually destitute. In each successive frontier, the pattern of brawling, debauchery, and drunkenness was repeated. Moral standards were lax; in certain
regions society itself seemed to be coming apart at the
seams. Measured by the standards of the older settlements
the raw backwoods seemed to many a moral desert. The
first clergymen who ventured to harvest these wild souls
were shocked by the enormity of their task and shaken
by the near-hostility which their none too tactful ap-
proaches evoked. Actually, however, even the newest
settlements contained God-fearing men on whom the
zealous missionaries could rely as a nucleus around which
the long slow task of taming the community could start.
Once initiated, progress was often phenomenal. The frontier settled down rapidly, but a new wave of settlement
was by then on ahead and pioneer clergy must hasten
to follow.[2]

Although the scene and time changed, the plot of the frontier drama remained unchanged. When the Methodist minister William Wood arrived at a Wisconsin lumbering outpost in the summer of 1848 he faced basically the same situation that confronted the Presbyterian leader, James McGready, in 1796 when he challenged the lawlessness and irreverent spirit of lusty Logan County in Kentucky. Preacher William Wood had come in response to a call sent out by twenty settlers who had felt the need for the gospel while drinking in the "Shanghai House" bar, the social center of the town. At his first service, held in the tavern dining room, he was obliged to interrupt a game of poker in the adjoining barroom so that one of the players might come in and pitch a tune for the congregation. Black River Falls "for fifteen years, . . . was about as rough and rugged a pioneer border town as the west could lay claim to."[3] Preaching under such conditions, circuit rider Wood was repeating the experience of Peter Cartwright, Benjamin Lakin, John Collins, and the long line of frontier missionaries who had been using saloons, dance halls, and tree stumps to give forthright gospel messages for the preceding four decades.

To these devoted churchmen, backwoods mores were appalling. Presbyterian historian Robert Davidson perceived in 1847 that

worldly mindedness, infidelity, and dissipation threatened to deluge the land, and sweep away all vestiges of piety and morality. The rising generation was growing up in almost universal ignorance of religious obligation.[4]

Hardened veterans of the Revolution swore that the Puritan Sabbath would never be established in their western settlements, and were prepared to defend that

oath. Churches were springing up here and there, but still
the Sabbath was profaned. This was the lament of Yankee
missionary John F. Schermerhorn, when he visited the
frontier regions of Pittsburgh and southwestern Ohio in
1813. An agent of the American Home Missionary
Society took a similarly jaundiced view of the religious
state of affairs in the Catholic settlement of Kaskaskia,
Illinois. After a ten-day residence he observed that all
the conversation he overheard concerned politics or dis-
sipations. "Wealth and publick offices," he concluded,
"are the reigning deities of the West."[5]

Why this religious apathy and low moral tone in the
western settlements? Many sociological and historical
explanations have been advanced. Among the forces to
be considered was the prevailing intellectual climate of
the times. In the years following the American Revolution, the low spiritual level of the cabin population merely
reflected that of the East, which was the dismay of all
church leaders. Playing a considerable role in the weak-
ening of spiritual forces in the new nation were the physical destruction of church properties, the loss of religious
leaders, the cloud of treason that hung over the Episcopal,
Methodist, and Quaker denominations for having supported the British cause, the church disestablishment
with its consequent de-emphasis on religion, the painful
process of creating national church organizations, and
the preoccupation with materialism. The pendulum was
at the far left; psychologically the "law of rhythm" was
evidenced in this nadir of spiritual oscillation.[6]

Undeniably, organized religion lost ground as rational-
ism grew in popularity. Particularly threatening was the
cult of Deism. This amorphous religion of reason threatened to sweep all before it in the West when two Revolu-

tionary heroes, Ethan Allen and Thomas Paine, lent their pens to the cause. In the late 1790's, Paine's *Age of Reason* was at the height of its popularity. Elihu Palmer, too, gave strenuous support when he contributed his organizational and propagandizing abilities to the war against religious orthodoxy. One Presbyterian visitor to the back country before 1800 was told by a Kentucky settler that "one-half" of the state's inhabitants were Deists; another farmer declared that "nine-tenths" was a more accurate estimate.[7]

Another key to an understanding of the lax moral standards on the frontier was the influence of the primitive environment. The homemaking pioneer's prime concern was the brute struggle for existence against an unfriendly Nature and often equally hostile Indians. Building a cabin, clearing land for crops, and hunting for game — these essential activities absorbed his energies. Spurred by the lash of necessity, the backwoodsman was likely to be preoccupied with matters material almost to the exclusion of matters spiritual.

Sickness was a constant threat. The early settler seldom escaped "woods fever" (ague) during the first winter in a new region; the lack of medical care made his plight critical. Alexis de Tocqueville in 1831 recorded one frontiersman's philosophy of survival: "They do like the Indians. They die or get well, as it pleased God."[8] Inadequate housing—the airy one-room cabin or the "half-faced camp"—often contributed to the pioneer's ill health. The net result of these hardships was mirrored in an early Methodist circuit rider's protest: "If you speak to some here about being descent [*sic*] they will plead up that they are in a New Country, and have many difficulties to encounter."[9] Fear of poverty, too, was very real in the western woods. Alerted to danger in all its guises, the frontiersman lived in an atmosphere of fear and insecurity. Such surroundings removed from man his inhibitions and laid bare his primitive nature.[10]

The simplicity and rawness of wilderness life can be seen in Peter Cartwright's account of Logan County, Kentucky, in 1793:

There was not a newspaper printed south of Green River, no mill short of forty miles, and no schools worth the name. We killed our meat out of the woods, wild; and beat our meal, baked our bread. . . . We raised, or gathered out of the woods, our own tea. We had sage, bohea, cross-vine, spice, and sassafras teas, in abundance. As for coffee, I am not sure that I ever smelled it for ten years. We made our sugar out of the water of the maple-tree, and our molasses too. These were great luxuries in those days.

We raised our own cotton and flax . . . our mothers and sisters carded, spun, and wove it into cloth, and they cut and made our garments and bed clothes, etc. . . .

Let it be remembered, these were days when we had no stores of dry goods or groceries.[11]

Population was sparse and settlements were few and far between. Lack of roads through the dark trackless forests increased the social isolation of the border people. The related sociological factors of monotonous existence, ceaseless hard labor, and limited sources of amusement also help explain the low moral tone.[12]

Hard liquor, plentiful and cheap, provided one release from a cheerless existence. Even professing Christians imbibed, and drinking was almost as common as eating. No one, according to a description of the Pennsylvania frontier of 1802, "seemed to think there was any harm or danger connected with its use, unless the user got drunk."[13] The proof of inebriation was either falling asleep or being unable to rise. To refuse to drink was an unpardonable incivility, and conversely, the good reputation of a family for hospitality might be forfeited if it failed to offer a drink to every visitor. In the West of that day it was "almost universally the custom for preachers, in common with all others, to take drams."[14] Such itinerants as Peter Cartwright and James B. Finley had to invent ingenious subterfuges to avoid taking a "social glass." Free whiskey was kept on the counter of the local store to treat customers. A man making a purchase amounting to fifty cents and failing to receive a free dram was not likely to return if he could secure the treat elsewhere. Liquor was essential to every social occasion from the birth of a child to the interment of a departed one. Overindulgence at log rollings, house-raisings, militia musters, cornhusking bees, weddings, and funerals was a subject of much comment by both foreign visitors and strait-laced easterners.[15]

A by-product of the excessive use of alcohol was brutal fighting. "Tearing, kicking, scratching, biting, and gouging each other's eyes out by dexterous use of thumb and finger" were common on the early Ohio frontier.[16] To Congregationalist Horace Bushnell, as well as to many later-day historians, these conditions indicated that the advancing frontier was always in danger of reverting to barbarism when the restraining and cohesive forces of established society were left behind.[17]

Albert J. Beveridge, the noted Lincoln scholar, concluded that in the Indiana backwoods of 1815

churches and schools were companion influences for decency, knowledge and morality in pioneer life and grave was the need for them. The drinking of whiskey, the fighting, and the swearing were accompanied by repellent conditions of living. . . . Social relations were loose and undisciplined.[18]

With neither convention nor law exercising its customary force, with rational discipline largely lacking, and social controls at a minimum, the environment molded man.

The West placed its mark upon its inhabitants; the resultant personality was a new man, the frontiersman.

The moral code of the frontier was also influenced by the makeup of the border society itself, a society often created in an explosive rush of settlement. The population was composed predominantly of young men, rough, driving, and bumptious. A tendency toward drunkenness, immorality, quarrelsomeness, gambling, and an exalted sense of personal importance were common faults. Yet other frontier characteristics were possessed as well: generosity, neighborliness, independent-mindedness, frankness, incurable optimism, and a resentment against all government. Almost all shared the conviction that American democracy was the work of the Almighty. These pioneers were energetic, restless ramblers,[19] "fond of chance," who seemed to have thought:

> If a path be dangerous known,
> The danger's self is lure alone.[20]

Undoubtedly a large lawless element was included. Like those who had described the border regions of thirty years earlier, traveler James Hall insisted that the outer settlements of Ohio and Kentucky in the 1820's were "often the refuge of loose individuals who if not familiar with crime, have very blunt perceptions of virtue." It often seemed that the settlers had left all moral restraint behind when they followed the trails westward. The professional classes, a moderating influence at home, scarcely existed in the pioneer communities. Thus the intellectual group that could serve as a self-disciplining force was relatively ineffectual in this new and wild country.[21]

Pioneer traits of the trans-Allegheny West were fairly representative of all frontiers. The first settlers were lusty hunter-farmers who labored hard and led simple lives.

Their formal schooling was slight and illiteracy was high. Inevitable by-products of that ignorance were narrowness of outlook, provincial-mindedness, and perhaps most important, superstitiousness that colored all the pioneers' thought on temporal and spiritual matters. In some important respects a kinship to the colonial mind is evident. The belief was common that extraordinary events in nature were the work of Satan. In their preoccupation with a personalized devil, ministers of the popular churches did not dissipate the belief; on the contrary, many encouraged it. Often the burden of their simple discourses was the message that God constantly intervened in the affairs of man to struggle with the Prince of Darkness. Free-lance evangelist Lorenzo Dow recounted a story of a "heavy shower drenching a neighborhood, while a small space, including a camp meeting was passed over and left entirely dry."[22] The implication was obvious. The Creator approved the Methodists' technique in the saving of souls and therefore operated to prevent the meeting's interruption.

Believing in witchcraft, numerous settlers advocated the use of a silver bullet to be shot at a "picture of a supposed witch . . . drawn on a stump or piece of board" so that the mortal spell of the fearsome one would be transferred to "that part of the witch painted on the board." Like their European ancestors, the frontiersmen had other vagaries of fancy as well. If a cock crowed before midnight someone was due to die before dawn; a strange black cat presaged an equally dire fate for some unfortunate. The small forked hazel rods used as divining rods by those desiring to sink a well were known as "water witches." Some hunters still clung to the notion that their rifles could be charmed by an evil one to prevent the killing of game. Other folks considered the moon a wonder-maker and regulated farming operations by its changes. To the pioneer, usually unversed in the natural and physical sciences, the invisible world was a fearful reality.[23]

Although alike in their superstitious beliefs, the frontier population of the upland South and the Ohio Valley revealed a rich diversity of nationalities and religions. There was almost everywhere a multiplicity of sects and hence a considerable degree of religious tolerance, accompanied at the same time by an intense rivalry. The Reverend George Shelton, an agent of the American Home Missionary Society, reported from northeastern Ohio in 1825 that the greatest obstacles to support of the gospel were "the numerous religious sects, which exist in almost every town in the western country."[24] Much has been written about the volatile emotions of the backwoodsmen which goes far to explain this unbrotherly feeling between the churches. In the view of Frederick Jackson Turner, the renowned frontier historian, all pioneers were "deeply responsive to the call of the religious spirit," and thus furnished "a foundation of emotional responsiveness to religion and a readiness to find a new heaven and a new earth in politics as well as in religion." This region of "high religious voltage," said Turner, was to be fertile soil for such democratic and emotional churches as the Baptists, Methodists, Presbyterians, and the later Campbellites.[25] Another scholar insisted that the westerner's daily life developed in him "a quick response to stimulus";[26] taking his religion in large evangelical doses, he was susceptible to not a little religious quackery.

The distinctive religious attitudes of the pioneer have been succinctly summed up as the product of a dual force: his independent and bold nature in revolt against society's restraints, and the leveling influence of poverty. Usually poor, the frontiersmen "accepted or produced anew the characteristics of the faith of the disinherited." Today as yesterday, the ethical and psychological traits of the religion of the poor include emotional fervor, a personalized religious experience, rejection of abstract creeds and formal ritual, lay leadership, a religious message that placed major emphasis upon such simple virtues as personal honesty, equality, sympathy with one's fellows, and the corollary urge of mutual helpfulness.[27]

Frontier churches attempted to breach the wall of irreligion that in part prevented the trans-Allegheny settlements from achieving a satisfactory social structure. Eastern missionaries alerted organized religion to the danger, and many westerners who had been faithful communicants back home sent out distress calls, which were soon answered. Different eastern church organizations joined forces in the more populous regions through interdenominational societies which sent men and money to the transmontane West. The emphasis was on instruction rather than castigation, for the societies realized that their agents' implied disapproval of the backwoodsmen's rough speech, crude manners, and customs was vigorously resented, and tended to make the westerners distrust them.[28] Such co-operation, for a time at least, softened the fierce rivalries which characterized pioneer Christianity, although much friction inevitably developed. Religious growth in the border areas was an interactive process in which the denominations of both sections participated and through which they were modified. In the opinion of one distinguished religious historian, the frontier exercised "perhaps its largest influence in the political, economic,

social and religious life in the nation" during the period
from 1800 to 1840. It was in those four decades that "the
great American churches were developing their peculiar
frontier techniques, which were to be used over and over
again, with variations, on succeeding frontiers."[29]

In the final analysis, the solution to the western challenge of intemperance, immorality, and disdain of the
world of the spirit lay largely within that section itself.[30]
Hard-working Methodist circuit riders, poverty-stricken
Baptist farmer-preachers, and self-sacrificing Presbyterian
teacher-preachers fought the battle for the Christian faith
in the border regions.

The Methodist Episcopal Church was one of the most
successful leaders in this struggle against godlessness. The
combination of a democratic theology which stressed the
Arminian doctrine of freedom of will and an autocratic
religious organization made it peculiarly suitable to
frontier conditions. It was fortunate, too, in having no
great historical traditions to restrict its innovating im-
pulses. Unlike the Presbyterians and Congregationalists
who looked for their own members cut adrift in the West,
the Methodists considered all men potential converts.
Through a transplanted itineracy system, changed into
rural practice by Francis Asbury in 1772, the church of
John Wesley was able to keep in touch with a people on
the move. The local ministry was composed of the located
preacher, class leader, and exhorter; the traveling minister, on the other hand, was attached to no one community. Through him the church was kept in the vanguard
of civilization.

Being a full-time worker, the circuit rider could devote
his whole attention to the task of ministering to scattered
settlements. Rival ministers found his zealousness exasper-

THE CIRCUIT PREACHER
was a familiar figure on the American frontier. This drawing by
A. U. Waud first appeared in *Harper's Weekly,* October 12, 1867.

ating at times, for the Methodists seemed to have knocked on all the doors first. One Presbyterian in Kentucky confessed:

I at length became ambitious to find a family whose cabin had not been entered by a Methodist preacher. In several days I travelled from settlement to settlement, on my errand of good, but into every hovel I entered, I learned that the Methodist missionary had been there before me.[31]

A Baptist clergyman overlooked partisanship to praise the Methodists in 1816:

... their complete system of mission circuits is by far the ablest for domestic missionary effort ever yet adopted. They send their labourers into every corner of the country; if they hear of any particular attention to religion in a place they double the number of labourers in those circuits, and place their best men there, and endeavor generally, to adapt the character of their preachers to the character of the people among whom they are to labour.[32]

When a spellbinder had won converts to the cause, a less flamboyant personality usually was assigned to that circuit to keep the new members on the right path. In these frequent changes of personnel the circuiteer and the community both benefited.

The Methodist hierarchy in America, closely resembling that of the Church of England, maintained a highly centralized authority. Only when this religious machine is seen with all its movable parts can one fully appreciate its high potential. The national leader was known as the "general superintendent," and he was clothed with vast powers. Governing bodies of the church were the "general conference," which met quadrennially, and the "annual conference." The latter was divided up regionally into districts and locally into circuits. In the 1820's "district conferences" were created. In practice, arbitrary features of Methodist church administration were made more palatable to democratic prejudices by the fact that the early church leaders, unmarried bishops like Francis Asbury, Richard Whatcoat, William McKendree, and Enoch George, and the district superintendents ("presiding elders") endured the rigors of pioneer life alongside the saddlebag preachers. These officials traveled almost continuously about the country, receiving the same pitiful salary as the humble itinerant.[33]

In the system of appointment to the itineracy the centralized character of Methodist church policy was also mirrored. A man who exhibited speaking ability in the local unit — the class — was encouraged by the class leader to "exercise his gifts." As an exhorter on trial, he was quickly offered a chance to prove his talent. If the local circuit rider and the presiding elder were favorably impressed he was awarded the title of "licensed exhorter" at the "quarterly conference."[34] This authority, effective for only one year, granted the recipient the power "to exhort" and little more. Perhaps he used his gifts of persuasion after the local preacher gave a sermon; often he assisted a traveling preacher on his circuit rounds. Frequently these laymen became itinerants themselves. Yet to enter the ranks of the traveling ministry was no easy task. The would-be itinerant had to obtain his license to preach from the annual conference, to which he was referred by either the local circuiteer or the presiding elder. He then worked "on trial" for two years but was not authorized to administer the sacraments. After serving that probationary period he was examined as to doctrine, conduct, and ability by a committee of the annual conference and then admitted into "full connexion."

With these preliminary obstacles surmounted, advancement was possible for the able preacher. After two years of satisfactory service he was eligible for ordination as a "deacon" by the presiding elder; with that advance he became qualified to assist the latter in the administration of the sacraments. He had now attained some stature in the Methodist hierarchy. At the General Conference in 1812 local deacons became eligible for "elder's" orders after four years of service, if approved.[35] That some itinerants progressed rapidly in this ecclesiastical system is illustrated by the case of Peter Cartwright. He was an exhorter at seventeen years of age, traveling preacher at eighteen, deacon at twenty-one, and a presiding elder at twenty-three.[36]

Among the many striking features of the itineracy system was the brevity of the average member's career and his woefully inadequate salary. The two circumstances were not unrelated. Before 1800 a circuit rider's yearly remuneration was but $64.00 plus a traveling allowance. That year the annual stipend was raised to $80.00, and in 1816 it was set at $100.00 a year.[37] Even this pay was not always collectible, since the pioneer communities being served were often so poor they could not raise sufficient funds to meet both the administrative expenses of the circuit and the preacher's salary. Benjamin Lakin told how his church people pooled their resources to buy a replacement for his worn-out horse. Other itinerants, less fortunate, had to stretch their own salary to provide this necessity.[38] Most of the men became "local supply" after but a few years of duty. This change usually occurred shortly after marriage, for the salary was hardly adequate for a bachelor, let alone a wife and prospective family. The hostility toward a wedded itinerant, fully aware as the settlers were that additional financial burdens had been foisted upon them, often reinforced the preacher's decision to settle down. Thus Asbury's lament was appropriate: "To marry is to locate."[39]

In addition to the uncertainty of receiving a regular salary, the saddlebag preacher never knew where he would next serve the Lord. He moved as directed by his superiors; every year he traveled to the annual conference sessions to receive instructions. According to a rule laid down in 1804, the maximum length of stay in a circuit for any one time was two years. Actually, the conference minutes show that itinerants frequently moved once a year and even every six months.[40] The meager salary and the nomadic existence facing the circuit rider made it certain that his loyalty had to be of high caliber.

Formidable indeed was the task confronting the Methodist preacher. In newly settled regions where the population was widely dispersed, his circuits covered a vast amount of territory, often three to four hundred miles. They were commonly referred to as "four weeks' circuits" or "six weeks' circuits," the number varying according to the time it took to tour them. Specific appointments, ranging from twenty to thirty in number, were marked out, mainly along the river courses. To reach his "charges" the traveling minister had to spend many wearisome hours in the saddle, often riding through thick woods on trails barely worthy of the name. He could look forward to speaking on an average of once each day with the possible exception of Monday, which was his usual rest day. A "son of thunder" like Cartwright might average two and even three speeches daily.

Most often traveling alone but sometimes accompanied by a younger hand, the circuit rider covered many thousands of miles during a single year to keep in touch with "society in motion." Filled with a prophetic zeal, he labored tirelessly to win frontiersmen to Methodism. In 1800 Henry Smith was the only Methodist minister for the entire lower part of the Northwest Territory.[41] Benjamin Lakin, riding the Miami Circuit in the new state of Ohio during the year 1806-7, had twenty-seven preaching sites. James B. Finley, traveling 475 miles to complete one round of the Wills Creek Circuit in the same state, would be so engaged for four weeks at a time.[42] The latter itinerant three years later rode a six-weeks' tour on the Barnsville and West Wheeling Circuit. In 1815 he had better luck and was assigned, along with a partner, to the Cross Creek Circuit in Ohio, which took only four weeks to cover, with an appointment every day and two on Sundays. He recalled they had to preach

thirty-two times every round, and meet fifty classes. Thus it will be seen that we had no time for "visits, modes and forms," to attend parties of pleasure, loaf around stores, offices, and shops, read newspapers and chat.[43]

In 1832, Michigan churchman James Gilruth had to ride four weeks to complete his Granville Circuit in the sparsely settled Michigan Territory. In twenty-two days, according to his own boast, he met twenty-five appointments, preached twenty-two sermons, supervised nineteen Bible classes, and never repeated the same sermon twice.[44] Every itinerant dreamed of his ideal: "Few preaching places, short rides, good accommodations, and sure pay."[45] Unfortunately, his hopes were seldom fulfilled.

Among the many duties of the busy circuit rider was that of co-ordinating the activities of the class leaders, exhorters, and local preachers in his domain. If the circuit were a large one he might share this work with a companion. The multiplicity of his tasks necessitated each visit's being brief. As one in the ranks phrased it, "The

Methodists were, in those days, like angels' visits, few and far between."[46] Other denominations, too, often found themselves spread too thin to be effective.[47] The circuit rider tirelessly delivered the word of God as he traversed his rounds; his message of hope reached hundreds at once when he called a camp meeting.

2

Seed Time

... the camp meeting project was orig-
inated by divine Providence to give a
mighty impulse to religious revivals,
and so produce amazing changes in the
moral world.[1]
— *Circuit rider Charles Giles, 1844*

T HE ORIGINS OF
the camp meeting, which seemed to have appeared on
the American frontier full blown in 1800 as the most
striking manifestation of the Great Revival, have long
been hid in obscurity. To many besides Charles Giles it
seemed to be of miraculous origin, like the sudden up-
swing of religious feeling of which it was a part. One day
the frontier was a godless place with little islands of
workers in the Lord, and the next it was all aflame with
religious zeal. No wonder that to those who knew it best
the camp meeting seemed an example of the sudden lifting
of God's hand to aid his servants in their Herculean task!

Nevertheless, there was ample precedent for the separate features of the true camp meeting as it was practiced
on the mobile frontier for half a century. The outdoor
meeting had held a place in Methodist technique ever
since the founding of that society. John Wesley was
preaching outdoors in England as early as 1739. As with
American camp meetings, the practice of open-air meetings was in part a result of necessity: when the Anglican

25

churches were closed to the Methodists, the latter took
to the fields. A striking parallel can be seen in the makeup
of the motley audiences facing Wesley and those who
made up the later American camp meeting. In England
"thieves, prostitutes, fools, people of every class, several
men of distinction, a few of the learned merchants, and
numbers of poor people who had never entered a place
of worship assembled in these crowds and became godly."[2]

With such a strange collection of listeners, these outdoor meetings were not always sedate affairs. Some folk
had come to hear and others to jeer the Methodist evangel,
and the first "field meetings" were marked by disorder.
Members of the audience amused themselves by throwing
stones or dirt at the speakers. At one service the spiritual
calm was shattered by the sudden appearance of a rampaging ox which had been untethered by a prankster. On
other occasions itinerants might find their discourses
drowned out by the noise of fife and drum as an anti-
Methodist parson led a marching group through the
grounds shouting the slogan, "Fight for the church!"[3]

The confusion and disorder, heightened by the shouts
and groans of worshipers who had been aroused by the
minister's spirited preaching, were striking features of
the open-air revival as an institution. Not a few were
physically affected by the preaching of the Word, giving
way to extreme bodily excitement. John Wesley recorded
in his *Journal* in 1739 that the Holy Spirit had surely
been the compelling influence.[4] The Methodist founder's
zealous use of the open-air rostrum has even led some to
the conclusion that he himself was the originator of the
camp meeting.[5] But the main features of the camp meeting—open-air preaching, emotion, and rowdy opposition
by outsiders — are as old as evangelism itself.

In America also, in the decades before 1800, preaching in the wooded clearing was common. The practice stemmed from both desire and necessity. The new settlers loved the out-of-doors, where natural beauty often turned their thoughts toward spiritual concerns. Church meeting-houses in the backwoods were also frequently too small to hold the numbers that attended. In some of the border regions the problem was not lack of space but the complete absence of a church building. In the frontier town of Pittsburgh, the Methodists had no place of worship whatsoever in 1810. In that year a subscription campaign was launched for the building or the purchase of a home for the use of their society.[6] Many other frontier denominations through necessity acquired the outdoor habit, precursor of the true camp meeting in America.

In the Virginia Colony during the first years of the Revolution — a period not celebrated for its emotional serenity — John Waller, a Separate Baptist minister, conducted meetings which he even called "camp meetings."[7] His protracted outdoor gatherings, like those of Samuel Harriss, James Read, and many other evangelists from the generating center of Guilford County, North Carolina, were in many ways similar to the later camp meeting. There were, however, at least two major differences. Camp Rules drawn by Waller made provisions for male campers only, women being forbidden to enter the grounds from an hour before sunset to an hour after sunrise. Moreover, the worshipers were not self-supporting, but dependent upon the people of the neighborhood for food. Yet of all the forerunners, this colonial prototype bore the greatest similarities to the later camp meeting. At Waller's woodland meetings were great crowds who had traveled far to attend. Here the unlearned preacher,

"raised up" by a divine call, preached earnestly and
emotionally with frequent whoops and hollers. Here too
was the emotional audience, often swept into frenzy by
the exciting sermons. The spectators wept and shouted;
many fell "roaring to the ground." The colonial revivalists, like the subsequent circuit riders, stressed in their
sermons correct living rather than formal creeds. Tents
and campers combined to make the continuous religious
services a time of social relaxation and companionship.
Finally, the camp regulations of the Separate Baptists
closely approximated those of the later camp meeting.[8]

A familiar feature of both American and English
Methodism was the circuit quarterly meeting (the "quar-
terly-conference"), which was often conducted in the
open. The size of the crowds attracted posed a serious
problem. One minister remarked: "Before camp meetings
we knew not what to do with the thousands who attended
our quarterly meetings. Sometimes we were forced to hold
our love feasts in the grove."[9] There were other opportunities for open-air services. Frontier sacramental occasions had been commonly observed outside the church
building during the summer for decades prior to the
Great Revival. Presbyterians, Methodists, and Baptists
met frequently in joint services, for there was an insuffi-
ciency of preachers and the church ordinances could not
be administered regularly in any other way. The Baptists,
however, observed communion by themselves at these
joint affairs. Such gatherings were great events in the
social as well as the religious life of backwoods America.
They afforded many churchgoers an opportunity for religious novelty and companionship; to others, who lived
out of reach of the regular circuits, they offered the sole
means of worship.

Some of the Methodist and Presbyterian "Union Sacramental Meetings" evolved into protracted outdoor revivals. This was the case on the Nashville Circuit in central Tennessee when, in 1799, services lasted ten and even twelve days. Yet the worshipers, who sometimes numbered as high as ten thousand, did not encamp but lodged in the neighborhood at night and returned to the grove early in the morning.[10]

Another forerunner of the camp meeting is to be found among the Germans. In the late eighteenth century German traveling preachers of both the Lutheran and Methodist denominations in the Pennsylvania back country took their congregations into a barn if attendance swelled beyond the capacity of the cabin. These *Grosse Versammlungen* ("Big Meetings") may also be considered the ancestors of the camp meeting, since they, too, often moved to forest clearings or fields when weather and need dictated. Joint communion services were conducted for a two-day period, with many preachers and exhorters from different communities addressing the thousands present. Another striking parallel was that the success of the *Grosse Versammlungen* was frequently measured "in terms of weeping and jubilation." Unlike participants in the later camp meetings, however, the German worshipers stayed overnight at the homes of local brethren, whose generosity also extended to the feeding of the large crowds.[11]

It is not surprising that historians are in disagreement as to the exact origins of the camp meeting, since the first participants themselves had only vague and contradictory ideas on the subject. Some writers have mistakenly credited its creation to the Methodists. Even the time of its initial appearance has been variously ascribed to the

1790's or the early 1800's, while the dates 1799, 1800, 1801, and 1803 have been frequently named.[12] Nor is there any unanimity as to the founder and exact place of the first camp meeting. Part of the difficulty is, of course, one of definition.

Among the numerous American claimants, the earliest to receive recognition was the Methodist Reverend Daniel Asbury of North Carolina. While his Rehoboth Church in Lincoln County was under construction in 1794, the congregation worshiped in the forest, their services continuing through the day and night.[13] Some have called this event the first camp meeting. At these sessions the sponsoring preacher was assisted in the pulpit by William McKendree, later a bishop, and others.[14] Perhaps the astounding success of this woodland revival with its three hundred converts encouraged McKendree to champion such a departure from established religious practice, for he later used the technique extensively. The year following Daniel Asbury's success, two more encampments were staged by him and his Presbyterian co-worker, James Hall, at Bethel, near "Rock Spring," and "Shepherd's Cross Roads" in Iredell County. The latter gathering was known as the great "Union Camp-Meeting." Both encampments produced a wealth of conversions. Similar services were repeated frequently thereafter by both the Presbyterians and the Methodists of the South Carolina Conference.[15] One historian listed the Carolinas as the first home of the camp meeting but conceded that it was in Tennessee and Kentucky that it was firmly established.[16]

A prominent Methodist itinerant and writer has acclaimed John McGee, a Methodist preacher of Smith (now Sumner) County, Tennessee, "the father of camp-meetings in America." The same authority set the time

and place as 1799 in Tennessee, adding that the credit
should be given to both John McGee and his brother
William, a Presbyterian preacher, with whom he worked
closely.[17] In point of fact, John McGee had earlier ministered in Guilford County, North Carolina, and it is
claimed that, greatly impressed by Daniel Asbury's near-
by camp meetings, he later transferred the technique to
the Red River area in Kentucky and to the Cumberland
River region. Lending credibility to this belief is the
participation of the two McGees in the sacramental
meetings which took place at the time of the camp
meeting's beginnings, and John McGee's later sponsorship of the first encampment to be held in Tennessee.
Yet John McGee in his several accounts of the first
encampments of the Great Revival never claimed credit
for originating them. A twentieth-century student of
religion observed, with considerable justice, that while
there exists no record of camp meetings' being attempted
in Kentucky or Tennessee before the opening of the nineteenth century, there are reports of them in the Carolinas.
Since several of the promulgators of the Cumberland
Revival had migrated from the latter states, it is conceiv-
able that they brought the plan with them.[18]

The difficulty of establishing the date and place of the
earliest protracted outdoor revival is apparent in the
writings of Jesse Lee, the first official historian of the
Methodist Episcopal Church in America. Lee, whose role
as a chronicler and leader of these early encampments
certainly qualified him as an authority, could only estimate that they were first introduced "about" 1801. He
added, "I never could learn whether they began in the
upper parts of South-Carolina, in Tennessee, or Kentucky."[19] Yet the dispute about dates is relatively unim-

portant; many camp meetings may have taken place in
the back country prior to the Second Great Awakening.
The significant point is that they did not achieve universal
popularity or standard form until after 1799. The story
of the seed time of the camp meeting is inextricably
connected with one man — the fiery Presbyterian minister, James McGready — and with the religious quickening he in so large a measure created, the Great Revival
in the West.

Of Scotch-Irish parentage, and a product of the Pennsylvania and North Carolina frontiers, James McGready
was one of the blazing lights on the evangelistic trail.
While ministering in Orange County, North Carolina,
where he initiated a great revival, he converted twelve
men who eventually themselves labored mightily in God's
calling. One of these was Barton W. Stone of later Cane
Ridge camp meeting fame. McGready preached a modified form of Calvinism. He continually dwelt on the
necessity of the "new birth" — a conscious spiritual
experience at a definite time and place. In his preaching
he took a leaf from the colonial revivalists' book and in
realistic terms depicted the wrath of an angry Jehovah
against impenitent sinners. No figure of speech was too
vivid to illustrate a theme.

McGready's appearance, combined with his powerful
oratory, made him a compelling personage. Described by
contemporaries as ugly and uncouth, he nevertheless
attracted the attention of all who passed. Barton W. Stone
was impressed by McGready's

remarkable gravity, and small piercing eyes. His coarse tremulous
voice excited in me the idea of something unearthly. His gestures
were *sui generis,* the perfect reverse of elegance. Everything appeared by him forgotten but the salvation of souls. Such earnestness,
such zeal, such powerful persuasion . . . I had never witnessed.[20]

While carrying on church work in South Carolina this fiery evangelist was accused of "running people distracted." In 1800 the opposition to McGready's florid and violent style of speech became so strong that he transferred the scene of his activities to southwestern Kentucky, where converts had written of the dire need of spiritual guidance.[21]

When this controversial preacher stormed into the scattered settlements of Kentucky in the early years of the American Republic, the time was ripe for a religious outpouring. The majority of the border settlers were Scotch-Irish, Celts whose emotions boiled "at a low temperature."[22] Theological argument and religious freedom flourished while the power of the church was atrophying. At the time of McGready's arrival in Logan County, this section of the Green River had already gained the rather dubious distinction of being nicknamed "Rogues' Harbor" — from the reputed number of horse thieves, runaway indentured servants, robbers, and murderers who sought to lose their identity there. It is a strange thing to relate, but these lawless backwoodsmen, unconventional and uneducated, who faced McGready reacted enthusiastically to the warm evangelistic temper of his preaching. McGready had found a home, and a task which was destined to raise him to greatness.

Dividing his tremendous energies among three congregations located on the Gasper, Red, and Muddy rivers, James McGready utilized the same techniques which he had found only partly successful elsewhere. Impassioned preaching, diligent pastoral work, and an artful prayer covenant were his main resources. The prayer covenant enjoined all signers to pray every Saturday evening and Sunday morning, and to devote the third Saturday of every month to prayer and fasting — all this to be directed at the generating of a religious awakening in the community. The campaign soon produced results.[23] In May, 1797, the Logan County Revival broke out in the Gasper River congregation.[24] Religious enthusiasm was tremendous and contagious, but organized opposition to the extremes of McGready's preaching slowed the spread of the revival idea. It did not reach its peak until the Red River sacramental service of June, 1800, which marked the prelude to the first planned camp meeting in America.

On that third week in June the little Red River church was filled to overflowing. Two fellow-churchmen, the Reverend William Hodges and John Rankin, aided McGready, and two Tennessee visitors, John and William McGee, were on hand as observers. While journeying to the Ohio country, the McGees had stopped off to see for themselves the already famous McGready technique for winning converts.

Although not a true camp meeting — for only one man reportedly came with his wagon filled with provisions and "lived on the ground" throughout the meeting — Red River was in many ways a harbinger of things to come.[25] Commencing on Friday, the services were scheduled to continue through Monday. On Sunday the sacrament of the Lord's Supper was to be observed.[26]

During the first two meeting days the audience was reduced to tears several times, but a still higher pitch was reached in the Sabbath service. Then, William Hodge's sermon caused one woman to scream, while many another fell to the floor crying, "What shall I do to be saved!" On the final day, after the formal service was at an end, the proceedings reached the ultimate. Three of the ministers left the church, but the McGee brothers remained behind with the seated congregation who were apparently deep in reflection. William McGee "felt such a power come over him that he quit his seat and sat down on the floor of the pulpit, I suppose not knowing what he did." John, trembling as he listened to the "solemn weeping all over the house," managed to compose himself for one final appeal.

I . . . exhorted them to let the Lord Omnipotent reign in their hearts, and submit to him, and their souls should live. Many broke silence. The woman in the East end of the house shouted tremendously. I left the pulpit to go to her. . . . Several spoke to me "You know these people Presbyterians are much for order, they will not bear this confusion, go back and be quiet." I turned to go back and was near falling, the power of God was strong upon me, I turned again and losing sight of fear of man, I went through the house shouting and exhorting with all possible ecstasy and energy, and the floor was soon covered by the slain.[27]

The news of this unusual happening spread far and wide, causing great excitement. The four to five hundred persons who participated at one time or another in this Red River service were themselves advertisers of its power. Visiting Presbyterian preachers were thunderstruck. Some were disgusted with the din, disorder, and crass emotional appeal of the service; others were as greatly impressed with its effectiveness in winning converts. Methodist and Baptist leaders who had been carrying on revival campaigns independently were encouraged to expend additional effort. McGready himself contrasted the preceding years of his evangelical work — "a few scattering drops before a mighty rain" — with the "overflowing floods of salvation" in the year 1800.[28]

Appraising the importance of the crowds that had come to the Red River communion, McGready decided to make

advance announcement of his next sacramental meeting
to be held at the Gasper River church in the last week
of July. Notices were sent out broadside and great numbers gathered in response, some coming from places as
far away as forty and even one hundred miles. There
were spectators from distant Smith County, Tennessee,
along with the Methodist preachers who had been specifically invited to attend. The McGee brothers and John
Page, also a powerful gospel minister, were among those
present.[29] McGready later recalled that "thirteen wagons
came to transport people and provisions" to the meeting.
Other estimates are much higher.[30] Thus, in the last week
of July, 1800, at Gasper River, where the planned practice of camping out was added to the continuous outdoor
service, the camp meeting was established in its fullest
sense.[31] In the staging of this sacrament, the fiery Presbyterian leader sponsored what was in all probability the
first planned "camp meeting" in the United States, if not
in the world.[32]

At Gasper River there was the usual frontier dilemma:
the number of worshipers exceeded the capacity of the
place of worship. To remedy this situation, woodsmen
cleared away the underbrush around the tiny church and
built a preaching stand and simple log seats. As the meeting progressed, religious services were held both in and
outside the church house.[33] Beginning on Saturday evening and lasting until Tuesday morning, with the Lord's
Supper observed on Sunday, this four-day schedule set
the pattern for the early camp meeting. Very little is
known about the operations of this first encampment,
but the fragmentary records are nevertheless revealing.
On the first night, after formal indoor services were over,
discussion groups of "seriously exercised Christians" spon-

taneously staged a revival of their own. The net result
was that most of the ministers and several hundred worshipers remained at the meetinghouse all night. Sleep
and all physical comforts were forgotten. Some pioneers,
more materially minded, who had carried along "victuals
mostly prepared," also set up makeshift tents of bushes or
branches, sheets or quilts, or rested in open or covered
wagons.[34] Thus the camp meeting came into being, a con-
venience if not a necessity in the American backwoods.

On Sunday evening, the spontaneous excitement manifested previously was repeated after a particularly vivid
sermon by John McGee. Toward the end of the message
the "cries of the distressed" grew in volume until they
almost drowned out his voice. Reported McGready:

No person seemed to wish to go home — hunger and sleep seemed
to affect nobody — eternal things were the vast concern. Here
awakening and converting work was to be found in every part of
the multitude. . . . Sober professors, who had been communicants
for many years, now lying prostrate on the ground, crying out in
such language as this: "I have been a sober professor: I have been
a communicant; . . . O! I see that religion is a sensible thing. . . . I
feel the pains of hell in my soul and body! O! how I would have
despised any person a few days ago, who would have acted as I
am doing now!—But O! I cannot help it!" . . . Little children,
young men and women, and old grey-headed people, persons of
every description, white and black, were to be found in every
part of the multitude . . . crying out for mercy in the most extreme
distress.[35]

Finally the penitents "obtained release" and joyfully
shouted of their deliverance. Even from this fragmentary
glimpse it is clear that Gasper River rivaled later camp
meetings in intensity of worship and rampant religious
zeal.

The sensational success of Gasper River quickly led
to the staging of other camp meetings by Presbyterian

and Methodist preachers who had marveled at its power. Encampment after encampment drew huge crowds. The pioneers, now awakened to their need of religion, were enthralled by this new religious device. With its sociability, its simplicity, its emotional magnetism transmitted through four or five days of fervent oratory, shouting, group singing, and the inspired prayer of preachers and worshipers alike, the camp meeting found a ready acceptance in the settled areas of Kentucky and Tennessee. Methodists, Baptists, and Presbyterians united to hold one successive high-voltage revival after another that summer. McGready declared that after his July meeting John and William McGee "carried home the divine flame, and spread it thro' the greater part of the Cumberland Settlements." At McGready's other two churches in Kentucky similar sacramental services were held during August.[36] More and more pioneers came prepared to encamp for the meetings' duration. It is no mere coincidence that this evangelical method sprang into popularity at the same time that the Second Great Awakening developed. While aided by the revival spirit that was abroad, the camp meeting itself was the generating impulse of much of that religious enthusiasm. The early history of the frontier camp meeting is, in large measure, the story of the Great Revival of 1800.

Almost as soon as the camp meeting became a familiar feature in the backwoods many explanations, some of a curious nature, were advanced as to how and why it arose. Contemporary opinion generally agreed that this new religious device was not the result of a preconcerted plan to promote revivalism, but arose logically out of the circumstances surrounding it. To one preacher of the Presbyterian faith, James Gallaher, it was clear that it was the settlers of Logan County in 1800, who had but recently made the long trek to the West from Virginia, North Carolina, and Pennsylvania, who originated the idea of combining the pleasures of camping out with a religious service.[37] Henry Smith, a Methodist circuit rider and veteran of the Cumberland Revival, did not hold to the theory that the camp meeting was the invention of newcomers to the region. Necessity, even more than the worshipers' predispositions, accounted for the outdoor revival. In the early days,

people went out far and near to sacramental or quarterly meetings, with no intention of staying on the ground, but intended either to return home or lodge somewhere in the neighborhood where the camp meeting was held; but so many were smitten to the ground, and continued in a helpless state, apparently insensible to everything around them and so continued for hours, some for twenty-four hours, that their friends had to stay and take care of them. . . . They had no provisions, or other accommodation. Yet some were detained in this way til they were suffering, if not in a state of starvation. . . . Many said "The next time I go to one of these meetings, I'll go prepared to stay on the ground." Others who were obliged to leave the meetings, soon returned with wagons or carts etc, to stay on the ground during their continuance, for many hundreds were obliged to go away.[38]

Jesse Lee also described the forest revivals as produced "through necessity, and without design." In the newly settled communities the crowds that gathered for a religious meeting were so huge "that no house could hold them and there were not neighbours enough to entertain them." To be able to stay until the meeting disbanded, which might be several days, the participants had to procure food and shelter. As the numbers of campers increased, the ministers thought it proper

to advise the people to come prepared so to tarry. In some cases public notices were given. . . . As the people were invited to come and to encamp on the ground, they soon gave to those meetings the distinguishing name of CAMP-MEETINGS. After that, when the name of a camp-meeting was heard of, the people knew what provision was necessary to be made for that purpose.[39]

The origin of the camp meeting, then, is not so complex and miraculous as it has seemed to be. It is one of those backwoods institutions which were so fertilely produced in that area — a striking and important element of the great frontier tradition of creativity. Its component parts are to be found in earlier secular and religious practices. The improvising genius of the frontier's dedicated preachers put various formerly-used techniques together and developed a new popular religious device of great power. That the final touches of this process of improvisation were accomplished in the course of one summer is the miracle and the measure of that improvising genius. In the year 1800 the camp meeting sprang into being, was almost instantly universalized along the southwestern frontier, and almost as rapidly standardized into a pattern.

3

Campfires in the Wilderness

*Upon the whole, sir, I think the revival
in Kentucky among the most extraordinary that have ever visited the
church of Christ; and all things considered, peculiarly adapted to the circumstances of that country. . . . Something of an extraordinary nature
seemed necessary to arrest the attention
of a giddy people, who were ready to
conclude that Christianity was a fable,
and futurity a dream. This revival has
done it; it has confounded infidelity,
awed vice into silence, and brought
numbers beyond calculation, under
serious impressions.*[1]
—The Reverend George Baxter, 1802

THE SETTING OF THE
early Kentucky camp meeting was "nature's temple"
— the forest clearing. Just one step removed from the
cabin meeting place, frontier encampments "offered nothing by way of worshipful environment save the natural
beauty of a grove of trees on a sloping green."[2] This very
lack of artificiality gave the open-air revival its great
religious power, a power that was never more explosively
demonstrated than during the era of the Second Great
Awakening (1800-1805).

The first encampments were cleared areas of the forest
close to meetinghouses which in their turn served the

41

several functions of worship centers, refuges for prostrate mourners, and lodging places for visiting clergymen. Since frontier churches were frequently located near waterways, it was only natural that camp sites were chosen near springs or creeks, and if possible on navigable rivers. Hence the distinctive names of the encampments of the Great Revival — "Muddy River," "Drake's Creek," "Red River," and "Cabin Creek." Aside from its aesthetic appeal, the chosen site had to provide drinking water, dry ground, shade, pasturage for the horses, and timber for tentpoles and firewood.

These desirable locations were not hard to find in the newly settled regions, and men with ax and sledge could quickly convert a two- to four-acre tract of forest land into an encampment. There was hectic activity as the prospective worshipers arrived at the spot, a week before or just prior to meeting time. Underbrush was cleared away, trees were felled, and preparations were made for a tent city.

Through the years encampments adhered to three general patterns: the rectangular, horseshoe, and circular forms. The last-named was by far the most popular.[3] Regardless of shape, tents formed the outer shell which enclosed the core of the camp meeting, the open-air auditorium. After a few years' experience, sponsors in the West urged that a supervisor be appointed to inform incoming wagoners of the encampment plan, so that much of the milling about on the first meeting day could be avoided.

Circular rows or streets of tents were irregularly arranged following the contour of the land on the edge of the area of cleared ground, with walks between. Camp

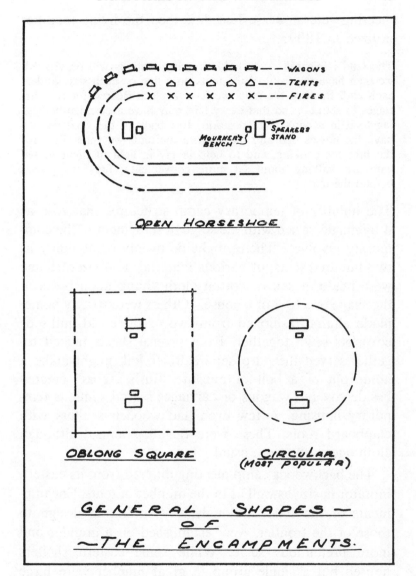

OPEN HORSESHOE

OBLONG SQUARE

CIRCULAR
(MOST POPULAR)

GENERAL SHAPES —
OF
—THE ENCAMPMENTS.

meeting veteran Jesse Lee described the living facilities utilized in 1809:

The land is cleared ... to hold as many tents as will be erected, we then have the front of the tents on a line on each side, and at each end. Back of the tents we have a place cleared for the carriages to stand ... so that every tent may have a carriage belonging to it in a convenient position. Just back of the carriages we have the horses tied and fed. Before the tents we generally have the fires for cooking, and to help in giving light at night to see who are walking about (if more convenient), fires are placed behind the tents.[4]

The number of temporary camp structures that rose as if by magic varied with the stage of settlement in the community involved. There might be twenty or as many as two hundred tents, of various materials and sizes.[5] Some were made of sail or cotton cloth "hung upon poles in the shape of a roof of a house." Others were strictly home-made affairs, fashioned from two or three old quilts or coverlets sewn together. Even several sheets tacked together served the purpose; wealthier folk might make a home out of a bolt of muslin. "Bush arbors" erected beside covered wagons or carriages served some as temporary housing. A few even had wooden shelters with clapboard roofs. These were the "log tents," although cloth ones were more usual.

The backwoods camp meeting differed from its eastern imitator in size as well as in the number of tents. Encampments of the East, although very similar in design to those of the frontier, were established on a grander and more pretentious scale. While some eastern shelters housed but a single group, a great number were large enough for many families. Perhaps twenty to fifty and even a hundred individuals found shelter under a single canvas. Mammoth tents were typical here. Likewise the eastern campers' furnishings included many of the comforts of home. The pioneer, by contrast, was lucky to have any piece of rude furniture. His bed might be of straw, or a makeshift one of poles and blankets.[6] Indeed, many at the Great Revival camp meetings slept on the ground, rolled up in blankets, when the homes of neighbors and the meetinghouse were full.

Preachers shared the same simple accommodations as the worshipers. Bishop William McKendree's quarters at the initial encampment in the Missouri Territory were "made by sewing the preacher's saddle blankets together and spreading them over a pole supported by forks in the ground like soldiers' tents." One end of the tent was closed with green boughs, while the other was left open, with a fire in front of it. Bedding arrangements were often as primitive. At one eastern campground six ministers slept in a huge bed made up of overlapping blankets, ingeniously arranged.[7]

The main physical feature of any camp meeting landscape east or west was the pulpit. Once a site was cleared, this was set up at one or both ends of the natural amphitheater, facing the parallel rows of seats. These stands were supplemented by fallen logs or wagon beds, from which ministers spellbound groups of listeners. Some of the pulpits were merely upraised platforms on stilts; others were sturdy, two-level affairs, often roofed to keep out the elements. Possibly ten feet square, the platforms were commodious enough to hold not only the speaker but also the several exhorters and ministers who were awaiting their turns to speak. Many were large enough to accommodate a dozen people. By standing in an elevated position four to eight feet higher than the milling crowds, a preacher had a better chance of being seen and heard.

Competing attractions gave the flighty a chance to wander from one orator to another, and the din and disorder gave even certain "sons of thunder" trouble.[8]

If the minister proved to be a pulpit thumper, members of the audience who seated themselves directly below the scaffold occupied a hazardous position. The Reverend James B. Finley recalled that more than once a front seat occupant was "suddenly aroused by the fall of a pitcher of water, or the big Bible upon the cranium."[9] Seats for the audience, where they existed, were merely felled logs cross-laid, or planks supported by tree stumps. The bark was dressed and the top adzed off to make them as comfortable as possible. This crude arrangement was not only the result of necessity; it was also consonant with John Wesley's rule concerning church seating: "Let there be no pews, and *no backs* to the seats." Also in accordance with the founder's wishes, the open-air auditorium was carefully divided, the women located on the right and the men on the left.[10] On some campgrounds a rail fence or wooden partition emphasized this demarkation of the sexes.

In both slaveholding and nonslaveholding regions, the Negroes were allowed to set up their own camps behind the preacher's rostrum. Because of the close proximity, their services often merged with those of the whites, adding no little to the general confusion and emotional excitement. The Negro housing area, with its crazy-quilt tents after the fashion of Joseph's coat, was a picturesque affair. As the camp meeting matured, the Negro camp section was sometimes separated from that of the whites by a plank partition. This barrier was torn down on the final meeting day when the two peoples joined together in a song festival and "marching ceremony."

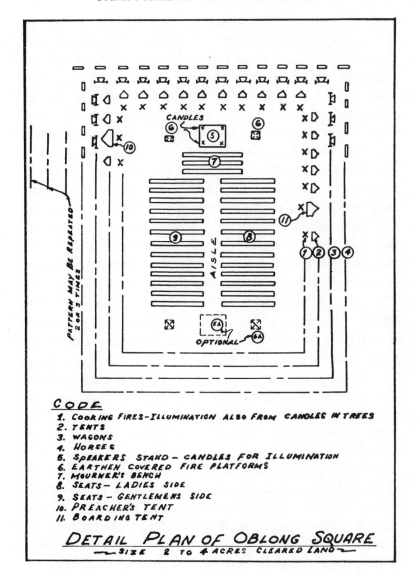

CODE
1. COOKING FIRES—ILLUMINATION ALSO FROM CANDLES IN TREES
2. TENTS
3. WAGONS
4. HORSES
5. SPEAKERS STAND — CANDLES FOR ILLUMINATION
6. EARTHEN COVERED FIRE PLATFORMS
7. MOURNER'S BENCH
8. SEATS — LADIES SIDE
9. SEATS — GENTLEMENS SIDE
10. PREACHER'S TENT
11. BOARDING TENT

DETAIL PLAN OF OBLONG SQUARE
SIZE 2 TO 4 ACRES CLEARED LAND

Illumination for the evening services presented no problem to the resourceful campers. At first, the lighting was provided by candles and pine knot torches affixed to preaching stands, trees, or other convenient places. Jesse Lee, writing of the first campgrounds, recalled seeing one hundred and twenty candles burning at the same time.[11] When campfires were located in front of the tents, they also helped light up the worship area. Gradually, fire stands known as "fire altars" came into regular use. These stands were erected in the four corners of the auditorium and consisted of earthen covered platforms on upraised tripods some six feet high. Bark, twigs, or "pine wood fires" burned on top of a layer of earth and sod. Later, oil lamps were utilized. At night the glare of the campfire, the flickering candles and torches, and the blazing fire altars all added an eerie touch to the colorful services.

The communion table set up at the initial woodland meeting in Missouri in 1809 was doubtless similar to those used during the Kentucky Revival. That sacramental table consisted of a "puncheon" split from a log, smoothed on the upper side, and laid on crossties supported by four forks placed in the ground. The whole was covered with a sheet, "for there were no table-cloths then."[12]

Usually no provisions were made for inclement weather; at the first Kentucky meetings enthusiasts worshiped out of doors in the midst of violent rainstorms. A few people could huddle in cloth or log shelters, but the western camp meeting was not noted for its comforts. The worshipers at the Goshen, Illinois, encampment of 1807 must have been surprised to find a large arbor in the form of an L erected there, an arbor spacious enough to cover seven hundred people.[13] In the East, by contrast, most campgrounds were dominated by huge tents that afforded privacy for prayer in good weather and shelter in bad weather. Kentucky accommodations in 1800 were crude but sufficient, and the pioneer settler did not complain. He had journeyed to the camp meeting expecting no great physical comforts; he had come to see for himself this religious marvel that was transforming men's lives.

The Second Great Awakening was the era of the gigantic camp meeting — the "General Camp Meeting" — where the unusual was the usual, where Presbyterian, Methodist, and Baptist ministers worked side by side, where the crowds were numbered in the hundreds and frequently the thousands, and where scores were swept into mass hysteria by the frenzied proceedings. These joint meetings were of two types, the "Sacramental" and the "Union" meeting, the former being so named because of the celebration of the Lord's Supper. When the time arrived for this ceremony Baptist leaders withdrew and the Methodists and Presbyterians conducted joint communion services. It was at the Union encampments, however, that the three denominations worshiped together most successfully. About these early meetings McGready could write glowingly that "bigotry and prejudice have received a death wound . . . Presbyterians and Methodists love one another."[14]

Among the Methodists, William McKendree looms large in the story of the "General Camp Meeting." He was assisted by a host of other traveling preachers, including William Burke, John Sale, Benjamin Lakin, and Henry Smith. McKendree had become enthusiastic over the camp meeting while an itinerant and district supervisor in southern Kentucky. In 1801 he overcame his denominational prejudice to co-operate with certain

Presbyterian leaders who were pioneering the innovation. Joint committees were set up, empowered to make camp regulations and appoint speakers for the outdoor sacraments. It was evident that enthusiasm for a new technique and the excitement of leading great numbers to the Lord were bringing about close co-operation among frontier preachers of differing denominations. The future of interdenominational harmony looked bright as the camp meeting enjoyed its first tumultuous surge.

During his union arrangement with the Presbyterians McKendree temporarily suspended the Methodist class meetings, the "love feasts," and the regular operations of the itinerant system. By 1802 the highly successful General Camp Meetings of Methodists and Presbyterians (and sometimes Baptists) were well known.[15] Yet rumbles of discontent with the practice were heard late in the very first year, indicating that the spirit of partisanship was still strong.

William Burke, speaking for the Methodists, complained bitterly that Presbyterians "were pressing in their invitations" to the sacramental gatherings but refused to support his denomination's open-air quarterly meetings, because of other appointments they had to meet. While the rivals of Methodism remained away from encampments on Friday, Saturday, and Sunday, continued Burke,

on Monday we generally saw some of their ministers in the congregation, but having our plans filled up for that day we consequently paid no attention to them; for we were fully satisfied that they only wanted the Methodists to shake the bush, and they would catch the birds. My advice to our official members in quarterly meetings was, to quietly withdraw from their meetings, and mind our own business. They did so.[16]

Actually, the co-operative arrangement did last several years longer, although the union grew weaker and weaker,

A VISITING
Frenchman's impression of an early American camp meeting.
From *États-Unis d'Ameriques*, by Jean Baptiste Gaspard Roux
de Rochelle, Paris, 1837.

terminating in the last year of the Great Revival, 1804.

Attracted by the forest revival's novelty, families of every Protestant faith mingled at these Great Revival encampments. Reports of the frenzied services had caused some to think the world was coming to an end; others anticipated a dreadful calamity about to befall the young country as a judgment of God on an impious people; still others saw meetings as "the work of the devil who had been unchained for a season . . . to deceive the ministers of religion and the very elect themselves."[17] The byways were alive with settlers, and the numbers in attendance were almost unbelievable. It seemed as if the entire population were hitting the camp meeting trail. Writing in the 1840's, Presbyterian Robert Davidson reflected upon the revival's lure:

The laborer quitted his task; Age snatched his crutch; Youth forgot his pastime; the plow was left in the furrow; the deer enjoyed a respite upon the mountains; business of all kinds was suspended; dwelling houses were deserted; whole neighborhoods were emptied; bold hunters and sober matrons, young women and maidens, and little children, flocked to the common center of attraction; every difficulty was surmounted, every risk ventured to be present at the camp-meeting.[18]

Participants in the 1800 and 1801 Kentucky and Tennessee camp meetings have insisted that the crowds numbered from three to twenty thousand at various times, according to the density of population in the neighboring territory. Although seemingly fantastic, these figures are borne out by more than one account. "Many thousands" met at Desha's Creek in August, 1800, to fall "like corn before a storm of wind." At the Cabin Creek Union Meeting in May, 1801, twenty thousand worshipers congregated; Point Pleasant had four thousand in attendance; and Indian Creek had ten thousand.[19]

Perhaps equally significant was the great number of frontier preachers who turned their siege guns on the campers. Peter Cartwright said the number of churchmen of different denominations who joined forces at any one of these woodland Bethels in Kentucky, Tennessee, and the Carolinas might reach "ten, twenty, and sometimes thirty." They preached, harangued, exhorted, and prayed "night and day, four or five days together," and often for a week or more.[20]

The immensity of the throng impressed a newcomer to a Cumberland Revival camp meeting — a "scene of confusion that could scarce be put into human language." There were not enough ministers present to keep the crowds seated or attentive; spectators walked about talking, laughing, smoking, and gesticulating during the services. Free of the restraint of a formal meetinghouse, the people indulged in complete emotional freedom and frequently reverted to herd behavior. If a particular sermon or song excited them, they cried, shouted, groaned, or repeated the spoken phrases over and over again in increasing tempo.

There would be an unusual outcry; some bursting forth into loud ejaculations of prayer, or thanksgiving, for the truth; . . . others flying to their careless friends, with tears of compassion; beseeching them to turn to the Lord; some struck with terror, and hastening through the crowd to make their escape, or pulling away their relations; others . . . fainting and swooning away.[21]

Preachers often found it impossible to maintain order when they themselves were physically exhausted from straining their voices so that thousands could hear them. At communion services their labors were intensified. The Reverend John Lyle, a Presbyterian, thought he was going to faint or die from the exertion of delivering the "action" sermon to about eight thousand at a Paint Creek meeting in 1801, "yet notwithstanding spoke above an hour."[22]

Competing with the preacher most of the day were the typical background noises — outbursts from the audience, sermons being delivered from other stands, and the offerings of praying and singing circles and groups. Largely unplanned, the service routine was most often spontaneous. At two separate stands, said one itinerant,

we had preaching alternately through the day. . . . Each public service was followed by a prayer meeting which was not to be broken off to make way for preaching, but the trumpet was sounded at the other stand, whither all who wished to hear preaching were wont to repair.[23]

The Reverend John Lyle reported that ten, twenty, and sometimes the majority of people under conviction offered up individual prayers simultaneously. Since this was a social as well as a religious occasion, whiskey had to be available to ease the parched throats of the participants. The "dissolute and irreligious were frequently more numerous than the serious minded," and to cater to their tastes, barrels of whiskey were hidden in the bushes to be retailed by the cupful later. Preacher Richard McNemar commented on the dregs of frontier society that took this opportunity to heckle and carouse. Even harsher judgment was expressed by Methodist historian Nathan Bangs:

It is admitted that in such vast multitudes, assembled in the open air, under circumstances of such peculiar excitement, and many of them not well instructed in science or morals, there must have been some disorder, some mingling of human passions not sanctified by grace, and some words and gesticulations not in accordance with strict religious decorum. Every action, therefore, and everything which was said and done [at these camp meetings], I am by no means careful to defend or pledged to justify.[24]

Immoral practices were frequent enough at these encampments to be commented upon by the camp leaders. Such immorality is not surprising when the mixed character of the pioneer audiences is taken into account. Certainly, the precedent-shattering size of the crowds and the emotional hysteria of the services did nothing to weaken such tendencies. Preacher Lyle, a sharp critic of the revival, stated that acts of immorality took place on the grounds under cover of darkness, or in the neighboring forest. He candidly told the facts of the situation concerning his own congregation. Some of the women who were the most persistent victims of the "falling exercise" were the ones prone to forget the edict of virtue. Thus "Becca Bell, who often fell, is now big with child to a wicked trifling school master of the name of Brown who says he'll be damned to hell if he ever marries her." Several other of Lyle's female parishioners "got careless," including "Polly Moffitt who was with child to Petty and died miserably in child bed." A preventive measure of indeterminate value was the "night watch" set up at the Sugar Ridge, Kentucky, camp meeting of August, 1802. This consisted of two men who patrolled the grounds and checked the meetinghouse to prevent any irregularities.[25]

Often setting the pattern of emotionalism was the camp preacher, himself overcome by the excitement and by his own success as a soul-saver. William McGee "would sometimes exhort after the sermons, standing on the floor, or sitting, or lying in the dust, his eyes streaming, and his heart so full that he could only ejaculate 'Jesus, Jesus.' " A Methodist minister claimed that Presbyterian leaders, not being accustomed to such noise and shouting, were particularly susceptible when they yielded to their emotions, and "went into great excess, and downright wildness." When preaching had ended, the service was frequently carried on by the audience — men, women, and even little children — who exhorted one another, prayed, wept, and even preached. One tale is told of a seven-year-old child who "sat on the shoulders of a man and preached til she sank exhausted on the bearer's head."[26] There was scarcely a moment when activity was not going on, whether staged by the minister or by his congregation. "When the shout of the King was in the camp" evening worship frequently extended until dawn. Old men who knew they could not spend the night awake brought "great coats" to keep themselves warm and took short naps on the ground with the sleeping children under the shelter of the trees while the worship surged around them.

The doctrines advanced during the Great Revival consisted of the preaching of universal redemption, free and full salvation, justification by faith, regeneration by the Holy Ghost, and the joy of a living religion. Often, the method used to convey this message created bedlam. A settler of sin-soaked habits was overwhelmed by electrifying tirades. The celebrated Presbyterian revivalist, James McGready, deliberately used strong language in classifying the erring members present. Blasphemers would be dragged by the fiends of Hell into the "liquid, boiling waves" only to fall to the "deepest cavern in the flaming abyss."[27] With the shrieks and yells encompassing him, the listener could well believe Judgment Day was upon him at that very moment, and that he himself, found lacking, was at the mouth of Hell. Such frightening preaching amidst eerie surroundings mowed the weary and overwrought sinners down in sheaves.

Less violent methods were also effectively used to bring

about conversion. Songs such as "Hark My Friend That
Solemn Toll" and "Pray Cast a Look Upon That Bier"
reminded the sinners sadly of the universal end of man.
The refrain of one song by John A. Granade, a contemporary camp meeting song writer, was aimed directly at the
wavering:

> Think on what the Saviour bore,
>   In the gloomy garden,
> Sweating blood at every pore
>   To procure thy pardon;
> See him stretch'd upon the wood,
>   Bleeding, grieving, crying,
> Suff'ring all the wrath of God,
>   Groaning, gasping, dying!
>
> 'Tis done! the dreadful debt is paid,
>   The great atonement now is made;
> Sinners on me your guilt is laid,
>   For you I spilt my blood.[28]

The first response of the crowds to the novel encampment conditions and the high-tension services was improvised and diverse. Later, these first responses tended to
become stereotyped and to be repeated in every meeting.
Most of the disorder and at least a part of the physical
excitement came under leader control as the camp meeting developed. These first camp meetings were tumultuous
almost beyond comprehension, and the effect upon the
participants was in proportion. It was almost impossible
for the worshipers not to feel that something great and
extraordinary — that is, the active participation of the
Lord — was going on.

The record of "acrobatic Christianity" at the Kentucky
and Tennessee revivals is the more understandable when
viewed against the backdrop of the awe-inspiring evening
worship, where candlelight and campfires lit the shadowy

scene, and where impassioned exhortations, prayers, and spirituals contributed to the extreme excitement of the "awakened sinners." From this high-voltage atmosphere burst forth many strange things. Five hundred or more would shout aloud "the high praises of God at once," and the "cries of the distressed . . . the rejoicing of those that were delivered from their sins of bondage" would rend the air. Women, particularly, would be affected. Some in the "transport of their feelings" hugged and kissed everyone in their vicinity.[29] As Methodist leader John McGee described the "Ridge" meeting of August, 1800:

The nights were truly awful; the camp ground was well illuminated; the people were differently exercised all over the ground, some exhorting, some shouting, some praying, and some crying for mercy, while others lay as dead men on the ground.[30]

Terror, distress, and despair seemed to overcome some congregations. Saints and sinners, young and old, white and Negro would, "with a piercing scream, fall like a log on the floor, earth, or mud, and appear as dead."

Along with the shouting, the "falling exercise" was the most common of all forms of bodily excitement. According to one participant, the "falling down of multitudes, and their crying out . . . happened under the singing of Watts's Psalms and Hymns, more frequently than under the preaching of the word."[31] When six or more hymns were sung simultaneously by different groups at a Providence, Kentucky, revival in 1801, there were accompanying violent motions of the body. Women in their frantic agitations sometimes "unconsciously tore open their bosoms and assumed indelicate attitudes." Those falling would be affected in varying degrees:

Sometimes, when unable to stand or sit, they have the use of their hands, and can converse with perfect composure. In other cases, they are unable to speak, the pulse becomes weak, and they draw a difficult breath about once a minute; in some instances their extremities become cold, and pulsation, breathing and all the signs of life, forsake them for nearly an hour. Persons who have been in this situation have uniformly avowed, that they felt no bodily pain; that they had the entire use of their reason and reflection, and when recovered, they could relate everything that had been said or done near them.[32]

When the "fallers" had recovered, they often arose shouting, "Praise God!" Soon those saved broke forth in a volley of exhortation. Some had seen visions, heard unspeakable words, smelled fragrant odors, and had "a delightful singing in the breast." The Reverend George Baxter reported that the first persons who lost consciousness at the Cane Ridge revival were a source of amazement for some of the Presbyterians in the audience, but after a little time "the falling down became so familiar as to excite no disturbance." In the summer of 1801, a Fleming Creek encampment had one hundred fallers, a Point Pleasant camp meeting two hundred and fifty, and at Indian Creek eight hundred persons were reported struck down.[33] When the falling reached such alarming proportions, to prevent those stricken from "being trodden under foot by the multitude, they were collected together and laid out in order, on two squares of the meeting house, til a considerable part of the floor was covered."[34]

Some were struck down at the camp meeting after exhibiting symptoms of "deepest impressions" and the shedding of tears; others fell on their way home, or while working in the fields. The Reverend John Lyle was more concerned about the aftereffects of these manifestations. He feared they would become habitual: "The oftener they fall they will more easily fall again, and will become at length the sport of lesser passions." A case in point was

Henry McDanal's wife, who had "swooned away" for two successive days at an 1801 encampment, "and since she came home has fallen again and again and still feels guilt and misery." Lyle's application of a "vial of hartshorn" to the fallen was without success in any case. The lancet was equally ineffective, although used to such an extent that according to one excited camper, the Gasper River meeting place "was crowded with bleeding bodies like a battlefield."[35]

In many cases toughs and scoffers fell at the services "as suddenly as if struck by lightening," sometimes at the very moment when they were cursing the revival. One unbeliever tried to prove that the fallers were shamming, and so prodded them with a nail on a stick, but to no avail. He had boasted that he would not fall, and so got liquored up, thinking that would pacify his feelings. In a short time, however, he too was struck down, and when able to speak "acknowledged himself a great sinner, and hoped for pardon through Christ."[36]

If the seizure was not so sudden, different manifestations might occur before exhaustion set in. Numerous leaders of the Kentucky Revival, including Stone, Baxter, Finley, McNemar, and Lyle, have described versions of nervous affection, in addition to falling—jerking, rolling, dancing, running, singing, laughing, and barking. The "jerking exercise" seemed to be the most common reaction to the stimulus offered at the Kentucky and Tennessee meetings, and the one that spread most rapidly through a congregation. Even preachers were not immune. The Reverend Samuel Doak insisted he was occasionally the subject of that bodily exercise for more than twenty years. The jerks varied in some degree from person to person:

Sometimes the subject of the jerks would be affected in some one member of the body, and sometimes in the whole system. When the head alone was affected, it would be jerked backward and forward, or from side to side, so quickly that the features of the face could not be distinguished. When the whole system was affected, I have seen the person stand in one place, and jerk backward and forward in quick succession, their heads nearly touching the floor behind and after.... I have inquired of those thus affected. They could not account for it; but some have told me that those were among the happiest seasons of their lives. I have seen some wicked persons thus affected, and all the time cursing the jerks, while they were thrown to the earth with a violence. Though so awful to behold, I do not remember that any of the thousands I have seen ever sustained an injury in body. This was as strange as the exercise itself.[37]

Peter Cartwright recollected that he had seen more than five hundred persons jerking at one time at Great Revival encampments. It would excite his "risibilities" to see the ornately dressed gentlemen's and young ladies' "fine bonnets, caps, and combs fly; and so sudden would be the jerking of the head that their long loose hair would crack almost as loud as a wagoner's whip." If one eccentric reporter is to be believed, some camp leaders in anticipation of this exercise cut saplings breast high to support the jerkers, who "kicked up the earth as a horse stamping flies."[38]

Then there was the "rolling exercise." Starting with a violent jerk that threw the person down, it doubled him up and rolled him over and over like a wheel or ball. According to a Great Revival minister, "this was considered very debasing and mortifying, especially if the person was taken in this manner through the mud and sullied therewith from head to foot."[39]

More socially acceptable was the "dancing exercise." This movement began with the jerking of the legs and feet, and proceeded to assume the characteristics of a dance, as the person affected "continued to move forward and backward in the same track or alley til nature seemed exhausted." Spectators seemed to think this was "heavenly." Some insisted that "there was nothing in it like levity, nor calculated to excite levity in beholders."

The "running exercise" was merely an attempt to escape the nervous affections. If any person tried to resist, the jerks would become more severe. One rowdy, feeling the jerks coming on, tried to escape to the bordering woods and fortify himself with some liquor, but the bottle was knocked from his hands and broken on a seedling. At this he became so enraged that he cursed and raved, but "at length he fetched a very violent jerk, snapped his neck, and soon expired, with his mouth full of cursing and bitterness." This fatality is the only one on record attributed to the jerks.

To preacher Stone the most unaccountable phenomenon was the "singing exercise." The subject, with a happy countenance, "would sing most melodiously, not from the mouth or nose, but entirely in the breast, the sounds issuing thence. . . . It was most heavenly. None could ever be tired of hearing it." Equally indescribable to Stone was the "laughing exercise." He stated that it happened frequently but only to the devout worshipers. Paradoxically, this loud hearty laughter indulged in by a few individuals was not infectious, but produced solemnity in saints and sinners. Other chroniclers called it the "holy laugh," but referred to it as a form of hysteria that gripped audiences most frequently after 1803.

The "barking exercise" was intimately related to jerking. It seemed that the disorder passed from the nerves and muscles to the mind. Men fancied themselves dogs, "went down on all fours and barked til they grew hoarse.

It was reportedly no uncommon sight to behold numbers of them gathered about a tree, barking, yelping, 'treeing the devil.' "[40] Preacher Stone discounted this dog delusion, preferring to believe that the grunts or barks resulted from the suddenness of the jerks. The name of the exercise apparently originated when an old Presbyterian clergyman in eastern Tennessee got the jerks and grasped a tree for support. Some punster who found him in that position reported he had found the minister barking up a tree.

The most fabulous of all Great Revival camp meetings, the one which seemed to incorporate and enlarge upon every excess of the previous revivals, was Cane Ridge. A "General Camp Meeting," the Cane Ridge sacramental services were staged some seven miles from Paris in Bourbon County, Kentucky. This camp meeting began on August 6, 1801, and continued for six long days. From Friday to Wednesday the frenzied worship continued night and day without intermission "either in public or private exercise of devotion." Even heavy showers failed to scatter the audience.[41] Although it was held under joint sponsorship, Cane Ridge seems to have been largely the work of the Presbyterian Reverend Barton W. Stone, a farmer-preacher. Another churchman of the same faith reported that he attended along with "eighteen Presbyterian ministers, and Baptist and Methodist preachers," although he could not recall the exact number of the latter two groups.[42]

Cane Ridge is important not only as a turning point in the history of the camp meeting, but as a phenomenon of the Second Great Awakening. In many ways atypical, it has been the model many critics have used to create their lurid pictures of the outdoor revival. Cane Ridge was, in all probability, the most disorderly, the most hysterical, and the largest revival ever held in early-day America.

Attendance estimates of Cane Ridge range from ten to twenty-five thousand, with most authorities placing the number somewhere between the two figures. Eager participants had boasted that "many had come from Ohio"— probably from the Miami River Valley.[43] While every shade of religious opinion was represented, there were many visitors whose religious convictions were nebulous. Tumult and disorder were inevitable when a heterogeneous group of such large proportions assembled, especially since the occasions for social companionship were so rare on the frontier.

If there is no agreement among participants as to the exact number that attended Cane Ridge, neither is there unity of opinion as to its place in history. Peter Cartwright insisted that Cane Ridge marked "the first camp-meeting ever held in the United States, and here our camp-meetings took their rise." The "Kentucky Boy" was not alone in this opinion. Confusing the issue was William Burke, Methodist participant at Cane Ridge. He insisted that this sacramental occasion was no camp meeting at all. While it was true that there were carriages and wagons on the grounds, "not a single tent was to be found, neither was any such thing as a camp meeting, heard of at that time." Burke himself had the only true tent, one he made on the spot out of poles and papaw bushes.[44]

The Cane Ridge services, if they can be dignified by that name, almost defy description. A visitor to the Sunday sessions reported four different groups meeting simultaneously at various crude speaker's stands about a hundred yards apart. One of the rostrums contained a colored exhorter addressing his race.[45] Another contemporary described the continuous preaching and exhorting. The attractions that caught his eye were the many "small [prayer] circles of ten or twelve," close together where "all engaged in singing Watts's and Hart's hymns." At the same time a minister would step upon a stump or a log, and would attract as many as could collect around him. William Burke's technique is a case in point. He mounted a log and

commenced reading a hymn with an audible voice, and by the time we concluded singing and praying we had around us, standing on their feet, by fair calculation ten thousand people. I gave out my text in the following words: "For we must all stand before the judgment seat of Christ," and before I concluded my voice was not to be heard for the groans of the distressed and the shouts of triumph. . . . Here I remained Sunday night, and Monday and Monday night; and during that time there was not a single moment's cessation, but the work went on.[46]

Peter Cartwright said that at times there were more than a thousand shouting at once, creating such a volume of noise that the sound carried for miles. The overwhelming impact of this deafening uproar and contagious bodily excitement has been depicted by James B. Finley, who was then, according to his own appraisal, somewhat of a free thinker in religious matters.

The noise was like the roar of Niagara. The vast sea of human beings seemed to be agitated as if by a storm. I counted seven ministers, all preaching at one time, some on stumps, others in wagons, and one . . . was standing on a tree which had, in falling, lodged against . . . another. Some of the people were singing, others praying, some crying for mercy in the most piteous accents, while others were shouting most vociferously. While witnessing these scenes, a peculiarly-strange sensation, such as I had never felt before, came over me. My heart beat tumultuously, my knees trembled, my lip quivered, and I felt as though I must fall to the ground. A strange supernatural power seemed to pervade the entire mass of mind there collected. . . . Soon after I left and went into the woods, and there I strove to rally and man up my courage.

After some time I returned to the scene of excitement, the waves of which, if possible, had risen still higher. The same awfulness of feeling came over me. I stepped up on to a log, where I could have a better view of the surging sea of humanity. The scene that then presented itself to my mind was indescribable. At one time I saw at least five hundred swept down in a moment, as if a battery of a thousand guns had been opened upon them, and then immediately followed shrieks and shouts that rent the very heavens. . . . I fled for the woods a second time, and wished I had staid at home.[47]

Probably the most intense excitement at Cane Ridge was experienced when the Sunday sacrament was served to some eight hundred to eleven hundred Presbyterian communicants and an indeterminate number of Methodists. Then the delivery of the impassioned sermons and exhortations prior to the sacrament resulted in some breath-taking spectacles. One preacher commented on the "one hundred persons of all classes, the learned and the unlearned, at once on the ground crying for mercy of all ages from eight to sixty years"; another reported that "undue excitement of animal feeling" resulted in at least one thousand persons' being swept into the falling exercise. The old campaigner, James Crawford, perhaps the "most reliable" of the Presbyterian frontier preachers, conscientiously counted the fallers and gave the higher figure of three thousand.[48] A regular system of caring for the afflicted was in force. When a person was struck down he was carried out of the congregation, and then some minister or exhorter prayed with him against the background of a hymn "suitable to the occasion."

At this largest of all encampments the greatest number of sexual irregularities occurred. After the Saturday evening worship, for instance, six men were found lying under a preaching stand with a woman of easy virtue. The following evening a couple were caught in the act of adultery. James B. Finley, present at Cane Ridge, observed that while the religious services were going on, "all manner of wickedness was going on without." "Men," he continued, "furious with the effects of the maddening bowl would outrage all decency by their conduct."[49] Camp sponsors declared that such carnal actions of "unclean persons" were deliberately aimed at bringing the religious revival into disrepute. Thus they discussed plans for supervision —having the stands watched and placing elders in the meetinghouse to make certain of the separation of the sexes in the sleeping arrangements.

There is no means of weighing the seriousness of the impression that Cane Ridge made upon the hearts and nervous systems of its thousands of participants. Certainly thousands were deeply moved. The number of those who professed conversion was estimated somewhere between one thousand and two thousand. The healing touch of revivalism was apparent on every hand. Among the happy converts were many men destined to be vigorous champions of the Christian life. James B. Finley, the celebrated circuit rider, dated his conversion from his troubled state of mind while a Cane Ridge visitor.

But what of the Kentucky Revival as a whole? Whether the majority of the conversions were lasting is problematical. Yet one contemporary historian, evaluating the movement in 1809, wrote:

The effects of these camp meetings were of a mixed nature. They were doubtless attended for improper purposes by a few licentious persons and by others with a view of obtaining a handle to ridicule all religion. . . . The free intercourse of all ages and sexes under cover of night and the woods was not without its temptations. It is also to be feared that they gave rise to false notions of religion by laying too much stress on bodily exercises, and substituting them in the place of moral virtues or inward piety. These are too often considered as evidences of a change of heart and affections, though they neither proved or disproved anything of the kind. After every deduction is made of these several accounts, it must be acknowledged that the good resulting from the camp meeting greatly preponderated over the evil. They roused that indifference to the future destiny of man which is too common, and gave rise to much serious thoughtfullness on subjects confessedly of the most interesting nature.[50]

Visible proof of the effectiveness of Great Revival camp meetings is offered also by the tremendous growth in church membership of those churches which used them. In Kentucky alone, between 1800 and 1803, the Baptists gained ten thousand members, and the Methodists about an equal number. The Presbyterians also added large numbers to their congregations during these years, although later evangelical schisms were responsible for the Presbyterian church's losing ground in the West. During the period in question the Methodists enjoyed an average increase of two thousand members a year, which necessitated a rapid division and redivision in church territories, districts, and circuits.[51]

The 1801 Bourbon County meeting at Cane Ridge not only helped multiply church membership, but also gave a powerful impetus to the revival itself. Richard McNemar declared that "the work breaking out in North Carolina resulted from people who had been to Cane Ridge."[52] As the movement continued, the charting of its progress became increasingly difficult, as it spread out in ever widening circles. A concurrent revival in the East, although mainly restricted to indoor "protracted meetings," made it appear that the "heavenly fire" from Kentucky had spread in almost every direction.

By the year 1803 the religious excitement had caught on in the Western Reserve District of Ohio, had spread back into western Georgia, North Carolina, and thence to South

Carolina, and was strong in other parts of the East. An ardent advocate of the camp meeting, the Reverend Henry Smith, staged one in Virginia while serving on the Winchester Circuit in 1803—this at a time when his constituents insisted: "It may do in the West, but it won't do here."[53] From Virginia the outdoor revival spread through neighboring Maryland, Delaware, Pennsylvania, and New York, and fanned out into Massachusetts, Connecticut, Vermont, and New Hampshire. The camp meeting even caught on in certain sections of Canada.[54] When settlers moved forward into the Mississippi Territory the open-air revival soon followed. In a short while evangelical Christianity blanketed the entire nation and found in the camp meeting its favorite method.

4

Camp Meetings Gain New Sponsors

*The people among whom the revival
began, were generally Calvinists; and
although they had been long praying in
words, for the outpouring of the Spirit;
and believed that God had "fore-
ordained whatsoever comes to pass";
yet when it came to pass that their
prayers were answered . . . they rose
up and quarreled with the work, because it did not come to pass that the
subjects of it were willing to adopt
their soul-stupefying creed.*[1]
— Richard McNemar, 1807

 GREAT DIVIDE
in camp meeting history was reached when the tumult of
Cane Ridge had died down. That revival, with its "muscular Christianity," its disorder and confusion, helped
fortify the convictions of the more conservative churchmen that camp meetings were a burlesque of religion.
Antirevival and prorevival sentiment soon divided western
Presbyterianism into two feuding groups. The camp meeting, begun on the promising note of interdenominational
co-operation, was now a cause of church discord.

One Presbyterian faction in the West, of an orthodox
temper, disliked the forest revival's unbridled emotionalism and condemned its infringement on the Calvinistic
creed. Most important, they wanted the new technique
discarded because they were unable to control it.[2] It was

69

soon obvious that this was the majority view of the western Presbyterians, a position in which they were supported by their eastern brethren. Congregationalists and Presbyterians, working together in the West under the Plan of Union of 1801, would sanction only "rational" revivalism in which there was "very little commotion of animal feelings." Such a definition obviously ruled out the young camp meeting. By 1805, the open-air revival had become mainly a Methodist institution discarded by its Presbyterian originators except for certain left-wing elements.

Yet the Presbyterian camp meeting picture is not crystal clear. One hears, for example, of a flurry of encampments staged by individual Presbyterian churches in collaboration with the Methodists in Illinois and Tennessee as late as the 1830's. This intermittent resurgence of revivals was great enough in 1832 to cause a physician-member of that church, Dr. Samuel Miller, to lament "that the use of camp meetings should be resumed in our body." He was particularly concerned about irregularities and immoral practices that he was sure were unavoidable "on the skirts and sometimes in the interior of such camps."[3]

While the reappearance of the camp meeting was perturbing Dr. Miller, four-day sacramental services, which in many ways resembled the earlier Presbyterian camp meeting, alarmed conservatives of the Erie Presbytery. These "four days' meetings," with their self-styled evangelist leaders and "Anxious Seats," caught on rapidly among the churchfolk of northwestern Pennsylvania and northeastern Ohio in 1831. Soon the fiery preaching of the traveling "revival men" aroused strong opposition. The revival flame again flickered out. The camp meeting, although discarded as Presbyterian practice, continued to make its influence felt in one form or another.

The revival faction of the Presbyterians which stubbornly clung to the new technique of mass conversion included many ministers and exhorters of little or no education. In their preaching they denied the aristocratic tenets of Calvinism, with its doctrines of predestination and election. Instead they emphasized an equalitarian theology which incidentally was the Methodist doctrine of grace. To be free to pursue such departures from established practice, these left-wing leaders broke away from the parent organization. Camp meeting revivalism, as a consequence, produced three schisms in western Presbyterianism. These schisms eventually resulted in the formation of the "Christian" church, also known as the "Stonite" or "New Light Presbyterian" church, the beginnings of Shakerism in the West, and the appearance of the "Cumberland Presbyterian" church. The first occurred in northern Kentucky and southwestern Ohio (1803-4), the second in southwestern Ohio as a result of the defection of several Stonite leaders to the Shaker faith (1805), and the third developed in southern Kentucky and north-central Tennessee (1803-6).[4]

Fifteen independent "Stonite" societies were functioning in Kentucky and southwestern Ohio by 1804. These little churches had renounced the Westminster Confession of Faith and the Presbyterian polity, taking the New Testament for their authority in both doctrine and practice. One harsh critic insisted that there was no set standard of doctrine in "this trash heap," each person being told "to take the New Testament, read it and abide by his own construction of it."[5] The camp meeting device seemed to fit in admirably with this nonorthodox approach to religion. The final rupture from orthodox Presbyterianism came in 1804, when every one of the revival-minded churches in the Ohio settlements, with but two exceptions, joined the "New Lights."

For the previous three years camp meetings had been staged north of the Ohio River. These New Light encampments were marked by the same rampant enthusiasm and animal excitement that characterized those in Kentucky— a condition that is understandable, since they were off-shoots of that same movement. The first camp meeting on record in the Ohio Territory was the one conducted at Eagle Creek in present-day Adams County beginning on June 5, 1801.[6] Visitors from neighboring states had returned home from Kentucky campgrounds to hold encampment after encampment; Barton W. Stone, Richard McNemar, Robert Marshall, and John Thompson were the guiding lights. The services were anything but calm, if McNemar's report is representative:

The custom of giving the right hand of fellowship was introduced, and the name of "brother" and "sister" applied to church members. The spirit of the Kentucky revival, especially in camp meetings was kept aflame. Praying, shouting, jerking, barking or rolling, dreaming, prophesying, and looking as through a glass at the infinite glories of Mount Zion [occurred]. . . . They practiced a mode of prayer, which was singular, as the situation in which they stood, and the faith by which they were activated. According to their proper name of distinction, they stood *separate* and *divided,* each one for one; and in this capacity, they offered up each their own separate cries to God, in one united harmony of sound; by which the doubtful might be directed, sometimes to the distance of miles.[7]

Use of the camp meeting after 1804 by the Stonites remains unchronicled in detail. Their leader, Barton W. Stone, although mentioning forest revivals which took place in the various autonomous church organizations through the year 1812, described no general camp meeting plan. After noting a joint encampment with the Separate Baptist's Annual Association Meeting in Meig's County, Ohio, in that year, he ceased reporting on the subject, thus ending even this meager source of information. When Stone led some of his congregations into a union with the Campbellites—"Disciples"—in 1832, the camp meeting was certainly not in good favor in those churches; for Alexander Campbell, their founder, was vehemently outspoken about the lack of scriptural authorization for such affairs.[8] Yet camp meetings did not disappear from the practice of other Stonite churches, if we can credit the report of one contemporary who described "Stonites" and Methodists as responsible for "most" of the camp meetings in the Northwest, particularly in Indiana, from 1830 to 1850.[9]

In the same year that the Stonites officially withdrew from the Presbyterian church, the "ministry" of the Shaker community located at New Lebanon, New York, some twenty-five miles east of Albany, decided to send missionaries to the West. Glowing accounts of Great Revival camp meetings in Kentucky, Tennessee, and Ohio appearing in the religious press of the East had matched the prophecy of founder Mother Ann Lee that great opportunities for the Shaker faith lay there. The Shakers were destined to play a brief but disruptive role in camp meeting history.

A cardinal tenet was set forth in their formal name, "The United Society of Believers in Christ's Second Appearing." The Shakers believed that the inspiring presence of Ann Lee constituted the second appearance of Christ. Ann Lee, after her unfortunate marriage experience, had developed an aversion to sex; celibacy thus became a major doctrine of the Shakers. Other tenets that attracted support from the lowly were their staunch opposition to war and their belief in the power of direct revelation, a power that had been demonstrated to their satisfaction. Shakerism had secured a tenuous foothold in America when the New Lebanon community was established in 1774; the church itself was not actually formed until after the founder's death in 1783. By 1805, the year Benjamin Seth Youngs, Issachar Bates, and John Meacham set out on foot to create a new moral order in the western country, there were eleven thriving Shaker communities, all situated in the East.[10]

Having started their journey on New Year's Day, these three hardy missionaries reached the scene of religious excitement, Bourbon County, Kentucky, some sixty days later.[11] One of the first encampments visited was a Cane Ridge camp meeting led by Barton W. Stone, whose earlier encampment had made him famous. There, on April 2, 1805, the representatives received a welcome that was lukewarm at best. Their peculiar doctrines and communitarian ideals were strongly disapproved. When Issachar Bates asked Stone for the right to preach, he was refused, although such action was in direct contradiction to the previous policy of allowing all sects to use the speaker's stand. Finally, on a Monday, after the formal camp services were at an end, Bates was granted the privilege of lecturing.[12] Other Kentucky encampments were visited by the "Three Witnesses," as they were called. Almost everywhere they had difficulty in gaining a hearing as opposition mounted against their unorthodox "testimony."

Moving northward to sparsely-populated Ohio the next year, the Shaker churchmen continued to use Stonite encampments as sounding boards. Stopping off at the Turtle Creek settlement in southwestern Ohio in March,

they made it a point to appear at all of Richard Mc-
Nemar's camp meetings, gaining converts through their
preaching. When the camp rostrum was denied them,
their campaign was carried into the homes of worshipers
in known "revivalistic" neighborhoods. Among the many
claims the Shaker spokesmen advanced was that they
could perform miracles. When challenged, however, by
Stonite ministers, they refused to demonstrate their
powers.[13] Such tactics aroused the ire of the Stonites, who
considered their hospitality rudely imposed upon. So in-
furiated was Barton W. Stone that he denounced the
Shakers as believers in "an old woman's fables." They
were "wolves in sheep's clothing [who] have smelt us
from afar and have come to tear, rend and devour."[14]

Not content with luring laymen to the millennial cause,
the Shaker missionaries reached out to win over a number
of Stonite ministers. Preacher Malcolm Worley, upon
becoming a convert, enthusiastically gave the society an
estate of five thousand acres. This tract formed the basis of
the main Shaker community west of the Alleghenies—
Union Village—which was founded near Lebanon, Ohio,
in 1805. Five other Stonite clergymen subsequently suc-
cumbed.[15] Of these, Richard McNemar's defection on
April 23, 1805, was the most significant. His congregation, like many of the others, also transferred their
allegiance. Thus camp meeting revivalism is inextricably
involved with the beginnings of Shakerism on the western
frontier.

McNemar waited but five days to hold his first encampment under new auspices. The ubiquitous missionaries
were on hand to assist in the preaching. A group of
Stonites journeyed from Springfield to the Turtle Creek
church to show the wayward members their folly and to

discredit the preaching there. The invaders soon made the campground a lively place. By no stretch of the imagination could the meeting be said to have contributed to interdenominational love and understanding. Again was demonstrated the camp meeting's ability to promote church discord. Issachar Bates, one of the Shaker spokesmen, described the hectic scene:

A great body of blazing hot New Lights with John Thompson . . . a preacher at their head determined to break down all before them. Thompson mounted the stand and began his preachment and undertook to show how much they had been imposed on by deceivers. . . . Now these Eastern men had come to tell us that Christ had made his second appearance, but they are liars, they are liars, they are liars. . . . For about half an hour it was one steady cry, glory to Jesus, glory to Jesus, glory to Jesus, and almost every other noise. . . . I was ordered back to the hell from whence I came and called all the bad names that they could think of. After the noise began to cease I stepped off the log and passed through the multitude and as I passed they cried out, see how his conscience is seared, as with a hot iron, he does not regard it at all.[16]

Although a few other encampments were held by the Shakers during 1805, once their new community at Union Village was firmly established they saw little need for more of them. Yet if these new western followers of "Mother Ann" abandoned the institution abruptly, their worship practices in Ohio retained vestiges of the camp meeting: bodily exercises sometimes broke out in the "Meeting House" and summer services were held in a forest grove which the Shakers picturesquely named "Jehovah's Chosen Square."[17]

The Cumberland Presbyterians, a product of the third schism in western Presbyterianism, utilized the forest revival far longer than either of the previously described splinter groups. Unfortunately, like the others they have little record of their camp meeting experiences; but the fragmentary evidence does reveal in outline a story of growth and decline, a story that was to be familiar elsewhere. "Father" Finis Ewing, a man inspired by James McGready's fervid and effectual preaching, set up and developed congregations in Kentucky and Tennessee during the years 1810-19, holding encampments "everywhere." When the Cumberland Presbyterians carried their proselyting campaign northward into the Old Northwest, the camp meeting was still proving an effective weapon for them. They frequently used the forest revival as an opening wedge in a campaign to create a church where none existed. As early as 1817 two Cumberland Presbyterian ministers appeared in southern Illinois. There, at Edwardsville, William Barnett and Green P. Rice staged a successful encampment on a Methodist campground. A Cumberland Presbyterian congregation came into being there as a result.[18]

At other times the establishment of a church preceded rather than followed a Cumberland Presbyterian camp meeting. This was the case when the first Cumberland Presbyterian encampment was held in Pennsylvania close by the Washington church in September, 1831.[19] The illustrious name of James McGready, founder of the camp meeting, is to be found high on the rolls of this meeting's sponsors. McGready, although associated with the group only a limited time, did noble work. In the fall of 1818 he had reported camp meeting successes from southwestern Indiana. At an Evansville encampment he declared: "I feel this day the same holy fire that filled my soul sixteen years ago, during the glorious revival of 1800."[20] Other outstanding Cumberland Presbyterian proponents of the camp meeting were John Morgan, R. D.

Morrow, and John Carnahan, to mention but a very few.

Late in the second decade of the nineteenth century and especially during the third decade, camp meetings were at the peak of their popularity within the Cumberland Presbyterian denomination. Then summer encampments were a regular feature. Finis Ewing described a Lebanon, Tennessee, encampment of June, 1818, as "literally a gospel sweeping shower." Working his way through Kentucky the next year, he was equally enthusiastic: "We have had and will have more camp meetings this season than any before since we were a Presbytery."[21] The open-air revival continued to be a success in the border South. In 1823 Mercer County, Kentucky, alone had five camp meetings in August; "powerful" encampments were reported from Tennessee, North Carolina, and Pennsylvania at the same time.[22]

By the mid-thirties the camp meeting device began to lose prestige among the Cumberland Presbyterians. Even camp meeting advocates wrote articles on the necessity of more careful management at encampments in order to avoid losing support among the parishioners. Friends of the revival expressed the hope that it was only a temporary setback, but the camp meeting "died a lingering death" in the Cumberland Presbyterian denomination during the years preceding the Civil War as successive encampments yielded proportionately fewer and fewer converts.[23]

Camp meeting revivalism was in part responsible for still another schism, this time in the German Reformed Church. In 1828 the Reverend John Winebrenner, a bilingual pastor of several small churches in western Maryland and eastern Pennsylvania, was excluded from his Harrisburg pulpit because of evangelistic activities. Expulsion led not to less evangelism on his part but to more, for he then became a roving gospel preacher. Winebrenner's oratorical talents combined with ardent zeal insured his success. In 1830 he founded a new denomination, "The General Eldership of the Churches of God in North America." Throughout his traveling ministry in central and western Pennsylvania he conducted many revivals, often uniting with the Methodists in camp meetings and in protracted indoor "prayer meetings."[24] His championship of revivalism and his staging of Winebrennerian camp meetings, which had already cost him a pastorate, continued to cause him to be castigated in print by conservative-minded theologians of the German Reformed Church. Too often, they claimed, participants at Winebrenner's gatherings surrendered themselves to the full sway of their emotions. And what was worse, only a barren crop of spurious conversions was harvested![25]

Other religious groups took to the woods upon occasion. Followers of William Miller, the millennial prophet, held frenzied camp meetings in preparation for the fast approaching Judgment Day. Miller's bizarre predictions had first scheduled the awesome event for March 21, 1843. Millerite forest services of that time in the eastern and middle states had little in common with the camp meetings of the other denominations unless it was in the degree of religious enthusiasm and moral earnestness. A hymnal published by this Adventist group during its brief heyday for use in "Prayer and Camp Meetings" remains a reminder of this ephemeral, frenetic movement.[26]

After the close of the Kentucky Revival, the Baptists, participants in the "General Camp Meetings," limited their use of the camp meeting technique to the annual meetings of the local "Baptist Associations," made up of several adjacent churches joined in voluntary union. At these Baptist Association sessions the delegates convened in the woods for worship and social companionship, remaining together for as long as three days. The gatherings with their large crowds and turbulent services closely resembled the Methodist camp meeting, for it was a "reviving time" of religion. By the late 1830's, however, the Baptists had perfected the "protracted meeting" device, which eventually again carried the revival indoors. Yet individual Baptist churches occasionally held encampments, as the Ohio, Indiana, and Mississippi record of the 1840's indicates.[27]

Camp meetings were carried on by a great number of denominations, large and small, in many backwoods vales. Their influence was evident in varying degrees in an afterglow reaching to the middle forties. The changing role that the camp meeting played in the economy of some sects in the West has already been delineated. Yet all these revival tangents were relatively insignificant when measured against Methodist utilization of the forest revival. By 1825 the camp meeting was almost exclusively a Methodist institution. One anonymous contemporary, a vitriolic critic of Asbury's followers, insisted that they "are accountable to the world and to their eternal judge for actually furnishing the occasion of [the evils] . . . by camp meetings."[28]

5

The Camp Meeting Matures

*My continual cry to the Presiding
Elders is order, order, good order. All
things must be arranged, Temporally
and Spiritually, like a well disciplined
army.*[1]
— *Bishop Francis Asbury, 1805*

At the same
time that the Presbyterians were discontinuing the camp
meeting, the Methodists were beginning to take it to their
hearts as their own. Under their sponsorship it reached its
harvest time. Actually, however, the outdoor revival was
never an "official" practice of the Methodist Episcopal
Church. No church body ever adopted it; no laws were ever
passed concerning it. There is no mention of this revival
weapon in the Journal indexes of the general conferences,
and but few references to it are to be found in the annual
conference reports between 1800 and 1845. Nor do the
many editions of the *Methodist Discipline* contain any
rules to govern the camp meetings. Circuit riders never
answered any formal questions concerning it in the quarterly conference.[2]

If further evidence were needed as to the official position of the Methodist church, there are the statements of
outstanding camp leaders on the subject. Jesse Lee commented in 1809:

Indeed these meetings have never been authorized by the Methodists, either at their general or annual conferences. They have been

81

allowed of; but we, as a body of people, have never made any rules or regulations about them; we allow them when and where they please, and to conduct them in what manner they see fit.[3]

Thomas A. Morris, editor of the *Western Christian Advocate,* similarly insisted that encampments were "not a part of the regular work prescribed in the rules of the church." Rather, they served as mere supplementary features of the Methodist system. He went on to list the advantages to the church and its workers of this freedom from official control: "Everyone is left free to say or write what he thinks on the subject, without being censured for inveighing against any rule in our church."[4] The way was made clear not only for constructive criticism of camp meeting practices but also for individual preachers to improvise new revival measures, many spiritually of a questionable nature. This freedom of action frequently ran over into license when some of the more flamboyant leaders attempted to add verve and excitement to achieve wholesale conversions.

The Methodists did not invent the camp meeting technique, and they never brought it under the supervision of their central legislative machinery. Nevertheless, the adopted child received loving care and became an integral part of the Methodist system. The American head of the church, Bishop Francis Asbury, who had played such an active role in the forest revival's formulative period, remained one of its staunchest advocates, which perhaps accounts for the fact that the open-air revival maintained its influence among Methodists long after the other major denominations had dropped it. Asbury spoke for himself as well as for his co-workers when he declared, "The Methodists are all for camp-meetings; the Baptists are for public baptizings."[5]

How fully Bishop Asbury appreciated the tremendous

popularity of the youthful revival can readily be seen in his *Journal* and letters. Every year his tour on horseback took him from the Methodist strongholds in the East in a wide circle through the expanding circuits in the West. These personal contacts were augmented by letter reports from the elders; thus, as principal overseer, he was remarkably well informed. The first time Asbury met the camp meeting institution was in October, 1800, when he and Bishop McKendree preached at the Presbyterian Drake's Creek meeting in Tennessee. But it was not until 1802 that he called such an occasion by the generic name of "camp meeting." Then he rejoiced that "the South Carolina and Georgia camp-meetings have been blessed to the souls of hundreds, and have furnished members to the Methodists, Presbyterians, and Baptist churches."[6]

Asbury well understood the need for a religious agency on the frontier that would carry the Word to great masses of people. In 1802 that need was partially met, for he said: "I think well of large meetings, camp and quarterly meetings. . . . We may hope for great things in the nature of things."[7] He urged the eastern Methodists to follow the western lead, advising them to build campgrounds for conference meetings, and to introduce camp meetings into all the eastern states. The initial efforts were successful, for the pioneer church leader stated in December, 1805, that his "northern letters" had brought news of many successful encampments in New York, Vermont, New Hampshire, and Virginia.[8] Two years later camp meeting enthusiasm was still running high in the East, as Asbury confided to the Reverend Elijah Hedding:

Mark well. I have either seen or heard, directly or indirectly, from most of the thirty-five Districts but some official letters are not come to hand. But from what I have collected, camp-meetings are as common now as Quarter meetings were twenty years back in many Districts, happy hundreds have been converted; in others happy thousands. Glory! Glory! Glory! Reputable report says, in the East of Maryland, last August, camp-meetings lasted eighteen days, 2,500 or 3,000 converted. Oh doubt not, the good news you bring will come to be general.[9]

As far as the Methodists were concerned the real testing ground for the new technique was in the East. It was not until August, 1807, that references to camp meetings in the West begin to appear in any number in the pages of Asbury's *Journal*. In that year and the next, the General Superintendent himself spoke at woodland gatherings in western Pennsylvania, Ohio, Kentucky, and the eastern region. In 1809 he rode the Ohio circuits during the mild months of August and September, and observed:

It appears that the bishops [elders] will hold a camp-meeting in every district; we are encouraged so to do: great power was manifested here, and much good was done. I will not say how I felt, nor how near heaven.[10]

About the same time the "pioneer bishop" confided to his *Journal*: "I pray God that there may be twenty camp-meetings in a week, and wonderful seasons of the Lord in every direction." It must surely have pleased him to receive the report from the presiding elders in the Western Conference that over seventy camp meetings were held that summer in their area alone.[11]

In sponsoring the woodland Bethels, Asbury revealed his resourcefulness, his indifference to narrow regulations, and his disregard of orthodox preaching style. But championship did not imply categoric acceptance of all the ramifications fanatical enthusiasm might bring about. While on his annual tour in 1809 he wrote to a fellow-itinerant:

Camp-meetings, camp-meetings, Oh Glory! Glory! But I fear a backsliding among the professors, and some sudden conversions, not sound or not lasting and many Methodist families have neither the form nor power of goodness! Yea, practical religion is pretty wanting. I have started for 2000 miles by Cincinnati to Charleston, there you will meet me with a letter if you get in a good harvest this fall in camp-meetings.[21]

Asbury's plans for 1810 were focused upon the attainment of "600 camp-meetings and thousands converted." This goal was largely realized, for in the year following he estimated that four to five hundred meetings were held.[13] By that year, his fortieth in America, the Methodist society had grown from 500 in 1771 to 86,734 in 1802, and 185,000 in 1811.[14] His faith in the forest revival was still strong, for he could happily announce:

Great and gracious signs follow our meetings at our annual conferences, our quarterly meetings and encampments. Never before did I witness such scaffolding for the divine building among us as there is at present. . . . The Camp-meetings provide a general blessing to both preachers and people.

At about the same time he wrote to circuit rider Jacob Gruber that camp meetings were held in practically every state of the Republic.[15] Even Asbury's optimism, however, could scarcely have envisioned the six hundred or more such meetings held throughout the country in 1816, the year of his death, and the nearly one thousand encampments in 1820.[16]

To Asbury's guiding genius can be attributed the fact that the camp meeting emerged as such an acceptable religious weapon, while at the same time preserving much of the spirit and fervor of the Cumberland Revival. "The outrider" affirmed that with such a method wonders could be accomplished. His statement was almost a command: "I believe, after we have established the credit of camp-meetings and animated the citizens, we must storm the devil's strongholds."[17] Thus it was that the Methodists consciously strived to erase the stigma that had been attached to the revival since the wild excesses in Kentucky and Tennessee. Under their management, the camp meeting experienced its harvest time, when conversions were plentiful and when membership in the church was mushrooming.

The keynote of the Methodist way was planning. Nothing was left to chance, from the scheduling of the meetings and their advertisement to the sharing of duties among the camp leaders and management of the camp services.

Mother Nature helped the churchmen in establishing a camp meeting season; when the weather was mild and sunny the open-air revival could flourish. Encampments were popular across the nation throughout the entire warm season of the year; but a meeting planned for the free interval after the wheat and hay harvests were in, and before corn-cutting time, could be assured of a much better attendance. Then, too, if the revivals were held in August and September, before the annual reports were due on the number of converts gained in each circuit, the preacher could undoubtedly present a list of new communicants that would impress his superiors.[18] Churchmen were also aware that if too many meetings were held in any one area the effectiveness of the device would be reduced.

The number of camp meetings staged each year depended largely upon the itinerant himself, the density of population, and the degree of enthusiasm among the settlers. Individual preachers co-operated in union-circuit meetings, and within a single circuit. By 1806 it became a fixed custom for the last quarterly conference to be held as an encampment.[19] This "yearly camp meeting," at which circuit business was handled, was always attended by the presiding elder of the district. Just as popular was the annual conference camp meeting, which likewise augmented the purely local ones.

"As was then the almost universal practice in the West," the 1808 Western Conference at Liberty Hill in Tennessee was held as a camp meeting.[20] The juxtaposition of revival time and conference time was a logical arrangement offering many tangible advantages. An army of preachers was on hand, including the very best speaking talent available—famous personalities who could attract hundreds from miles around. Various church leaders could compare notes as to service routines and could pick up new ideas. Many a circuit rider left the campground spiritually uplifted, full of zeal to resume his arduous labors for another year.[21]

The annual camp meetings came to be looked upon as great social events, and many a family organized their farm tasks so that they could make the yearly trek to the old campgrounds. But even the "extra occasions in the economy of Methodism" were advertised well in advance by their sponsors. News of them reached the settlers several weeks and even more than a month ahead of meeting time. In the religious newspapers of the 1820's announcements appeared thirty days prior to an encampment date. Only rarely were such notices printed in the secular press. One such example, the Ohio *Delaware Patron's* advertisement in 1823 of a four days' camp meeting "to be holden on the lands owned by Col. Moses Byxbe," carried the admonition: "Brethren will make preparations for their own accommodations on the ground."[22]

The good word was also spread by the itinerant as he went from cabin to cabin on his regular rounds or by

correspondence with those he could not visit. Often meeting notices tacked to trees bordering the road to the
encampment served to guide the worshipers on their
way. A camp announcement in Whitewater County,
Indiana, during 1809 threatened disorderly persons with
a fine of $3.00 to be imposed by the Justice of the Peace.
Not appreciating the warning, one pioneer paraphrased it
into a popular bit of doggerel whose every stanza ended
with the admonition "three dollars fine!"[23] Early notifica-
tion by one or all of these means was necessary to insure
a successful meeting, for anticipation increased attendance.

Shortly after the end of the Cumberland Revival, adherents of Methodism in the Midwest began the practice
of donating land for the use of the campers. As a result,
encampments soon bore the name of their benefactors,
such as "Baxter's Camp Ground" and "Pierce's Grove"
in Illinois, "Windell's Camp Ground" and "Turner's
Camp Ground" in Ohio, "Windrow's Camp Ground" in
Tennessee, and "Tait's Chapel Camp Ground" in Alabama.[24] One donor, a Mr. Winchell, provided the ground
and most of the pasturage for the transient livestock and
horses, by turning them into his meadow. He also set up
a large tent where a great number of visitors were fed
and lodged.[25] When queried whether he did not worry
about the loss of his pasture grass, the Methodist layman
replied: "The Lord makes the grass grow as fast as it is
eaten off." Not only the faithful, but "respectable world-
lings" let the campers use their land. In some cases semi-
permanent installations (preacher's stands and seats)
were built on the farmer's land. In all the more settled
regions, however, the trend was toward permanent camp
installations maintained by "Camp Meeting Associa-

tions"; many of these lasted for decades after the Civil War.[26]

As time passed, the length of the forest revival became relatively fixed. Four-day camp meetings, beginning on Friday afternoon or evening, taking advantage of the Sunday crowds, and continuing until Monday noon, became the rule.[27] During the early revival the term "four days' meeting" was synonymous with "camp meeting," and by the 1830's the phrase "protracted meeting" was also used to describe this evangelical device.[28] Six-day meetings, however, were not uncommon, and in the East some encampments were even held for eight or nine days. Possibly more camp meetings could have been so extended, since the backwoodsmen enjoyed quantity in religion; but the saddlebag preachers were often worn out from the prolonged camp work, and circuit schedules had to be met.

In keeping with the Methodist system of supervision over the outdoor revival, duties were carefully apportioned among the camp leaders to achieve maximum effectiveness.[29] When the presiding elder was absent, the senior minister assumed the leadership. Work schedules were arranged in shifts so that some preachers slept while others labored in the pulpit "pouring hot shot into Satan's ranks."[30] Both traveling and "located" preachers were assigned speaking hours and places. Service leaders took their places on the speaker's stand, the exhorters were strategically located in the audience, and aides to the penitent stood waiting at the altar. This division of labor was based upon each man's specialty, for naturally the participating ministers were of uneven ability. The campers, on their part, could classify the orators by the hour of their appearance. There were the "eight o'clocks" and

the "eleven o'clocks." The former, the early morning leaders who might also lead the opening service of the camp
meeting on Friday night, were third-rate platform per-
formers. The "eleven o'clocks" were the "intellectual
Samsons of the occasion."[31]

Definite rules of order were adopted by individual revival leaders in the East as well as the West sometime
prior to 1809, making orderly proceedings realizable.[32]
While any schedule might be discarded when the "spirit
ran high," preventing the carrying out of a set plan, most
of the camp leaders devised camp codes that outlined the
order of service, retiring and awakening time, hours of
eating, and the prescribed rules of personal conduct.
Little is known of the exact origins of the regulations,
although Henry Smith claimed credit for devising "the
first rules I ever saw or heard on a camp ground," while
planning an encampment on a Virginia circuit in June,
1804.[33] Smith may rightly be considered the innovator of
Methodist camp rules, although as early as 1775 a Baptist
revivalist had drafted a similar set of regulations. John
Early, Methodist preacher, also presented himself as the
originator of Virginia Camp Rules in 1813.[34]

The "Order of Meeting" at a Wilson County, Tennessee, encampment of five days' duration in July, 1820,
is illustrative of the early nineteenth-century service
pattern:

Friday
    2 P.M. — Sermon, announcement of the order of meeting, and
                invitation to the altar.
    7 P.M. — Candlelight service and invitation to the altar.
Saturday
    5 A.M. — Prayers preceding breakfast.
    8 A.M. — Sermon, to be followed by another sermon or
                exhortation.
  11 A.M. —   ”   ”   ”

3 P.M. — Sermon, to be followed by another sermon or
        exhortation.
7 P.M. — Candlelight service.

Sunday

5 A.M. — Sunrise service.
8 A.M. — Sermon, to be followed by another sermon or
        exhortation.
10 A.M. —   "   "   "
11 A.M. —   "   "   "
             (no formal afternoon or evening services)

Monday

7 A.M. — Baptism and Sacrament of Lord's Supper
12 M.   — Sermon
             (no formal afternoon or evening services)

Tuesday

8 A.M. — Sermon
12 M.   — Meeting ended.[35]

Following Asbury's counsel "to be wise as serpents" in
the management of their meetings, energetic camp leaders
prescribed rules that covered every phase of activity.[36]
Nathan Bangs generalized on these particulars when he
listed the laws applicable in the 1830's:

1. The times of preaching are 10 o'clock, A.M., and 3 and 7
   o'clock, P.M., notice of which is given by the sound of a
   trumpet or horn at the preachers' stand.
2. The intermediate time between preaching is occupied in prayer
   meetings, singing, and exhortation.
3. In time of worship persons are prohibited from walking to and
   fro, talking, smoking, or otherwise disturbing the solemnities
   of the meeting.
4. All are required, except on the last night of the meeting, to be
   in their tents at 10 o'clock, P.M., and to arise at 5, A.M.
5. At 6 o'clock, A.M., they are required to take their breakfast,
   before which family prayer is attended in each tent occupied
   by a family.
6. In time of preaching all are required to attend, except one
   to take care of the tent.
7. That these rules may be observed, they are published from the
   stand, and a committee appointed to enforce them.

8. A watch is generally appointed to superintend the encampment at night, to keep order, to see that no stragglers are on the ground, and to detect any disorderly conduct.[37]

Through the printed and spoken word, camp rules were made known to the worshipers. They were announced from the speaker's platform at the initial session, sometimes circulated in broadsides, or perhaps read by respected laymen to the campers. Even the illiterates, of whom there were many in attendance, could not remain ignorant of the regulations. At one Kentucky meeting in 1806 the preacher posted the laws on trees along the road to the encampment.[38] That numerous other camp leaders followed the same practice is evidenced by the reference of one denominational opponent to the Methodists' "peculiar love of legislation" which compelled them to convert trees into "lettered pillars . . . inscribed with the twelve tables of a camp code."[39]

To preserve the religious impact of the forest revival while at the same time curbing the excesses of emotionalism proved to be a Herculean task, but one not impossible of attainment. There was less opportunity for meetings "as wild as an autumn storm" when camp rules forbade night-long services, and less opportunity for promiscuity when women were forbidden to leave the encampment after dark. Lamps, torches, and candles illuminated both the camp area and tent interiors through the night to prevent disorderly conduct; camp guards with distinctive armbands or "white peeled rods" (as Asbury suggested) toured the encampment to make sure that all visitors who had not provided tents for themselves were excluded until morning.[40] As the Prussian traveler Frederick von Raumer declared after noting the Methodists' efforts to eliminate the conditions under which licentiousness could flourish,

"And who can doubt but that they contend with all their strength against the irregularities which creep into these meetings, held by night as well as day."[41]

All these precautions to insure a truly orderly and religious meeting did not prevent historians from speculating as to the post-Great Revival's probable role in contributing to immorality. In the absence of concrete data, the question of the extent of immoral practices remains unanswerable. Little or no evidence has been uncovered to substantiate the cynic's canard that "more souls were made than saved at a camp meeting."[42] That is not to say, however, that sexual irregularities did not take place at later encampments. The woodland gathering was a product of the times. Frontier society was primitive; hard liquor, imbibed furtively, inflamed emotions. Crude extemporaneous sermons and exhortations of backwoods orators raised passions to a high pitch. "Wild-fire songs, processions, blowing of trumpets . . . and other imitations of military operations" made the participants feel that they were truly about to enter battle with the unbelievers.

Even some of the devout could understandably have thrown restraint to the winds when they became an integral part of such tumultuous crowds. A Methodist adherent declared in 1823 that the incidental evils "ought not to be attributed to the meetings themselves, but to the native wickedness of the human heart, which, pervading many individuals now collected together, appears in concentrated force."[43] For surely the dregs of society were there. The "profligate people flock to them for the worst of all purposes" and their influence was always felt.[44] The truth lies somewhere in between the blind insistence of the revival's sponsors that the services had nothing to do with the carnal acts that occurred there, that they "have a tendency to inspire a spirit of devotion," and the equally sweeping generalization of later-day writers that the emotional hysteria of the camp meeting was chiefly responsible for the disorderly practices.

To John Humphrey Noyes, the nineteenth-century eccentric philosopher who tried to reason out the close connection between emotional preaching and the breaking of the prevailing moral code, the conclusion was apparent that:

In the conservative theory of Revivals, this power [of God] is restricted to the conversion of souls; but in actual experience it goes, or tends to go, into all the affairs of life. . . . Religious love is the very near neighbor to sexual love and they always get mixed up in the intimacies and social excitements of Revivals. The next thing a man wants, after he has found salvation of his soul, is to find his Eve and his Paradise. A worldly wise man might say that these facts show that Revivals are damnable delusions, leading to immorality and disorganization of society. I should say they show that Revivals, because they are divine, require for their complement, a divine organization of society.[45]

But for the circuit riders, whose aim was solely to bring the wavering sinner into communion with God, and not to found a utopian community, the emotionalism engendered by the camp meeting had to be harnessed. Their own sense of self-restraint proved to be the keynote of the effort. Sound psychologists as well as showmen, they often curbed excesses by crude jokes, gibes, or anecdotes. Peter Cartwright declared: "The Methodist preachers generally preached against this extravagant wildness. I did it uniformly in my little ministrations, and sometimes gave great offense."[46]

As a result, one of the distinguishing characteristics of the woodland gathering's second phase of development, its maturity, was the lessening of bodily excitement. Much evidence exists to support the conclusion that physical manifestations of extreme excitement became the unusual at the backwoods revival after 1805. The proof lies both in the omission of reference to nervous affections and in the concrete statements of the men best qualified to know: the circuit riders themselves. Thomas S. Hinde, untiring reporter of western Methodism in its earlier years, did not make a single mention of "barking, running, jumping, or falling" taking place after the Great Revival.

Time after time reports of camp meetings appeared in the "Revival Intelligence" columns of the *Western Christian Advocate* from 1834 to 1844, carrying the same refrain: "Good order and solemnity prevailed throughout." Circuit rider William Capers, one of the later bishops of the Methodist Episcopal Church, South, noted in his "Autobiography" the vast difference three years of management made in the revival pattern of the Sumter District of South Carolina. In the 1802 and 1803 camp meetings "strange and unaccountable bodily exercises" prevailed, while

such exercises were scarcely, if at all, present among the same people at the camp-meeting of 1806. And yet this camp-meeting was not less remarkable ... for the suddenness with which sinners of every description were awakened.[47]

Sixteen years later, a camp meeting near Charleston was reported in the *Wesleyan Repository* as being attended by a large crowd "uncommonly attentive; and they were as orderly and decorous, with one or two exceptions, as if they had been in church." In the Frederick Circuit of Virginia, the Reverend Enoch George, conscious of the revival's bad reputation, reported late in 1804 that he was "encouraged to find, in most places, our jumping is changed to tears and prayers, groanings and supplications."[48]

If the jaundiced view of a Methodist itinerant of fifty years' service is accepted, the "jerks" were the peculiar property of the Kentucky and Tennessee settlers, some of whom journeyed north of the Ohio River after the Cumberland Revival and carried their strange habits with them.[49] Another veteran camper asserted flatly in 1873 that these manifestations of nervous affections "disappeared soon after . . . [the camp meeting] came under Methodist management or at least lost some of its distinctive features."[50]

The same changes were noted in other parts of the East as well. One participant, after attending some four gatherings in Pennsylvania and Maryland in 1823, declared:

Though I have been in the habit of attending camp-meetings for nearly twenty years, I have never seen so little disorder. The oldest and most vigilant managers have expressed the same opinion. This orderly behaviour has been accompanied, too, with a corresponding degree of seriousness and attention to the word.[51]

Fragmentary evidence in the Old Northwest and the Old Southwest is also of the same piece. Shaker missionaries from New York, no enemies of bodily excitement, while visiting southwestern Ohio in 1805 observed that

in Kentucky and Ohio the exercises have much abated, but in the lower parts of Tennessee, particularly Blount County . . . and also in the old Cumberland South of Kentucky . . . they are still prevalent, though not so much in the latter as in the former.[52]

In 1809 Henry Boehm wrote to a comrade in the ministry of "more than seventy great camp meetings" occurring that year in the Western Conference at which "good order and decorum prevailed." This statement was based upon reports received from the presiding elder of each district.[53] In Tennessee one camp leader of the Nashville District boasted a net gain of 1,305 members for the year 1820, adding:

The character of this revival is the least mixed with what is called irregularities or extravagancies [*sic*] of any that I ever saw. We have had nothing of what is called the *jirks,* or *dance* among us. The work of conviction in the hearts of the sinners has been regular, powerful, and deep . . . their rejoicing scriptural and rational.[54]

From the pastor's reports, bodily exercises formed a general pattern, with the unmarried women and young children most frequently affected. Jerking and falling seem to have been largely supplanted after 1805 by the more understandable "leaping" and "shouting" activities. Bodily exercises of course did occur at the later camp meetings, but the infrequency of their appearance underscores the change from the conditions of the Great Revival. In the relatively settled section of southeastern Indiana in 1830 the laughing exercise made a brief appearance at circuit rider Allen Wiley's camp meeting, and then disappeared almost as fast as it had materialized. Wiley, writing in the mid-1840's, remarked that one worshiper who had attempted to resist this nervous exercise was "well nigh thrown into the 'jerks' of a former day."[55]

So greatly had the revival changed, that in 1836 a Unitarian minister could denounce a Methodist encampment in Ohio for trusting "too much to sympathy . . . to a merely physical or nervous imitation," and yet cite as his only example the case of a girl who had fainted "from anguish of heart or fervor of devotion." Even a Presbyterian contemporary grudgingly reported that the camp meeting of that day was "reduced to some degree of order, and subject to specific regulations."[56]

Through these years the camp meeting had undergone many changes. Like a growing child to whom maturity adds dignity and grace, the forest revival exhibited a strangely sedate character after its boisterous infancy had passed. An ever evolving institution, it was intimately connected with the prevailing intellectual climate of the times. On successive frontiers it passed through three distinct phases of growth—primitive disorganization, orderly regulation, and gradual but inevitable decline. When the sponsoring community was new and raw, the meetings it held were largely unplanned, extremely disorderly, and highly emotional. Months and even years later the camp meeting might enter the institutional phase, distinguished by planning, more effective audience management, and a notable decline in emotionalism. Then the meetings were smaller and highly systematized as to frequency, length, procedure of service, and location. Both man and nature had effected this systematization; its attainment had been not only possible but unavoidable.

6

Methodist Harvest Time

Camp-Meetings! Camp-Meetings! The
Battle axe and weapon of war — it will
break down the walls of wickedness,
forts of hell.[1]
— Bishop Francis Asbury, 1811

W ITHIN ITS KEN-
tucky birthplace the camp meeting device which had been
engendered in the Great Revival faced an uncertain future. The rash of revivals had dissipated most of the
religious energy of the Kentuckians. In the central region
of the state the camp meeting had been practically abandoned by 1808, when two Methodist preachers tried with
little success to revive the practice. Ten years were to pass
before it regained its former utility there.[2] To add to the
Methodist worries, the Baptists appeared to be "opposing
and triumphing" on every hand. In spite of the defection
of some former friends of the revival, an 1819 encampment at Versailles, Kentucky, did produce good results.
Benjamin Lakin recorded in his "Journal":

The Lord visited us at our meeting. Sinners were convicted and
some converted — from this time our prospects began to be
better and a new society was raised about Seven miles from Town
— our Campmeeting I have reason to believe went to remove
much of the prejudice from the minds of the people in Town and
Country and appeared to lay a foundation for good to be done.[3]

At near-by Cynthiana, meanwhile, an 1818 camp meeting generated a religious upsurge which resulted in the

conversion of some four hundred persons. The presiding
elder of the district, Jonathan Stamper, told Methodist
historian Thomas S. Hinde that

it was almost impossible to conceive the good effects resulting
from this glorious *camp meeting*. Many of the young converts
began to preach; and several of them are now distinguished
travelling preachers. Subsequently, camp meetings have regained
their former standing in this part of the country.[4]

While the evidence concerning the state-wide use of the
revival weapon may be contradictory and inconclusive,
if the situation in the southwestern section was any cri-
terion the camp meeting had become an annual habit in
Kentucky by the early 1820's. Peter Cartwright, one of the
backwoods revival's champions, was put in charge of the
Cumberland District comprising some eight circuits in
southern Kentucky and northern Tennessee. Speaking of
a Logan County encampment of 1822, he declared that
here "camp-meetings started in modern times; and they
had been in progress for twenty-two years, every year
more or less."[5]

The camp meeting fires previously lighted in Kentucky
continued to burn brightly in section after section of the
new nation as the traveling ministry followed migrants
toward other frontiers. Some adventurous Methodist circuit riders had felt called to penetrate the Old Southwest,
while others from the Upland South were moving northward into the Ohio and western Virginia regions, bringing the revival weapon with them.

The camp meeting institution did not, however, experience parallel growth on a nation-wide scale. Being a part
of community life, it reflected the social forces at work.
At any one time it could exhibit maturity in one area and
primitive disorganization in another. Thus while only a

few isolated cases of "falling" occurred at early Methodist encampments in Ohio,[6] the first camp meetings during the year 1807 in the Illinois region of the Indiana Territory near Edwardsville and Shiloh found "many present" affected with "that strange movement, the jerks" and "falling."[7] Earlier encampments held in Ohio by other sects when the country was less settled, however, were not noted for their sobriety. The tone of the forest revival was an accurate reflection of the population tide and level of social development of a particular region. As the environment of the pioneers grew less frustrating, so did the spirit of animal excitement at the camp meeting diminish.

Almost without exception, first encampments held in a newly settled area, whether in the Old Northwest or Southwest, displayed scenes of frenzy rivaling those of the Great Revival. In these first meetings, where vast and often disorderly crowds of backwoodsmen mingled, there were confusion, frenzied preaching, and an abundance of "muscular Christianity." In 1803, for example, during the high tide of the Kentucky Revival, the initial camp meeting in western Pennsylvania drew an enthusiastic crowd of three thousand. These worshipers were ministered to by fifteen traveling and located preachers. A major reason for the encampment's attraction in addition to the novelty of the occasion was that the indefatigable and ubiquitous Methodist leader, Francis Asbury, had promised to lead the meeting. From Asbury's hastily scribbled letter to a friend we get an intimate glimpse of the scene:

August 19, 1803 [Friday] This day I came to camp a very feeble man, the camps upon a most agreeable mount under a Noble Lofty Shade 2000 hears [hearers] at the sound of the trumpet came to the big stand; to hear the little preacher Francis, several have been striken 6 hopefully brought through oh there may be hundreds. This night General Fleming with many others will lodge in camp. . . . I hope we shall have 2 if not 3000 tomorrow. I am very unwell I mean to go and fire a Gun each Day and retreat. . . . Oh to see old men and old women dwelling in tents, the waggons and horses put away not a trifler upon the Ground but many fainting and falling for mercy. . . .

Monday 22. I preached again Corinth XV: 58 it was an open season the exercise continued. The greater part of the nights many powerfully striken we guess at near one hundred, how many converted we know not, several sermons, and exhortations by night and Day. . . . Great order was observed we had watchmen by Day and night to guard the camp. A poor Roman brought whiskey to give away but some of the guard secured his bottle. Tuesday the provisions of many families failed and [as] they had been 6 or 7 days from home, they struck their tents and moved their waggons, but as we were coming away many were coming.[8]

In this way did Asbury describe the enthusiastic response to the first camp meeting in that pioneer region — a response so overwhelming that even after seven nights and days of tumultuous services, the encampment was prolonged to accommodate the new arrivals.

In the Ohio Territory, although the first Methodist camp meeting held in 1804 had received only a lukewarm reception, the Deer Creek encampment staged four years later was in the true Kentucky tradition. An estimated 125 tents and wagons circled the grove. A battery of twenty-three preachers made ready to preach to some two thousand persons. Rainy weather did not halt the services, which continued night and day with "blessed results."[9] A contemporary church chronicler of the Mad River settlements described the years 1803-7 as difficult ones. Not until 1808 did the pioneers there have "an opportunity of spending their time profitably together, and camp meetings began." At one of these early encampments General Simon Kenton, celebrated fighter, hunter, and traveling companion of Daniel Boone, was "caught in the

Gospel net" after praying at the altar the whole night through.[10] Likewise, the first camp meeting southwest of Tennessee, held in the Mississippi Territory, was a rousing revival. At this December, 1804, meeting, the eccentric Lorenzo Dow presided. In his typical fashion he made the innovation a startling success by announcing from the speaker's stand that he had the latest authentic news from Hell.[11]

The initial woodland revivals held in the Illinois Circuit during the summer of 1807 were also marked by rampant enthusiasm. James Gwin, leader of the Three Springs camp meeting, was able to subdue certain "lewd fellows of the baser sort" who combined whiskey with their religion. Gwin's preaching and hymn singing at the three o'clock service penetrated the conscience of at least one of the drinkers, who ran up to the preacher entreating:

"Are you the man that keeps the roll?" I asked "what roll?" "That roll," he replied, "that people put their names to when they are going to heaven." I supposed that he meant the class-paper, and sent him to Brother Walker. Turning to Brother Walker, he said, "Put my name down, if you please," and then fell to the ground. Others started to run off, and fell; some escaped. We were busy in getting the fallen to one place, which we effected about sunset. . . . Looking around upon the scene, and listening to the sobs, groans, and cries of the penitents, reminded me of a battle-field after a heavy battle. All night the struggle went on. Victory was on the Lord's side; many were converted, and by sunrise the next morning there was the shout of a King in the camp.[12]

This same success story was repeated in the Indiana Territory six years after the first camp meeting there. At the Sunday morning worship session of a Christian Circuit encampment in 1813 Peter Cartwright reported "several hundred" falling in five minutes' time, a record rivaling that of the earlier exercises in Kentucky.[13] And so the pattern continued, as the circuit riders followed adventurous pioneers into new areas, holding primitive camp meetings whenever a substantial group of settlers were within riding distance of a camp site. In the Louisiana Territory the first camp meeting took place in 1806; in the Arkansas Territory, 1819; in the Michigan Territory, 1822; in the Minnesota Territory, 1836; and in the Wisconsin Territory, 1838.

Beyond the bald facts that old manuscripts, containing dates, names, and circumstances, can give us concerning the first camp meetings, certain themes can be read between the lines. Over and over again in the fragmentary reports certain years or months are recounted as "good years," "frustrating days," or "harvest times" of the camp meeting. Categorically, it can be stated that when new frontiers were being carved, the inscrutable forces of nature seemed almost to overwhelm man. He then turned instinctively to religion; his camp meetings, admirably suited to the primitive conditions of settlement, were frenzied and emotional. With a return to normalcy, his worldly nature resumed dominance. Thus in the early days of settlement unusual natural phenomena such as fierce storms and earthquakes influenced many to join a religious society. The superstitious pioneers believed such strange occurrences were not the result of natural forces, but the machinations of either a wrathful God or the devil. When a hurricane struck in the middle of a Chillicothe camp meeting in May, 1809, the preacher found his dire predictions for the sinners being reinforced. As the storm raged, John Sale preached on about the evils of horse racing, with the result that many were eager to confess Christ.

The young converts exhorted, shouted and sung the praises of their Redeemer amidst the raging elements, and the tumbling forests! whilst darkness and horror were on the brow of the enemies of the cross of Christ.[14]

The unprecedented earthquakes of 1811 and 1812 were a time of great terror to sinners. For almost four months the central Mississippi River region was subjected to recurrent shocks, numbering over a thousand in all. Brick houses cracked, chimneys toppled off, and yawning chasms opened up. Settlers hastened to atone for this visitation from God that had most certainly come as a punishment for their sins. An Indiana itinerant happily noted that "some men were converted and became preachers, whose conversion I had been in the habit of regarding as almost as hopeless as the conversion of the devil himself."[15] In Ohio scores of people flocked to church meetings who had previously paid no attention to the subject of religion.[16] Methodist membership in the Miami District doubled within the single year of 1812; the Baptists likewise reaped a harvest. Even if the conversions were short-lived, a startlingly auspicious beginning had been made in the new state. Fear may have been the precipitant, but the preachers made full use of nature's aid. This

work began and ended with earthquakes, in the counties; and the whole strain of preaching by the Baptists and Methodists was, that the end of all things was at hand, and if the people were not baptized, or did not join societies, there was no hope for them. . . . It is also a fact that many, who had joined their societies, have already left them. Some have been excluded from communion, and others are under censure.[17]

One preacher sadly noted that after the return to normalcy "half as many as our present membership" had become backsliders.[18] Natural catastrophes were always highly useful to the frontier soul-savers. Even as late as 1833 a burning comet dipping near the earth so that its tail was visible even by daylight caused great consternation. It was long remembered as "the year the stars fell." Considered prophetic of the end of the world, this striking phenomenon, like those of twenty years earlier, stampeded many into conversion. Camp meeting orators, influenced by millennial doctrines then popular, turned these happenings to good use. If divine intervention were to transform the world and establish the Kingdom of God on earth, let no man be unprepared![19]

Conversely, religious ardor was considerably diminished by the more tangible "agents of the Devil," the Indians and the British. From 1795 to 1812 the midwesterners lived in comparative peace with the partly dispossessed Indian tribes. The disturbing times leading up to the War of 1812 and the war itself hampered religious progress on the northwest frontier. Talk of Indian war councils sometimes kept the Ohio settlers on edge. Bishop Asbury commented in 1807 that the rumor of an expected attack by the red men had caused many inhabitants of that state to flee. Again, when itinerant Benjamin Lakin visited the Wyandots in Upper Sandusky town on a missionary tour in 1810, he learned the whites were feeling "considerable alarum in consequence of the Sinneca Indians and others, holding councils in the night ... [showing] an inclination to go to war with the Winedotts."[20] The tribes that allied with the British a few years later did make forays into southern Illinois. Some Methodists believed that missionizing would effect a change in the Indians' savage ways, but Lakin was skeptical; he had little hope that the plan under consideration for sending missionaries to live with them was feasible, for "Indians are much prejudiced against the Christian name." "And no wonder," continued Lakin; the evil practices of whites in robbing the Indians of land and fur, of undermining their character with drink so as to make the robbery easier, made missionary work among them seem hopeless. He suggested "no trade," urging instead frequent visits "to show them there was a difference between a Christian and a white man."[21]

The camp meeting did not escape the devastating impact of the War of 1812. For two years the Maumee River Valley in Ohio was a scene of hostilities, and war hysteria gripped circuit riders as well as the Methodist faithful. Lakin complained at the 1812 session of the Ohio Conference: "I felt my mind pained at the spirit of war that appeared in some of the Preachers. Three had left their circuits and gone—volunteers for thirty days in the army —But the Conference thought proper to give them [back] their stations."[22]

Attendance at the forest revivals, east as well as west, dropped off so sharply that few circuits planned on having their annual meetings. A spirit of patriotism rather than devotion prevailed. The impingement of war preparations was evident at Lakin's Strait Creek, Ohio, camp meeting in July, 1812. After the close of the first day's sessions,

a man came to call the people together to see who would volunteer to carry relief to DeTroit to our army who were in distressing circumstances. All that ensued was comotion. . . . [next day] We had but few to preach too, and not more than 20 or 30 to attend the sacrament.

Two days later the circuit rider lamented that "at my last camp and quarterly meeting, we were frequently interrupted by the returning volunteers: Yet some souls were converted." Undoubtedly there was excitement in the air, for on occasion a staff officer, such as General Meade, would mount the rostrum and order the soldiers to comply with the camp meeting rules.[23]

The outbreak of war had not hindered Bishop Asbury, however, from traveling six thousand miles in an eight-month period, supervising nine conferences, and attending ten outdoor revivals. He rigorously observed the principle he had laid down for his ministry "to be careful to preach to the soldiers, wherever opportunity offers."[24] Volunteer troops were marched in a body to the campgrounds. In September, 1812, Asbury addressed Marylanders at two forest meetings where five thousand and ten thousand persons had gathered. At a Uniontown, Pennsylvania, encampment his sermon concerning the evils of a nondefensive war was heard by a company of soldiers about to move on to the eastern front. Henry Boehm, a bilingual itinerant, was also busy giving camp sermons. His were delivered to German worshipers throughout the year 1812.[25] War might drastically alter the outdoor revival, but it did not change its primary goal—the saving of souls.

By the year 1815 lean times for the camp meeting were over. Summer encampments were a normal feature of Methodism in Ohio; Asbury reported that he personally attended five there that year. By the first year of peace the forest revival was again all-powerful in the young republic.

Wherever the camp meeting had sunk its roots, the character of the revival changed, almost magically. While the frontier stage of settlement was passing in a given area, the camp meeting techniques were taking on respectability. Reports of 1816 clearly indicated that Ohio encampments were reflecting the institutional stage of the outdoor revival. The greatest examples of excitement included only the customary loud prayers and songs, the groans of those under "the felt burden of guilt," the joyous shouts of the saved, and "the crying of youths." On the Pickaway Circuit, a chronicler noted that even with an all-night service "the order of this meeting was good." Local magistrates had aided by enforcing the ordinances against the rowdies.[26]

Methodism's rapid progress in this area can be charted in the multiplication of circuits and the increase in church membership. When the Western Conference was created in 1800 only three circuits existed in the Ohio Territory.[27] Then the total Methodist membership in the entire Northwest Territory was only 364 whites and 2 colored. By 1811, the year before the Western Conference was divided into the Ohio and Tennessee conferences, eighteen circuits had been formed in Ohio; the church's enrolment had grown to include 10,028 white and 76 colored communicants. Explanation for this phenomenal growth lay in the tireless activities of the itinerants and the rapid settlement of the state. In the ten-year period after 1800 the population had jumped from 45,365 to 227,843 persons.[28]

Most of the revivals north of the Ohio after 1815 were reported to be orderly affairs, where "the greatest decorum was observed." "Powerful times," however, still attended the encampments. "Notwithstanding the calls to farm and workshop" a White Oaks Circuit camp meeting of 1841 sparked such excitement that it continued for ten days.[29]

By 1829 the Pennsylvania backwoods revival had outgrown its frontier habitude. The southwestern area of the state had by then become a thickly populated region of considerable wealth; tenting had lost much of its old appeal. In the Pennsylvania camp meeting sociability had largely supplanted soul-saving as the primary interest. Camp leaders found it necessary to urge the campers to discontinue bringing their best beds, bedclothing, and gear, and to return to the frontier way of Spartan simplicity. Circuit rider Robert Boyd detailed this change in emphasis:

Great preaching was in high demand; and as a speedy reward, a good dinner, prepared *during the sermon,* was in waiting for the preacher as soon as the sermon closed. . . . There was usually a respectable group of visitors whose *only* business was to hear a good *sermon* and share a good dinner.[30]

As the population of Indiana grew from 24,000 in 1810 to 64,000 in 1818, and 348,000 by 1830, the camp meeting underwent alterations, settling into the customary pattern of annual encampments.[31] Allen Wiley noted:

There were two good camp meetings on the former camp grounds on the [Lawrenceburg] circuit this year [1817]. When, however, we say they were good, I could not be understood to say they would compare with the former meetings. There was much more preaching talent at those meetings than the former; but there was not the same zeal in the preachers or people.[32]

Although the passing of time may have altered certain aspects of the camp meeting, Indiana folk continued to be fascinated by this open-air religious technique. They still flocked to campgrounds in the 1820's and 1830's. Even the wintry winds of October could not quench the religious ardor at one meeting during this period. The worshipers had to build huge log fires to keep themselves from freezing.[33] The camp meeting tradition was firmly rooted in Hoosierland.

The Illinois country was filling up with people by 1809, and opportunities were increasing for the revival institution to spread throughout the new territory. In 1820 church leaders proudly announced the camp meeting season as especially prosperous, listing two or three encampments in each charge, at which "large numbers were converted."[34] With population skyrocketing from 12,282 in 1810 to 55,211 in 1820, civilizing forces affected the camp meeting.[35] Preacher William Beauchamp commented on the 1821 encampments in the Upper Wabash region. They were, he said,

remarkable in regard to seriousness, solemnity, and good order. In this respect I can truly say, that, although I have been at many camp-meetings, I never saw such as these before. We had no guard; and at the last meeting no rules, for the regulation of it, were published. We needed none. God was our defence and salvation. . . .

The presiding elder who attended this meeting, informed me that many camp-meetings had been held in this district, and that they had been generally blessed with great displays of divine power.[36]

Peter Cartwright's spritely reporting dispels the idea that all was peace and quiet at these camp meetings. As presiding elder of the Illinois District from 1825 to 1829 he had been leader of some lively sessions. He reminisced: "We always had good times; there was, however, considerable opposition and persecution" from the rowdies.[37]

In the decade of the thirties, the Michigan region, like the rest of the Lake Plains — northern Indiana and Illinois — was settled in a rush, mainly by migrants from New England and the Middle States. Whereas it had once been considered "poor, barren, sandy land on which scarcely any vegetation grows," a veritable "interminable swamp," the pioneers who followed the Erie Canal route of trade after it was opened in 1825 found the land anything but forbidding. With the expansion of population, conditions were ripe for the growth of the camp meeting. Michigan revival practice closely followed that of Illinois, Ohio, and Indiana; the encampments were sober in character, exhibiting the maturity stage in every aspect. In the pages of James Gilruth's daily *Journal* this pattern can be seen. When Gilruth presided over the quarterly conference held as a camp meeting in 1835, representing the co-operative efforts of the three circuit leaders from Ann Arbor, Tecumseh, and Ypsilanti circuits, he made the following observations:

Frid June 5. . . . Reached Home about 3 P.M. as the afternoon was showery I concluded to remain at home and not attend our Camp Meeting till next day —

Sat June 6 Rose a little after day — as soon as convenient I set out with my familey for camp meeting — reached there about 9 — during Morning sermon — our qM conference was held at 1 P.M. in which Joseph Smith a local Pr was expelled for sowing and maintaining unitarianism and enveighing against disciplines—while q conference (for Ann Arbour cir) was in session Dr. Sayre preached and conducted a Prayer M in wich 7 or 8 experienced peace. From this time the work began to advance — Day cloudy and some rain — to bed about 12.

Sund June 7 Rose about 5 — preached at 8 from luke xiv: 16-24. There was much people on the ground today — the good work was powerfull at night — day cloudy — to bed say 2 A.M.

Mond June 8 Rose about 5 took a vote of the people concerning continuing meeting till Tusd which was carried — a good work to day and to night — some rain in the morning — day cloudy — to bed about 2 A.M.

Tusd June 9 Rose about ½ past 5 — About 10 our camp meeting closed. A fairwell sermon and the reception of Members . . . there were it was supposed between 40 and 50 converted — some also professed sanctification — We had some disagreeable wether in the fore part of the Meeting: but we had verry little disturbance from the Ungodly — This meeting will tell in eternity.[38]

By 1838, if not before, the outdoor revival institution had become accepted in all the areas of the Old Northwest. Permanent campgrounds dotted the landscape, and annual encampments were held universally. The whole section, with a population of 4,500,000, was passing beyond the frontier stage by 1850, with the exception of northern Michigan and Wisconsin.[39]

In the Old Southwest, however, primitive religious conditions prevailed generally until 1860 in the half-circle of states that girdled Kentucky and Tennessee to the south in the trans-Allegheny West. Without permanent church buildings, many rural localities were served only by itinerants. As late as 1849 the Methodists in the Old Southwest had 1,476 traveling preachers as compared to 3,026 located preachers. Naturally, the camp meeting was a popular device; since the winters were mild there was never an end to the camp meeting season. As the region of the Great Appalachian Valley, covering parts of eight states, was not economically and topographically an entity, so the forest meetings held there cannot be generalized to fit a single mold. Where slaveholding was not a prominent feature of the culture pattern, different social classes were dominant: the tradesmen, yeomen farmers, and poor whites. The local revival was adapted to the character of the audience at the same time that it cut across class lines. The camp meeting proved to be a common denominator, appealing to all but the class-conscious who viewed the democratic gospel of Methodism with contempt.[40]

There was a distinctively western flavor to these religious efforts, although the slavery institution made certain alterations in the national revival pattern inescapable. In the slaveholding sections the masters were encouraged to bring their slaves with them to the camp meeting. Benjamin Lakin, for example, thought of the slaves' welfare first when it was suggested that Sunday camp services be discontinued because of the disorder on that day.

It would "effectively cut off the Black people from the benefits of the meeting which I think ought never to be done," said Lakin.[41] Most of the slave owners were of the opinion that religious instruction would keep their workers servile and obedient. And as for the bondsmen, there was no question of their love for camp meetings.

By no class is a camp meeting hailed with more unmixed delight than by the poor slaves. It comes at a season of the year when they most need rest. It gives them all the advantages of the ordinary holiday, without its accompaniments of drunkenness and profanity . . . they can jump to their hearts' content.[42]

Largely unplanned, Negro participation in the white camp meetings was usually spontaneous. Slave camp services received official notice in 1846 when the recommendation was made by the Methodist Episcopal Church, South that prayer meetings for slaves should be conducted back of the pulpit by one or more of the regular preachers, with the aid of colored leaders when available.[43] This procedure had been generally followed, and sometimes a board fence made the segregation more definite. In an 1834 camp meeting, while the services were being conducted, the Negroes separated themselves and

sought their own preacher and anxious seat. A stand was presently fixed between two trees; a preacher was seen, appearing and disappearing between them, as his violent gesticulation caused him to lean backwards or forwards. The blacks had now things to their mind, and they pressed round the speaker, on their feet or their knees, with extended hands, open lips and glistening eyes. . . .

As the scenes on either side the stand were not dumb-show the evil was, that the voices of the parties speaking met each other, and made confusion; and as either party raised his voice to remedy the evil, it became worse.

At another encampment a camp official tried vainly on two successive days to convince a group of slaves that

AN UNUSUALLY
sedate Methodist camp meeting in the backwoods, *circa* 1849.
From B. W. Gorham's *Camp Meeting Manual, A Practical Book
for the Camp Ground,* Boston, 1854.

their "convulsive outbursts [were] wrong, and disturbing both to themselves and others." Irrepressible as they were in their expression of religious feelings, the Negroes never seemed to feel entirely free to work in their own way until the white people closed their services and went to their tents. In a Georgia meeting when the 10:00 P.M. curfew had been sounded, and after the altar fires had burned low and the smoke hung in mists over the trees, from the other encampment

the singing of hymns still ascended, though much lower; still the class-leaders exhorted; . . . Some oppressed souls still lay bowed upon the counter and still were the preachers giving consolation either by word or song.

The slaves gradually dispersed and carried on individual penance in the tents. They pounded their chests, cried out with great pathos, and danced the "holy dance," although the last was forbidden by the preachers.[44]

Legislation was passed after the Nat Turner insurrection of 1831 in Virginia which forbade separate meetings, but this rule was only temporarily observed.[45] Indoor meetings and outdoor gatherings, held separately and in conjunction with the whites, permitted the slave to express himself in his own manner. Revivalism gave to the Negro a rare opportunity to express his higher life, an opportunity denied him in most other spheres. Socially and psychologically it gave him release.

The religious behavior of the slaves centered around the preacher, the music, and the frenzy.[46] The pastor was usually one of their own, a bondsman or a "free citizen of color" who received his piecemeal training from a master, from attendance at church services, or from the white clergy. Plantation Negroes were usually allowed to hold prayer meetings twice a week in addition to Sunday services, and on certain plantations Methodist and Baptist ministers were allowed to preach to them. Henry Francis of Georgia and "Preacher Jack" of Virginia were fortunate enough to have their freedom purchased by white ministers who recognized their unique oratorical talents.[47] As early as 1800 the Methodists provided for ordination of local Negro deacons where colored churches were established. By 1824 traveling Negro preachers were authorized.[48]

Exhorting in their own idiom, the Negro churchmen led their flocks in devastating attacks upon sin. One concluded a "Religious Testimony" meeting with this personal experience:

Some eleven years ago, I came to de old camp-ground (pointing his finger) down yonder in the bottom, in de devil's barge (meaning a canal boat). As we come in de range of de guns of Zion, dey give us a broadside. I was wounded and fell overboard; but dey sent out de lifeboat, and took me aboard the old ship Zion; and I bless God, I on de old ship yet, and I spect to stay dar till she ride safe into harbor.[49]

Immediately after his speech, the preacher began to sing the song "Old Ship Zion," in a "full and sonorous tone of voice." The audience could not be restrained; a "universal shout of triumph rolled up to heaven."

The principal characteristic that made the Negro camp song unusual was the pattern of delivery. The statement of a theme by a leader was repeated by a chorus, or a choral phrase was balanced as a refrain against a longer melodic line. It "may be affirmed that . . . they are beautiful, childlike, simple, and plaintive: they are the Negroes' own songs." The passionate ardor with which they were sung made the songs "melodious, burning sighs." Dramatic bodily gestures accompanied the singing:

These are all sung in the merry chorus-manner of the southern harvest field, or husking frolic method of the slave blacks; and also very greatly like the Indian dances. With every word or so sung, they have a sinking of one or the other leg of the body alternately; producing an audible sound of the feet at every step and as manifest as the steps of actual negro dancing in Virginia. If some in the meantime sit, they strike their hands alternately on each thigh.[50]

A combination of primitive persons of little or no education, the Negro revival-spiritual, and the "Hell Fire" oratory of a son of thunder resulted in instances of bodily excitement at the slave encampments. The tide of enthusiasm on the Negro side of the campground would mount and intensify, reaching its climax on the last evening when the rules regarding a curfew for the slaves were generally suspended. All night the hymns poured forth: "Roll, Jordan, Roll," "O' Sinner, Run to Jesus," "Hark, From the Tomb the Doleful Sound," and many others.

When a thousand negroes keeping time with foot and hand, with arms and body, poured out their souls upon the night air in a camp meeting chorus . . . the weird and solemn grandeur and grotesqueness were indescribable.[51]

The services were most frenetic when shouts of "Amen!" "Hallelujah!" "Help, Lord!" "Send the Power, Lord!" "Only hear that!" "Is all that a-coming sure enough?" and more unintelligible plaints for salvation would roll like thunder from the bondsmen's section. Bodily exercises followed:

A sort of suppressed terror hung in the air and seemed to seize us . . . that lent terrible reality to song and word. The black and massive form of the preacher swayed and quivered as the words crowded to his lips and flew at us in singular eloquence. The people moaned and fluttered, and then the gaunt cheeked brown woman beside me suddenly leaped straight into the air and shrieked like a lost soul, while round about came wail and groan and outcry, and a scene of human passion such as I had never conceived before.

Those who have not thus witnessed the frenzy of a negro revival in the untouched backwoods of the South can but dimly realize the religious feeling of the slave; as described, such scenes appear grotesque and funny, but as seen they are awful.[52]

Too much credence, however, should not be given the reports of the visiting foreign travelers whose genteel prejudices hampered their objectivity. Too often their observations are the only written records of the slave camp meetings. Being largely illiterate, the Negro participants themselves were not able to record their impressions. There is no reason to believe the meetings would have been allowed by the slave owners if no control over the proceedings were possible. Nor would religious instruction have been continued if some beneficial results had not been seen. To what degree the moral preachments were understood and observed is, of course, debatable. One famed northern traveler, after conscientiously studying southern religious efforts, concluded:

I have not been able to resist the impression, that even where the economy, safety, and duty of one sort of religious education of the slaves is conceded, so much caution, reservation, and restriction is felt to be necessary in their instruction, that the result in the majority of cases has been merely to furnish a delusive clothing of Christian forms and phrases to the original vague superstition of the African savage.[53]

A sensitive European visitor, however, was much impressed by the fact that most of those who had been converted at camp meetings and who subsequently had joined a class continued to remain orderly members of society.[54]

The story of the spread of the camp meeting from section to section would not be complete without the mention of the outdoor services held by another component of American society, the Indians. Indian missions were part and parcel of the Methodists' crusading zeal, and it became the practice to hold camp meetings at the settlements. The first Indian mission had started the trend. After the Ohio Conference took over the Sandusky Valley, Ohio, mission started by John Stewart, a freeborn Virginia mulatto, the task of supervising it fell to James B. Finley. From 1819 on Finley's camp meeting innovation met with success.[55] In the South even earlier circuit riders had extended a welcome to various tribes that were camped near the revival sites. In 1807 Jacob Young had successfully incorporated Choctaws in southwest Mississippi camp meetings. Before that tribe was pushed west, religious encampments were conducted among them from 1828 to 1834. Red men became missionaries to their own people as well as converts. William Winans Oakchiah was admitted on trial at the Mississippi Conference in 1831, and continued to preach the white man's religion for years.[56]

Falling, jerking, and holy dancing made some of their meetings as frenzied as those held during the Kentucky Revival, and this in spite of the Indians' reputed stolidity. However, most reports of Indian camp meetings stress the serenity of the atmosphere and the attentiveness of the participants. The Shawnee Methodist Mission camp meeting of 1843, for example, combined eloquence with an inspiring pastoral setting. A migrant to the Missouri frontier from North Carolina wrote home his impressions:

I visited on Monday last — this is Wednesday — an Indian Methodist camp meeting about 20 mile from here Independence. If I had of gone on sunday I should have been more interested as I should have seen a much larger crowd however as it was I saw much — very much — to please. The first sermon in the morning was preached by a white man — one sentence at a time — and interpreted by an Indian who was decidedly the better orator of the two. After this a large Indian man of fine appearance preached for about 15 or 20 minutes and as far as I could judge — saving a little to much ranting — preached well and eloquently. I was very sorry not to be able to understand there language. The whole was concluded by a sermon and a prayer from an Indian woman of about 40 who had no scarcity of words to express every thing she wished. Strange indeed was the scene. Stretching out west for thousands of miles was the beautiful prairie dotted with herds of horses and Cattle and occasionally a company of Indians. To the East might be seen beautiful Indian farms in a high state of cultivation and only a short distance from us flowed the waters, collected from a thousand streams, of the mighty Missourie and to crown the whole in a clump of trees where the camp ground was situated was worshiped in sincerity and truth the God of the white man by Deleware, Wiandot, Shawnee, Kaw, Seneka, and Canzas Indians.[57]

Only in America did the camp meeting reach the peaks of popularity. One reason was no doubt demographical. Such a means of personalized religion could not have flowered without the existence of a vast area of open land and a temperate climate. The temper of the people here also furnished fertile soil for its nourishment. The English might logically have been expected to use the device extensively, since the American Methodists espoused it so heartily, and the mother church had no prejudice against preaching outside the church building. Nevertheless, the attempt to transplant the camp meeting to England met serious opposition.

Jesse Lee recommended its use at an English Conference but was given no encouragement; the visiting American evangelist and wife, Lorenzo and Peggy Dow, aided by two local Methodists, Hugh Bourne and William Cleves, went on the road using the open-air revival technique to preach the gospel to the poor and uneducated.

For their pains, the two overzealous Englishmen were expelled from the ranks of the English Methodists. The 1807 Wesleyan Conference rather pointedly declared:

It is our judgment that, ever supposing such meetings to be allowable in America, they are highly improper in England, and likely to be productive of considerable mischief, and we disclaim connection with them.[58]

It was the highly stratified class structure of the mother country which precluded acceptance of the outdoor meeting. The inclement climate and the equally dampening official censure discouraged even the usually irrepressible Dow. A small group persisted in using the camp meeting method, and in 1811 formed a new church organization calling themselves "Primitive Methodists."[59] Their unrestrained singing of American camp meeting songs and their own spirited tunes in the English, Scotch, Irish, and Welsh revival circles earned them the distinctive title of "Ranters."[60]

Thus it was that the New World alone used the camp meeting and adapted it, little by little, to the character of its people and the changing frontier environment. The "camp meeting" was many things to many people. The social milieu in which it was incorporated must always be considered when an evaluation of its worth is to be made.

7

A Camp Meeting Day

Being at a camp meeting was like
standing at the gate of heaven, and
seeing it opened before you.[1]
       — *Frances Trollope, 1832*

IN ANY GROUP OF
homeward-bound campers, there were always those who
felt, like Frances Trollope, that they had glimpsed a bit of
heaven. Others knew that they had undergone an emotional experience that would keep them talking about
the camp meeting for days. From the minute they had
arrived on the grounds a sense of urgency had gripped
them. Their camp leaders had wasted no time in starting
the proceedings, for they realized the wisdom of
immediacy:

Let us draw near the stand and get into a devout frame of mind.
Our object is to do good and get good. Let us give ourselves to
prayer at once. . . . It is *salvation* we want. We must spend no
time in vain conversation. No time to visit, to talk of politics or
commerce. We are here to worship God. . . . Get into the work
at once. There is no sense in waiting three days to get warmed up.
It will be harder every day you wait. O, may the power of God
rest upon preachers and people at the beginning of the meeting.[2]

Returning home, the campers could attest that no time
had been lost at the camp meeting; they had participated
in a dawn-to-dusk revivalism. The pace set at the afternoon opening was maintained each day in a typical camp

meeting of the Old Northwest in the 1820's. The worshiper's first full day began when he was "blasted up by a
trumpet call" at daybreak. The second sounding of the
horn was the signal for family prayers at each tent or a
short prayer meeting around the altar before breakfast.[3]
Having attended to his personal needs and straightened
out supplies unloaded the previous day, before the sun was
high in the sky the camper was prepared for a day of public devotions. Services were held at eight, ten (or eleven),
and three o'clock, and an evening meeting began at the
hour of candlelight, while prayer meetings filled in any
free intervals.[4]

The 8:00 A.M. service of the typical camp meeting day
was likely to be as brief as the initial one held the previous
afternoon. As in the morning prayer session, proceedings
began with the "lining of a hymn." The preacher read two
lines and then everyone sang them; he continued in this
way until the many verses had been sung. Of course,
if the selection was a camp meeting favorite like Isaac
Watts's "Am I a Soldier of the Cross," prompting was
unnecessary.

Customarily the same person who presided at the
encampment's opening gave the early morning address,
one which was not calculated to be of great import, but
only an indispensable preliminary. Thus when John C.
Havens preached the opening sermon "in rather a teeter-
ing manner," little excitement was aroused in the congregation.[5] The Reverend Charles Giles, with his "brow set
against wickedness — alcoholic wickedness in particular," was more effective. Taking a highly favored Methodist theme certain to nettle the hard drinkers in the crowd,
he "shook the rod of truth over the distillery, the rum
shop, and the intoxicating fluid as it ran down the drunk-

ard's neck." In the preacher's words, "It was plain pointed work. . . . Knowing that truth and reason were on my side, I was not anxious about the judgment of men."[6] The ministers themselves and agents of the local and state organizations of the American Temperance Society used the camp platform as a sounding board for temperance. Thousands of "tee-total" pledges were taken there. Here is evidence that the woodland revival was yet another medium of the humanitarian crusade that was growing in power during the thirty years which preceded the Civil War.

Less disturbing to the predilections of the listeners than temperance talks was Robert Paine's discourse from the text, "Why stand ye here all the day idle." He portrayed idleness as a sin against self, society, church, and above all, as a sin against God. There was "dignity in human labor" and "glory in the work of Christ." With a voice "like a trumpet" he concluded with the demand:

> Go work in God's vineyard. Go *work today*.
> To postpone is ruin, to neglect is death.[7]

The early morning sermon was followed by a number of exhortations, delivered not infrequently from several sides of the preacher's stand — and behind it as well, if Negro worshipers were in attendance. Ohio Conference circuit rider James Gilruth found it necessary when he exhorted at this time one day to reprove sharply "some of the Methodists for setting a table and eating in time of preaching and others for driving wagons through the encampment."[8] After a hymn, the meeting came to an end, leaving the camper to his own devices until the eleven o'clock session.

When a presiding elder was present at the fourth quarterly meeting held as a camp meeting, it was common practice to hold a "love feast" and to observe Holy Communion. On Sunday or Monday both of these ceremonies took place before the late morning sermon. The "love feast," preceding the Lord's Supper, included singing and prayer, religious testimonials by the participants, and the symbolical partaking of bread and water by church members and "serious persons who are not of our church." New members were inducted. In the Communion procedure the ministers first received the sacrament while kneeling within the altar, and then administered it to successive groups of campers kneeling outside the railing. At an 1836 camp meeting all this went on while a choir of ministers were singing "some of the most touching of the Wesleyan Hymns."[9]

Camp leaders considered the eleven o'clock sermon the principal one of the day. The introductory attractions — a short prayer and the singing of a few songs of praise — were quickly offered. Then the heavy artillery was drawn up, the most gifted speaker in the camp. Until he "warmed up" he relied on brief sermon notes, for this was customarily the occasion for a prepared address.

One might have been subjected to a fearsome message made up almost exclusively of "hell-fire and damnation." This was certainly the most popular topic with the frontier churchmen at any time of the preaching day. Yet the visitor might have chanced upon Bishop William McKendree, speaking after a Sunday sacrament from the text, "Come, let us reason together." McKendree forcefully sounded his subject of "atonement, the great plan of salvation, and the love of God."[10] Or possibly Benjamin Lakin, veteran itinerant of the Old Northwest, would be the speaker. His addresses evidenced great power of close reasoning. Using as a text I Cor. 15:34, "Awake to righteousness," he outlined man's need for acquiring a knowledge of God:

1st. Take notice of the knowledge of God. Knowledge can only be obtained by experience and all experience we can have of God must be by revelation of himself to us and by inspiration of his spirit to give us understanding . . . of the operations of his nature.

2nd. The helps God hath given us, and what is required of us in order to attain this knowledge: (1) the Scriptures (2) the preaching of the Gospel (3) the influences of his grace and operations of his Spirit (4) living witnesses etc. — our duty (1) to awake out of our slumber (2) cease from sinning (3) turn to righteousness.

3rd. The great impropriety of our remaining destitute of this knowledge.[11]

Backwoodsmen were beyond doubt "discombobulated" when one Methodist bishop exhibited his breadth of learning by opening a talk with these words: "My beloved hearers, I shall in the first place speak to you of the things which you know; second, of what I know; third, of the things neither of us know."[12] Bitterly sectarian sermons were common at the eleven o'clock meetings, as western preachers were loquacious and dogmatic on matters of creed. At a Goose Creek encampment of 1822 in Kentucky, Peter Cartwright held his audience of an estimated ten thousand long past their lunchtime with a three-hour discourse ridiculing Baptist opposition to infant baptism. His acid remarks caused a visiting Baptist minister to depart in haste before the talk was finished — much to Cartwright's delight, for an elderly lady had promised the Methodist churchman a suit of clothes if his opponent could not stand his ground.[13] Camp services were likewise jarred off schedule by visits from denominational rivals who used the speaker's stand to attack Methodist theology.

The inevitable exhortations came after the conclusion of the prepared address at the eleven o'clock session. These enthusiastic and often nonintellectual discourses of the licensed preachers and exhorters wounded the feelings of some by their pertinacity and raucousness. An Indiana itinerant credited one exhorter with such powerful lungs that it seemed as if he could be "heard distinctly one mile in every direction on a still night." People attending a Hockhocking, Ohio, camp meeting complained to Benjamin Lakin that a particular evangelist pleaded with such vigor that "nobody could heare [sic] for him." Lakin's characteristic response was that while he agreed the man should have been less noisy, he would leave the matter "in the hands of God."[14]

An exhorter's remarks as he reprimanded members of the audience for slight or serious misdeeds undoubtedly subjected certain individuals to great embarrassment. In one talk, the Reverend James Axley upset daydreaming worshipers by pointing an accusing finger at a little girl who had been giggling and chattering during the preceding sermon, by reprimanding a man for sleeping during the service, and by sharply criticizing "that dirty, nasty, filthy tobacco-chewer, sitting on the end of that front seat" for spitting all over the floor.[15] Other exhorters, using the "Homeric epithets of early Methodism," alternately issued sharp warnings of impending doom and impassioned pleadings to flee from the wrath that was to come.

With the singing of a hymn the morning services were concluded. For some, the end of formal worship meant but the beginning of private prayer services in special tents or in living quarters, services which lasted until the noonday meal. Dinnertime around the open fires was a happy visiting time for all except a few "mourners" and friends who remained by their side to comfort them with prayer, song, and counsel.

More informality was to be encountered at the afternoon meeting than at any other camp session. Frequently it began with the "handshake ceremony" — one of the many features of camp meeting religion that permitted the worshiper to participate directly. With all the congregation standing, "you turned to the right, and then to the left, shaking hands with whosoever stood next to you."[16] There was also audience participation that was spontaneous. It took a hardy voice to be heard over the chit-chat of the bystanders and the fervent shouts of "Hallelujah!" "A-a-men, A-a-men!" and "Praise God!" While the minister could accept such heartfelt enthusiasm as a token of his effectiveness, he was negatively impressed with the talking, whistling, and strolling about of the less serious-minded. Most disturbing were the activities of the whiskey vendors illicitly operating on or about the grounds. The consumption of their wares inevitably led to high-spirited rowdiness when some spectators engaged in gay repartee with the itinerants or attempted to start a free-for-all.

Another trial to the ministers were the "religious crackpots" drawn to these well-attended woodland Bethels. Cartwright told of one mystic at an 1822 encampment who wanted to preach the novel doctrine that "a Christian could live so holy [a] . . . life, that he would never die, but become all immortal, soul, body, and all." The rostrum was denied him, although he flattered the backwoods preacher by informing him he had been revealed as one of the elect in a recent heavenly message. As Cartwright put it, he felt himself "accountable to the people as well as to the Lord, for the doctrines advanced from the stand."[17]

Camp meeting preachers not only had to be fiery orators, moving their audiences into raptures or instilling in them an overpowering sense of guilt and fear, but they also had to be mentally agile, for they never knew when someone would take exception to their preachments. Years of service usually qualified them to deal with the most unlikely contingency. Cartwright, when confronted with a large, disorderly Sunday crowd at a Roaring River Circuit encampment in Tennessee during the summer of 1821, put them in a receptive mood by relating a few anecdotes. His humorous stories aroused interest and made many laugh. This manner of preaching so irritated one man sitting down front that he shouted at the circuit rider, "Make us cry — make us cry; don't make us laugh." Cartwright vehemently retorted: "I don't hold the puckering strings of your mouths, and I want you to take the negro's eleventh commandment; that is, Every man mind his own business."[18]

On Sunday, the banner day, camp leaders arranged for two consecutive afternoon sermons. No particular topic was considered most appropriate, and the themes varied from time to time. If the worshiper had been present at the Randolph Grove, Illinois, encampment of 1831, he might have his prejudices appealed to by an evangel's denunciation of eastern missionaries and correspondents who

represent this country as a vast waste and the people as very ignorant; but if I were going to shoot a fool, I should not take aim at a Western man, but would go down by the seashore and cock my fusil at the imps who live off oysters.

As soon as the first speaker sat down, another began to

rail against the popular vices of the campers; horse racing
came in for the severest censure. "There is a class of
people," said the itinerant, "who can't go to hell fast
enough on foot, so they get on their poor, mean ponies
and go to the horse-race."[19] Many a worshiper would
have liked to answer him derisively, although all but a
few restrained themselves. They had long since become
reconciled to harangues against their shortcomings. Some
bystanders, however, did talk back to the preacher, who
in turn tried to argue them down.

With a large crowd in attendance, fund raisers who
were given the rostrum became particularly eloquent in
the hope of furthering some favored enterprise. Money
was taken up for Bibles, tracts, and all other religious
purposes.[20] Superannuated preachers and building funds
for new churches were recipients as well. Amounts collected at these gatherings were exceedingly modest, often
totaling less than five dollars.[21] Pioneers and hard cash
were comparative strangers, as the circuit rider's own
income testified. The platform technique of the minister
of Wyandot Mission fame, James B. Finley, was especially
effective for fund appeals. He solicited funds for his work
by presenting a converted Indian chief, "Between-the-
Logs," whose weird English phrases were supplemented
by the remarks of an interpreter. Thus many camp
audiences were thrilled as were the Marylanders at the
Baltimore and Severn encampments in July, 1826, when
they listened to a "powerful financial appeal to thousands
on behalf of the poor Indians . . . starving for the bread
of life."[22] An 1843 spokesman even exhibited "Texas
horned toads in alcohol" to arouse interest in proposed
church buildings for Galveston and Houston in the Lone
Star Republic.[23]

Considerable church business was conducted at encampments. Deacons or presiding elders were ordained, disputes between class members arbitrated, and circuit policies made. Circuit missionary societies and class meetings convened there.[24] Through all these many activities the people waited, some patiently, some impatiently, for the main event — the spontaneous appeal that would be aimed at moving the heart of the most hardened sinner. It was for this that they had come, and seldom were they disappointed. The ministers prepared the way by moving sermons, which ranged from a one-word text like "Mercy" or "Justice" to an elaborate discourse that sketched in overpowering detail the torments of hell and the joys of heaven.[25]

At an Eagle Creek, Ohio, campground James Quinn delineated the Judgment Day, using as a text Ps. 1:3-6, which included the frightening words: "For the Lord knoweth the way of the righteous: but the way of the ungodly shall perish." Quinn described the sacrificial offerings of Jesus Christ, the atonement by which "rebel man" was permitted to make a covenant with his God, and the final judgment scene. Confronted with this luminous picture of a dissolving firmament, "few could retain their seats."[26]

The exhorters who aided the regular circuit preachers did not mind using unconventional means to press home a point. Joshua Thomas, who was attending an island camp meeting off Maryland's Eastern Shore in the early thirties, arose and cast his low-crowned hat aside; his longcoat went the same way. Then he turned to the expectant audience and said, "It seems to me I must first shout." Jumping up and down, he clapped his hands, saying over and over again, "Glory, Glory!" until he was in

a mood of deep religious fervor. The audience wondered
at first about this strange action. Then some ventured an
"Amen!" Soon shouts of "Glory, Glory!" "Amen!" and
"Praise the Lord!" reverberated from the sides of the
stand. Exhorter Thomas, satisfied with this emotional display, launched an earnest appeal. At an early Ohio
camp meeting, one mother felt so strongly the need to
awaken fellow sinners that she exhorted for several hours
even though she had started to nurse her baby.[27] Emotionally aroused, other worshipers started to sing spontaneously. Enthusiasm mounted as a refrain was sung out
lustily from all parts of the clearing. It has been truthfully said that in the early days of Methodism, congregational singing was worship and the beginning of prayer.

The time had now come for the altar service, the core
of camp meeting religion. The people "set more store"
by this worship form, whether occurring in the afternoon
or evening, than any other. Worship at the altar offered
the greatest opportunity for audience participation; it
was as much a property of the people as of the preacher
on the rostrum.[28] At the end of formal worship pulses
inevitably quickened when the circuit rider issued the call:

> Come all the world; come sinner, thou,
> All things in Christ are ready now.[29]

Never elaborate, the setting of the altar event varied
in simplicity according to the facilities the encampment
provided. There were the "mourner's benches," "mourner's tents" or "praying tents," and "praying circles." In the
larger camp meetings the center of interest was the mourner's bench located directly in front of the pulpit. To the
godly this structure was also known as the "altar"; to the
scoffers, because of its similarity to a hog enclosure, it
was the "pen." By the 1820's the title "anxious seat"

also came into use. In composition the altar ranged from an allocated first row of seats for mourners to a spacious enclosed area, often twenty or thirty feet square, down the center of which ran a rail fence segregating the men from the women. By definition, a mourner was "one who, becoming alarmed about the state of his soul, began to pray and seek deliverance from the bondage and domination of sin."[30] Thus the sinners who wished to be "instructed" were isolated from the saved persons and sinners not yet moved. Here they could find "peace."

Mourner's tents began to appear only after 1820 and were complementary to the altar worship. Canvas shelters, sometimes as large as fifty feet long and thirty feet wide, they were especially popular in the East. On some campgrounds they were pitched within the altar area; on others, they were set up on the edges of the open-air auditorium. Lights were kept burning within through the night, and a drawn curtain separated male and female compartments. As in the altar area, the floor was covered with straw. Frequently, as at an Indiana camp meeting of 1829, bundles of straw were piled up next to the outer walls to serve as seats but "at that moment . . . were used to support the heads and the arms of the close-packed circle of men and women who kneeled on the floor." At that same encampment Negro mourner's tents were set up. Private worship was also carried on in them when all other services had ceased.[31]

The "praying circles" or "prayer rings" materialized when a group of respected laymen and preachers joined hands to form a circle and asked all who felt themselves sinners to enter therein. This "circle of brotherly love," as it was also known, appears to have been mostly an eastern camp meeting custom, since the backwoods circuit riders made little mention of it, but emphasized the mourner's bench. The prayer ring was evidently a substitute for the altar area device.[32]

Such was the setting for the afternoon altar service. The religious content of this form of worship almost defies description. There was a bewildering complex of simultaneous prayers, of heartfelt shouts by the penitent, of impassioned appeals to the sinners by fervent preachers who shouted, stamped, and gesticulated with great effectiveness, of heart-searching testimonials, and of inspiring hymns and chants.

Song played a major role at the altar services, for camp songs helped light revival fires. A considerable number of song texts were written during camp meetings by two Great Revival alumni, John A. Granade and Caleb Jarvis Taylor. One Methodist chronicler explained that although these creations possessed little poetry, they "served to excite the feelings of devotion," and "entered into a description of it."[33] Does not this narrative of personal religious experience by Granade graphically describe the altar devotionals?

> Sinners through the camp are falling;
> Deep distress their souls pervade
> Wondr'ring why they are not rolling
> In the dark infernal shade.
>
> Grace and mercy, long neglected,
> Now they ardently implore;
> In an hour when least expected
> Jesus bids them weep no more.
>
> Hear them then their God extolling,
> Tell the wonders he had done;
> While they rise, see others falling!
> Light into their hearts have shown.[34]

Compositions by other camp meeting song writers had similarly suggestive lines: "Pray on, my brethren in the Lord," and "Come, saints and sinners hear me tell, the wonders of Immanuel."[35] If one released sinner shouted joyfully, "I'm converted, glory hallelujah!" the whole audience might respond with the spiritual "Shout Old Satan's Kingdom Down."[36] Testimonial songs revealed the happy state of the penitent at the altar:

> When I hear the pleasing sound
> Of weeping mourners just converted,
> The dead's alive, the lost is found,
> The Lord has healed the broken-hearted.
> When I join to sing his praise,
> The heart, in holy raptures use;
> I view Immanuel's land afar,
> I shout and wish my spirit there.
> ·Glory, honour and salvation;
> What I feel is past expression.[37]

The emotional impact of the more mournful type of song was exhibited at a camp meeting on the Fishing River Circuit near Liberty, Illinois, in July, 1823. Two Methodist ministers had preached and exhorted in turn. One of them began leading the hymn and when he came to the second verse — "Soon as from earth I go, What will become of me!" — the power

of the Almighty came down in such a wonderful manner as is seldom witnessed. Brother Harris fell back in the pulpit, overcome by the influence of the Holy Spirit, and called upon me to invite the people forward for prayers. . . . The invitation was no sooner extended than the mourners came pouring forward in a body for prayers till the altar was filled with weeping penitents.[38]

The meeting continued that afternoon and all night.

Another glimpse of the altar service is given by an English traveler who attended an Indiana encampment of 1819. At eleven o'clock in the morning the altar was already crowded with mourners. The preacher gave a soulful prayer, followed by a thought-provoking sermon based on the reflection, "What will become of the church when we are dead and gone?" His address being interrupted by the aroused audience, he left the platform. Then

a tune was struck up and sung with grand enthusiasm. The worship now proceeded with a new energy; the prompter in the pulpit had succeeded in giving it an impulse, and the music was sufficient to preserve emotion. The inclosure was so much crowded that its inmates had not the liberty of lateral motion, but were literally hobbling *en masse*. My attention was particularly directed to a girl of about twelve years of age, who while standing could not be seen over her taller neighbours; but at every leap she was conspicuous above them. The velocity of every plunge made her long loose hair flirt up as if a handkerchief were held by one of its corners and twitched violently. Another female, who had arrived at womanhood, was so much overcome that she was held up to the breeze by two persons who went to her relief. I never before saw such exhaustion. The vertebral column was completely pliant, her body, her neck, and her extended arms, bent in every direction successively. It would be impossible to describe the diversity of cases; they were not now confined within the fence, but were numerous among the people without. Only a small proportion of them could fall within the observation of any one bystander. The scene was to me equally novel and curious.[39]

Yet altar services were often solemn, prayerful occasions. Such was the case of a Portsmouth, Ohio, encampment of August, 1818. After delivering a sermon, the circuit rider exhorted his listeners to attend to their religious impressions. Those mourners who had found by experience that the tumult at the altar lessened their convictions were advised to go to the grove to seek God in secret. "Many tried the experiment. The lonely valley soon became vocal with bitter lamentations; and although they could not hear the cries of each other, they could not refrain their own. Many were thus converted in the woods."[40]

While the afternoon altar period was a disquieting time for many souls, for others it was a highly amusing form of entertainment. Peter Cartwright had to contend with "idle professors" and "idle spectators" who were overcrowding the altar at his Russellville, Kentucky, camp meeting in 1822. Fearing that sincere seekers, particularly the ladies, were kept from coming forward, he directed that the avenues leading to it be kept clear, forbade "standing on the seats and . . . around the pales of the altar," and sharply circumscribed the number of persons authorized inside the enclosure.[41]

With the cessation of the afternoon program the campers again had a chance to visit and time to prepare and enjoy the evening meal. Yet by now there were many who were beyond caring for sociability or physical comforts. This was especially the case if it were one of the concluding days of the encampment. Tension had been mounting steadily, and mourners who had failed to find "release" in the afternoon worship were still being attended by earnest friends. For them the day had been one continuous religious battle. And now night was falling.

The forest setting of this solemn hour was both mysterious and awe-inspiring. Flickering lamps and candles were attached to the trees, while flaming elevated tripods and smoking campfires also helped illuminate the woodland auditorium. To one visitor all the lights seemed to have but one effect, "everywhere more was hidden than seen." Circuit preacher James B. Finley experienced the same reaction. He described the "innumerable lamps hung out, casting their lights among the branches," the "village of snowy tents," and then the novel sight of hundreds of campers with torches passing to and fro in answer to the trumpet's summons. As a hymn was sent out into the night air, the total effect was "to awaken the most solemn reflections."[42]

At candlelighting time devotions might open with a joyful refrain:

> Come my Christian friends and brethren
> Bound for Canaan's happy land:
> Come unite, and walk together,
> Christ the Saviour gives command. . . .
>
> Here's my hand, my heart and spirit
> Now in fellowship, I'll give; . . .
>
> Now we'll preach and pray together,
> Praise, give thanks and shout and sing,
> Now we'll strengthen one another,
> And adore our heavenly King.[43]

If a Peter Cartwright were present, the best in frontier pulpit oratory could then be heard. On one occasion he spent some forty minutes on waggish talk, in which "shafts of ridicule, bon mots, puns and side-splitting anecdotes sparkeled, flashed and flew like hail, til the vast auditory was convulsed with laughter." Then gradually his manner changed, his face grew serious, his voice earnest. Soon "tears came to his eyes and he descanted on the horrors of hell til every shuddering face was turned downward, as if expecting to see the solid globe rent asunder." When he made his call for the mourners to come to the altar, five hundred persons pressed forward.[44]

If the opening of an evening meeting revealed a noisy, antagonistic crowd, a different technique was called for. Desiring to prevent disorder and to channel mischievous energy into religious enthusiasm, one minister at a Fredonia, Illinois, encampment spoke on civil and religious liberty. He appealed to all those in whom flowed the "blood of the patriot sires of '76" to join with the leaders to prevent the rabble from endangering the camp meeting's religious rights and privileges. As a result, the evening services were carried out successfully.[45]

Often a rip-roaring, hell-fire sermon paved the way for a spirited evening session. The enormous depravity of man and the last judgment were portrayed. Here the pulpit thumper would describe the day of reckoning in vivid detail, as did the Presbyterian James McGready when he depicted the "fork-like cloven flames, the thunder, the general destruction of all things." "As yet, indeed, I have not felt the earth tremble under my feet; it seems to stand firm," he added as he stamped on the pulpit floor, "and as yet I hear not the rolling of the thunder of doom; but it may, nevertheless, be at hand."[46] Then would come the offer to help "anxious sinners to wrestle with the Lord."

Evening altar services began as the formal worship ended, although the aroused participants noted no sharp break in the continuity. As seekers came forward, the impromptu proceedings commenced. Elder church members and preachers mingled with them, and soon the air was filled with singing and shouting. Frequently, women were chosen to sing for those under stress in the altar area or mourner's tents. Housewives were said to be particularly "good shouters." With all this activity the camp meeting was aglow with life.

By its very nature, the evening worship conformed to no set pattern. James Gilruth's candlelight service at a Granville Circuit, Ohio, camp meeting of 1831 was brief. After he preached from Matt. 11:28, "Come unto me, all *ye* that labour and are heavy laden, and I will give you rest," there followed only one exhortation. The campers then went to their tents and "spent the evening til about eleven o'clock singing and praying—then the signal of rest was given and all retired to sleep."[47] Again, short devotionals at the altar sometimes permitted song-fests in the mourner's tents to be held far into the night.

If the spirit ran high, however, night altar exercises were prolonged by testimonials of personal religious experiences. In an age when a person was not ashamed of exhibiting his inner feelings, one man after another eagerly told of his sinful past and spiritual rebirth, as he urged others "to git religion." Weeping and repeated shouts of "Praise Jesus!" "Hallelujah!" and the like punctuated these volunteer exhortations. Walking back and forth one happy soul chanted, "I have been a great sinner, and was on the way to be damned; but I am converted now, thank God—Glory, Glory!"—occasionally turning around on one heel and giving a loud whoop.[48] Affirmations were more restrained when the leaders asked for recitations of favorite Bible verses. In the space of half an hour, forty to fifty Scripture texts would be spun forth. From time to time the circuit riders intervened with telling comments on particular selections. Itinerants often encouraged the penitent to "cry aloud and spare not."[49] In their exhortations these soul-melting ministers preached the certitude of eternal damnation for the unrepentant sinner and the joy of salvation. The tenor of their remarks is indicated by the opinion of one convert that no one was saved until he "could first smell fire and brimstone."

As in the afternoon altar service, songs were selected with care for the purpose of "encouraging and instructing the seeker in the way of mercy." Preacher Finley fondly recalled "Father John" Collins lining a hymn at one Eagle Creek, Ohio, camp meeting when "all could tell that his

heart was filled with emotion too big for utterance." And
when the song was sung, "as only the Methodists in early
times could sing at camp meetings," it seemed "as if the
soul of the entire encampment was in the sound, and went
up to heaven as an offering of praise."[50] Even the biased
Englishwoman, Frances Trollope, conceded that an evening hymn in a forest setting had a "solemn and beautiful
effect." A popular technique of the preachers was to step
down from the platform and circulate through the crowd
while giving out a hymn. One counseled his listeners:

> Now the truth is gaining ground,
> By their testimony,
> Weighty testimony saved,
> Sweeter than the honey:
> Humble souls begin to see
> In the heavenly mystery;
> And they hold and preach and sing,
> Christ the great salvation,
> Let their testimony ring
> Through the whole creation.[51]

In addition to rendering old favorites, a song leader
was often inspired to improvise new tunes on the spot by
simply furnishing several lines to which the audience
responded with a simple chorus. After the congregation
had sung that, he was ready with another hastily-devised
line or two, and so on indefinitely.[52] The altar services—
with their conflict of souls in torment—were often advanced on a wave of song.

When the services were at their height, every tent
became a "bethel of struggling Jacobs and prevailing
Israels," every tree "an altar," and every grove "a secret
closet." The campers were held fast in the grip of religious
ardor. Dozens of prayers were offered up simultaneously
and a stranger might infer "that the one praying assumed
that God was deaf."[53] Sinners and church helpers labored

together in prayer and exhortation, and frequent were the loud shouts as penitent after penitent "crossed over into Beulah land."

A sensitive Universalist minister, while visiting one Indiana encampment in the 1840's, was repelled by the "noise, uproar, and fanaticism." He watched with disgust the evening marching ceremony, the fiery preaching, and the unrestrained exhorting. He noted that "some seemed to be suffering intense agony, others as happy as clams at high water; some kept their seats, while others were hopping, skipping and jumping." Leaving the campground at midnight, he queried himself, "Is this the proper way to worship God?"[54] On the other hand, an English clergyman, while decrying the excessive use of invitation to the "anxious seat," was favorably impressed with the preachers' appeals to the heart and understanding. He described a Monday evening service:

The singing . . . now showed results. Two or three young women were fainting under the exhaustion and excitement; and one, who was reported as a Methodist, was in hysterical ecstasy, raising her hands, rolling her eyes and smiling and muttering. It appeared that she courted this type of excitement as many do the dram, and was at frequent meetings of this character, for the sake of enjoying it. . . . The regular service began. It was composed of exhortation and prayer; and it was excellently conducted. . . . The first address referred to the past, the effort which had been made; the results which ought to follow, but which had not followed. . . . The next exhortation was on conversion. Some skillful and orthodox distinctions were established on the subject, as it involves the Agency of the Spirit, and the Agency of man. It . . . threw all the responsibility of perversity and refusal on the sinner. It made a strong impression.

The third exhortation was on indifference and despondency. The subject was well timed and well treated. . . . Exhortation and singing were renewed; and it was proposed that they should go down and pass among the people, for the purpose of conversing with them and inducing them to come forward; and fervent prayer of a suitable character was offered in their behalf. . . . Other exhortations, of a lower but more noisy character were made, with endless singing; favourite couplets would be taken up and repeated without end. The effect was various, but it was not good. Some with their feelings worn out, had passed the crisis, and it was in vain to seek to impress them; while others were unduly and unprofitably excited.[55]

Yet with all the confusion and excitement, provision was still made for carefully ascertaining the number of converts gained and church members admitted—two distinctly different matters. The custom developed of tallying in the converts either during the two altar services or by the visitation of appointed persons to the campers' tents the following morning. As early as 1806 Jesse Lee observed that the ministers took great pains to report accurately the number who "openly professed." He described the procedure at a Maryland meeting where laymen were stationed in the congregation to keep an accounting. They may have mistaken emotion for penitence,

but the Christians who were acquainted with the people while they were careless about their souls, and were present with them while they were under conviction, and at the same time they professed to be converted, can tell pretty well whether they were deceived or not.[56]

Lists were prepared and then turned over to the appropriate saddlebag preacher or to the class leader to present to the next itinerant who took charge of the circuit in which the penitents lived.[57] Thus did the Methodist church keep in contact with a society in motion.

When present, the presiding elder talked to the converts who were applying for church membership. He strengthened them in the faith, or, as an open-air revival critic phrased it, fixed them "inflexibly in the Methodist peculiarities and connexion."[58] Outlining the six-months' probationary period that preceded full connection with the church, he stressed the requirement of regular attendance at class and circuit quarterly meetings. At a later camp session the applicant sat in the altar area during a ceremony in which his name was added to the Methodist rolls; he was again counseled in his duty to attend class "according to rule and order."[59] These instructions underscored the church's view that altar conversion was not an end in itself. Once accepted into a class, the neophyte came under the strict supervision of the *Methodist Discipline*.

The fervor of conversion under rowdy circumstances, which is all that many observers saw, was only the initial step. After that there was the stern discipline exercised by a pious but rigidly uncompromising clergy. The camp meeting experience heralded the beginning of a new life for the happy convert, a Christian way of life that might have remained unknown to many but for the existence of the forest revival institution.

8

Evangels of the Backwoods

*The Lord called them and made them
ministers, and as* polished shafts, *hid
them in his quiver.... And where did
Washington and his brave fellows learn
the dreadful trade of war? Where, but
on the toilsome march, the tented field,
or battleground? And yet were there
ever better soldiers...? And where
and how did the Methodist preachers
learn to preach? By preaching. The
answer to these interrogatories should
be clearly given by the historian. And
then it may be asked, where or when
has there been a better or more successful set of truly-evangelical preachers?*[1]
— *Circuit rider James Quinn, 1840*

THE WHIPPING BOY
of many writers on frontier history, the Methodist circuit
rider has been most often portrayed as illiterate, un-
trained, and undisciplined. A "giver of violent and senseless harangues," he has appeared as a humorless person,
steely eyed, with grave and unrelenting expression. His
aim was supposedly to sweep the listener into an emotional frenzy and through bodily exercises — viewed by
him as a manifestation of God's power — to terrify the
poor sinner into repentance (and the Methodist fold).
The preacher of this caricature was "deplorably ignorant, bitterly sectarian and wildly fanatical"; "often as

145

illiterate as those who listened" to him.² His frantic speeches, gesticulations, and outcries "set them dancing, laughing, barking and jerking." He could fell "a group or a crowd with the sweep of his arm."³ In the somber costume of his calling, broad-brimmed hat, round-breasted frock coat, and breeches, his hair falling down to his shoulders, "the very looks of a Methodist preacher would strike terror to the sinner's heart."⁴ One historian grouped all circuit riders together as men who "induced in themselves 'possession' by sleepless nights, lack of food, [and] long journeys with physical discomfort." The churchmen, more zealous than devout, "broke down the critical senses of their congregations by the primitive devices of singing, shouting, and stamping in rhythm, just as the savage used the rhythm of the drum and the dance to produce an hypnotic effect."⁵

It is not difficult for the student to see that this picture has been produced by concentration upon the eccentric few — with the result that caricatures, not portraits, have been drawn. So much attention has been paid to unorthodox leaders like "Fighting Parson" William G. Brownlow, "Father" John Collins, and "Crazy" Lorenzo Dow, that the ordinary saddlebag preacher is often overlooked. It is not the speakers who specialized in sober doctrinal sermons who are remembered, but those who warned their audiences, "You are hair-hung and breeze-shaken over Hell." Actually, there was no circuit rider "type." Frontier ministers, like other mortals, were individuals. It is impossible to fit them into the one mold so many historians have fashioned for them.

In the ranks of the selfless itinerants were the uncultured "son of thunder" and the educated minister, "the weeping prophet" and the rational orator, the vain show-

BISHOP FRANCIS ASBURY.

This earliest known portrait of Methodism's first bishop, painted in
Baltimore in 1794, was lost for many years. When found in 1866,
it had been used as a fire screen and a hole had been cut (at the
upright hand) for the stovepipe. The painting is now in the Lovely
Lane Methodist Church, Baltimore, the "Mother Church of American Methodism," and is reproduced here by permission of the
Reverend Kenneth R. Rose.

man and the humble introvert who had difficulty finding "liberty" in preaching. Jacob Gruber, veteran of many circuits in Virginia, North Carolina, and Ohio, was "a character" who "copied after no man." His customary outfit was a gray suit of Quakerish cut and a broad-brimmed hat, beneath which his long bobbed hair peeked out. One of the biggest if not the most impressive of circuiteers was James Gilruth. Possessing an exhaustive knowledge of the gospel, he had also mastered farming, carpentry, shoemaking, and veterinary medicine. This Jack-of-all-trades was so robust and indefatigable that he needed two horses to carry him on his long journeys around the Ohio, Michigan, and Illinois circuits. He would ride the horses alternately, allowing the tired nag to follow behind.[6] Jovial, Virginia-born Jesse Lee could match Gilruth in size. Lee weighed all of two hundred and fifty pounds.

James Axley was remarkable for his down-to-earth habits. A habitual tobacco chewer with crudest manners, Axley once amused the governor of Ohio, at whose home he was a guest, by throwing half-eaten chicken bones on the floor for the waiting dogs. His travels took him through Ohio, Indiana, Louisiana, North Carolina, Kentucky, and Tennessee, and wherever he went he was accepted on the virile frontier as a man among men. James B. Finley, an Indian fighter and hunter-farmer product of the Ohio, Carolina, and Kentucky frontiers, wrestled with sinners both mentally and physically, as did so many of his cohorts. Individualistic colored preachers and exhorters, Ohio's John Stewart and Alabama's "Ned," had distinctive traits that appealed to their Negro audiences.[7]

The backwoods preacher was by nature a democrat.

Speaking the frontiersmen's language, he won respect. He did not look down on the pioneers, for he was one of them. With his unsophisticated manners and simple emotional appeal, he met the settler on his own level, exerting a powerful influence for good upon frontier life.[8] Staunch champion of the moral order and the decent life, the saddlebag preacher sought to improve man by the double-edged sword of word and deed. Peter Cartwright, although a rough and ready preacher, was the exemplification of this type of minister. He vividly portrayed the necessity for a roughhewn preaching technique:

The great mass of our Western people wanted a preacher that could mount a stump, a block, or an old log, or stand in the bed of a wagon, and without a note or manuscript, quote, expound and apply the word of God to the hearts and consciences of the people.[9]

Like Cartwright, the average circuit rider joined the itineracy as a young man, before his arteries were hardened by caution.

This rough, tough man of the gospel considered himself not chosen by man but "called by God" to enlist in His service. His spiritual qualifications included a compelling sense of inner conviction, a ready tongue, and an eagerness to hunt souls. One circuit rider who "located" only to return to the traveling ministry stated he did so in the belief "that God hath called me to travel." The reasoning was interesting:

My belief is founded on (1) a conviction of duty. (2) on seeing some fruits of my labours (3) on the accomplishment of God's promises to supply my wants and to make my way clere [sic] before me, and giving me all the satisfaction in the enjoyment of the comforts of life ... (4) that when located though God gave me the comforts of life he took the enjoyment of them from me — I cannot see that I could now locate in faith because (1) I am sensible that I am called to travel (2) I am not sensible that this call is reversed by a call to locate (3) if I locate without a call, thereto, I shall be out of the order of God (4) in that situation cannot expect the blessing of God.[10]

The backwoods evangel, often highly introspective, searched his soul for purity of thought and motive — sought to purge himself of vanity and selfish ambition. The writings of Bishop Asbury, Henry Smith, and Benjamin Lakin are filled with this self-perfecting struggle. Henry Smith during a reflective moment wrote Asbury that while performing his duties on the Winchester, Virginia, Circuit in 1803 he "enjoyed perfect love," but added, "Ah, how secretly and securely did pride, self-will, vanity and many other hurtful desires and unholy things lurk within me." Constantly beset by doubts as to his spiritual state, circuit rider Lakin noted in his "Journal" in 1809 that he "had not been as faithful" as he should have been. Resolving to talk less, read, and pray, he begged God "to keep me little and make me unknown to the world."[11] Self-indulgence was frowned upon; in fact, many backwoods preachers fasted one day each week. The morning of the fast day was spent in reading, prayer, and meditation.

As befitted a man in close kinship with God, the minister was of grave disposition. Some, like James Gilruth, were utterly lacking in a sense of humor. Unusually puritanical, he was a rabid abolitionist and an ardent temperance man. Moreover, he was always extremely conscientious in the utilization of time. Others, like the irrepressible Peter Cartwright, James B. Finley, and Jacob Gruber, did not let otherworldliness blunt their sense of humor. They found time to enjoy a good joke, particularly of the practical variety that was then in vogue. Cartwright at an 1827 camp meeting demonstrated his

love of a good farce. Plagued by a rowdy threat to break
up the services, he donned old clothes and late in the
night mingled with the toughs to learn their strategy.
Later when the lights were out in the campers' tents,
reported Cartwright, he

slipped down to the brook, and filled the pockets of the old
overcoat that I had borrowed, with little stones; and as I came
up to them, they were just ready to commence operations on the
preacher's tents; but before they had thrown a single stone, I
gathered from my pockets my hands full of stones, and flung
them thick and fast right in among them, crying out, at the top
of my voice, "Here they are! Here they are! take them! take
them!" They broke at full speed, and such running I hardly ever
witnessed.[12]

The task of the God-seekers was the ingathering of
souls, and consequently they believed their conversation
must be conducted in a serious vein. The Reverend James
Quinn's description of an 1802 party honoring the visiting Bishop Asbury underscores this mental attitude. As
soon as the men got together Asbury sanctified the occasion with a short prayer. The Ohio elder drew this picture:

The prayer concluded, the company resumed seats; and what then?
Light chit-chat, mixed with peals of laughter, in which all persons
talk and no one hears? No, no; it was "the feast of reason and
the flow of soul" in a free flow of conversation and on a variety
of interesting topics, chiefly of moral and religious character. The
state of the old world, in religion and politics, occupied a part
of the time. The revolutions in Europe, the shaking of thrones,
the fulfillment of prophecy . . . infidelity in Europe and America;
the spread of the Gospel . . . the glorious 1836, which — according to some — was to usher in the glories of the millennium, these
together with the state of affairs in our own America . . . entered
largely into the social entertainments of that pleasant day.[13]

An anecdote by the same clergyman reveals the moral
earnestness Asbury transmitted to his followers. Quinn
remarked to the General Superintendent that the ferry-

man at the Little Hockhocking River in Ohio always carried bakers and Methodist clergymen across the river free of charge, believing "if they do no good they do no harm." "Ah, that is not true of ministers," responded Asbury, "for the minister who does no good does much harm." The traveling clergy measured its reward in the eyes that were opened, the hearts that were comforted, and the souls that were saved.[14] To them, the struggle was its own reward. Their faithfulness became so well known that the saying on a stormy day became proverbial: "There is nothing out today but crows and Methodist preachers."[15]

A striking characteristic of the frontier ministers was their lack of formal education.[16] Their cultural deficiencies — only partially a handicap in the backwoods society of the early nineteenth century — have aroused the scorn of recent students of history. While the preachers in homespun were men of limited schooling in a western society where illiteracy was a common possession, they were not ignorant. Many were former lawyers, doctors, and schoolteachers who had been converted, possibly at a camp meeting. Moreover, if the circuiteer had been a stranger to "book larnin' " when he joined the cause, he later endeavored to remedy this lack through a process of self-education.

Francis Asbury himself had left school after the sixth year. James Quinn had "six or nine months schooling" which enabled him to "read pretty well and write some" by the time he was eight. Like so many of the circuit riders, he came from devout parents who taught him to read the Bible. Other pioneer evangelists whose formal schooling was almost nonexistent at the time of their entry into Methodism included James Axley ("unaccustomed to the free use of the pen"), Samuel Parker, Peter Cartwright, and Jesse Walker. The last-named could recall only twenty days of schooling.[17] A Presbyterian missionary on a western visit in 1813 significantly characterized the circuit riders as men of "little learning, though when they preach, they begin to study, and many of them improve considerably."[18]

In 1805, a Methodist churchman offered a biblical defense against the objection that the camp meeting's principal advocates were "ignorant and illiterate Methodists." His rebuttal was that if the charge were true, which he denied, they were simply following St. Paul's instructions to Timothy on preparation for the ministry: "Give attendance to reading, to exhortation, to doctrine. Neglect not the gift that is in thee." He added that the Apostle Paul had not demanded of Timothy that he be educated, but only that he give voice to his spiritual feeling and that he preach with a sense of absolute conviction.[19]

This educational handicap, however, must have caused many preachers moments of doubt about their vocation. Benjamin Lakin, in one of his frequent moods of faltering confidence, admitted in his "Journal": "I many times feel so ignorant that I ought not to preach yet I think God hath called me to the work and I must go on."[20] Itinerants usually made up in moral earnestness what they lacked in formal training and instruction. It has been said that "religion is not taught but caught." If this generalization is at all true, then it follows that there are a few men so alive with spirituality as to be transmission agents; the circuit riders belonged to this select group. Their religious enthusiasm, their inner compulsion, swayed many a pioneer; they possessed an inner fire which often swept all before it.

The worldly success enjoyed by innumerable Methodist preachers when they left the ministry reveals the fallacy of the generalization that they were of low intellectual caliber. The record, on the contrary, shows the saddlebag preacher not only a democrat, but a man of parts. Leaders in the spiritual field, an imposing number with educational qualifications achieved pre-eminence in other spheres as well. James B. Finley, a classical scholar, doubled as professor of languages at Augusta College, Kentucky, and as a lifelong circuit rider. Jesse Lee, first historian of American Methodism, was elected four times in succession to the chaplainship of the United States House of Representatives. Circuit rider William H. Milburn twice won that same post and later served as chaplain of the Senate. He knew intimately the political greats of his day, including Clay, Webster, and Calhoun, as well as such distinguished men of letters as Washington Irving, William Cullen Bryant, and Henry Wadsworth Longfellow. Popular as both preacher and lecturer, Milburn, known as "Blind Man Eloquent," had a facile pen, as his many books demonstrate.[21]

In his excellence of literary style, Milburn did not stand alone. Two western poets and famed religious song writers, Jarvis Taylor and John A. Granade, belonged to the itineracy. Peter Cartwright and James B. Finley wrote autobiographies that rank high in the field of early frontier literature. Many of their traveling brethren also took time to record their frontier preaching experiences. Thomas S. Hinde, an English-born resident of Newport, Kentucky, was a striking example of versatility. He was a doctor, local minister, compiler of a popular western camp meeting hymnal, and church historian of considerable ability.[22]

Edward Tiffin, the first governor of Ohio, had served earlier as a "local supply." He was not the only clergy-man who engaged in politics along with or subsequent to a religious career. William G. Brownlow, veteran of Ten-nessee circuits, served as Union governor of Tennessee during the Civil War. Peter Cartwright was a shining example of the preacher-politician. He was twice elected to the Illinois legislature. The one defeat of his public career occurred in the Congressional race of 1846 when his campaign efforts to prove Abraham Lincoln an infidel failed. Thomas Scott, one of the many who were forced to leave the traveling ministry after marriage in order to support their families, was elected chief justice of the Ohio Supreme Court in 1810. Many other instances could be cited of early western preachers who left their calling because of financial pressure and made their mark elsewhere.[23]

Circuit riding demanded that a man have a hardy con-stitution fit to bear the countless physical hardships he encountered. The frontier apostle bore these burdens with little or no complaint. His attitude recalls to mind the apt phrase of William Penn, "No Cross, no Crown." Confronted with almost unbroken wilderness, the back country minister, like his parishioners, was exposed to all the privations incidental to the setting up of a new com-munity. The great distances on his circuit meant days and even weeks of long riding. Those who carried the gospel to the front lines of settlement were men of vigor, strength, and great self-reliance — or they did not outlast the year's appointment. They undertook, often alone, long and perilous journeys over blind paths, over trails marked only by the blazes on the saplings, or over roads hardly worthy of the name. The saddlebag preacher often outworked the farmer, outrode the hunter, and out-distanced the fur trader.

If married, the frontier preacher frequently had the additional burden of working a small farm to keep his dependents alive while he traveled the rounds. Farm labor had to be done during the intervals between circuit tours (perhaps a week); farm chores were carried on in his absence by his wife and children. In that way he attempted to circumvent the condition of poverty forced upon him by his pitiful salary. Cartwright observed with characteristic forthrightness that married circuit riders were "starved into location."

While Bishop Asbury did not want his preachers to suffer because of their monetary distress, he felt that the presence of too many worldly goods would cause a diminution of zeal and spirituality. On one occasion he is reported to have "prayed to the Lord to keep the preachers poor." According to historian Bangs, this prayer was not necessary, for "it was very congenial to that covetous disposition so natural to men, to withhold when they are not compelled to pay."[24] Not the least of the circuiteer's difficulties was the matter of provisions. Since he had little cash of his own for this essential, he was most often dependent upon voluntary contributions from the faithful. "Donation" parties had become customary by the forties. "Jerk," dried strips of venison or beef which did not spoil easily, was the backwoods minister's staple stock of food, while he begged oats and corn for his horse. One of his favorite songs depicted this economic deprivation:

> No foot of land do I possess
> No cottage in the wilderness[25]

Asbury himself never bought a home, and once confessed,

"I can hardly command my own coat on my yearly allowance."[26] The circuit rider's living conditions were much the same as if he had taken the vow of poverty.

The problem of lodging added to the physical hazards of his occupation. Often he slept on the floor of the pioneer's cabin, or in taverns or other places of entertainment. Not infrequently he spent the night out in the open. Lakin noted that many times he had knocked on a settler's door to ask for a night's resting place only to be curtly turned away. Several days of "riding through the rain and sleeping in damp beds" brought him down with sickness. A former member of the traveling ministry observed that the bare earth was their bed three-fourths of the time winter or summer, with "a saddle their pillow and the sky their coverlet."[27] When free lodging was furnished by friendly frontiersmen, whether of Methodist or of non-Methodist persuasion, it often meant a restless night in an overcrowded bed with bugs and fleas. While terming the border people "the kindest souls in the world," Asbury added:

But kindness will not make a crowded log cabin, twelve feet by ten, agreeable: without are cold and rain; and within, six adults and as many children, one of which is all motion; the dogs too, must sometimes be admitted. On *Saturday* at Felix Earnest's, I found that amongst my other trials, I had taken the itch; and, considering the filthy houses and filthy beds I have met with . . . it is perhaps not strange that I have not caught it twenty times. . . . But we must bear it for the elect's sake.[28]

Even were there a clean cabin and a relatively private bed, a night's lodging did not represent complete relaxation for the religious visitor. He always led the pioneer's household in Bible reading and prayers before retiring. Cartwright told of staying with a family in a Kentucky cabin in 1821. Though they were Baptists, "Uncle Peter" led them in devotions, and was gratified to hear two young women sing some of the "Methodist camp-meeting songs." Before leaving, the minister customarily had morning prayers with his host. One day visitor William Colbert forgot to call a family to prayer for the first time in his career. Much distressed, he attributed the oversight to fatigue, haste, and "a want of faithfulness to God."[29]

Welcome havens for the traveling minister were the "Methodists Preacher Harbors." These were the known homes of Methodist adherents which were always open to an itinerant; they afforded him a chance to rest up for a few days, to mend and wash his threadbare clothes, and to write letters. Asbury termed them places at which he could "get refitted." An itinerant, speaking from experience, sketched the typical circuit rider's housing and food problems:

[He] . . . lay out all night, wet, weary, and hungry, held his horse by the bridle all night, or tied him to a limb, slept with his saddle blanket for a bed, his saddle or saddle-bags for his pillow, and his old big coat or blanket, if he had any, for a covering. . . . [He] ate roasting ears for bread, drank buttermilk for coffee, or sage tea for imperial; took, with a hearty zest, deer or bear meat, or wild turkey, for breakfast, dinner, and supper, if he could get it. . . . This was old-fashioned Methodist preacher fare and fortune. Under such circumstances, who among us would now say, "Here am I, Lord, send me?"[30]

This outdoor life, working, riding, and sleeping in the open in season and out, occasionally broke the devoted churchman's health. The famous contemporary portrait of the itinerant traveling on horseback with cape and umbrella through the driving storm is not only picturesque but factual. Fording swollen streams on horseback or on foot in all kinds of weather with saddlebags slung over his shoulder, the itinerant often was prey to chills and fever ("the ague"), the chronic frontier sickness. Alfred Brunson was stricken with "the quinsy" in the spring, and went without a tie in the summer to "get browned in face and neck." In the winter, leggings, a big coat, and an umbrella were useful as protection from the elements. Such primitive preventive medicine did not always suffice. His own practitioner, the circuiteer was limited to the known and available remedies of the time. One reported, "In a few days I let blood again, and supping the barks and wine freely broke the ague."[31]

Frontier evangelists continued their rounds as long as they were able to move. Asbury, the "outrider," was often so ill that he had to be hoisted into the saddle and tied on when he started a journey to his appointments, frequently too weak to speak audibly; his adherence to duty was paralleled by that of many others. Benjamin Lakin, on the Hockhocking Circuit in September, 1809, described his experience of crossing the Scioto River as follows:

... my horse plunged into deep water and came out the same side I went in at; and in getting up a steep bank lost my [saddle] baggs and was some time before I could get them again. Just as I got my baggs the ague took me. I rode about ten miles with wet clothes on shake and puking til I puked blood. On the next morning I attended the meeting and preached.[32]

His "Journal" entry two days later read "in bed with the ague and fever." Rarely did the men miss an appointment. Ill health seemed merely to intensify their will to win converts. William Colbert, speaking of traveling while "very unfit," summed up the point of view of his whole profession: there was "no rest for Preachers while so many are flocking the downward road."[33]

When the minister's camp meeting labors — long hours of preaching and praying on the rostrum, in the "prayer rings," or in the hot tents — are added to his ordinary circuit duties, the good health he usually enjoyed seems little short of miraculous. Exposure to the night air, inclement weather, and infrequent changes of clothing made a life "well calculated to wear them out." A camp leader commented on the hardy circuit rider in the same vein: "We have been ready to say truly, 'They are immortal till their work is done.' "[34]

For some of the traveling clergy the work load was too great. Captain Frederick Marryat, the English visitor, quoted one man to show that the laity tyrannized the leaders of the democratic churches by constantly demanding the new and unusual. He also related to his readers that it was "a well-known fact that there is a species of bronchitis or affection of the lungs peculiar to the ministers of the United States, arising from their labours in their profession." Another observer, the Reverend Andrew Reed, was even less restrained in his commentary. He told Marryat, "It is these excessive, multitudinous, and often protracted religious occasions, together with the spirit that is in them, which have been for some years breaking up, and breaking down, the clergy of this land."[35]

Yet many itinerants thrived on the rugged regimen. Peter Cartwright had seventy-one years in the traveling ministry, Henry Smith sixty-five, and James B. Finley more than thirty-four years. Such service records demonstrate the weakness of the sweeping statements made by some that camp meeting leaders were soon physically and mentally debilitated by the religious practices of the "shouting Methodists."

In common with the pioneer hunter-farmer, these prophets in the wilderness had the Indian peril to combat. They took their chances of meeting with an Indian arrow or tomahawk. Alarms were frequent even in the pacified regions. A story is told of the Reverend John Strange's journeying from blockhouse to blockhouse in the newly formed Brookville Circuit of the Indiana Territory during the troubled year of 1812. Upon arriving, if all the settlers were still safe from the marauders, he led the singing of a hymn that began "And are we yet alive."[36] The circuit riders gloried in the endless tasks and the hardships and dangers incurred in the Cause of the Kingdom. Their reward, as quaintly expressed by preacher William Burke, was a selfless one: "We were gratified in having souls for our hire, and rejoiced to see the wilderness blossom as the rose."[37]

Unquestioned loyalty to the Methodist church and iron obedience to superiors in the true military tradition were demanded of them. Their method of appointment and advancement, already described, was indicative of the rigid supervision. It was likewise demonstrated in the day-by-day operation of the circuit rider system and in the training program laid out for the neophyte. The disciplinary techniques the church exerted over its hard-riding spokesmen constitute another of the many topics slighted or ignored altogether in many studies of western society.

Strict adherence to the *Discipline* was enjoined upon the backwoods evangel. The Prince of Darkness would find little opportunity to communicate with the traveling preacher who followed the regulations closely. The "First Discipline" of 1784 included these admonitions:

1. Be diligent. Never be unemployed. Never be trifling employed.

Never while away time; never spend any more time at any place than is strictly necessary.

2. Be serious. Let your motto be, "Holiness to the Lord." Avoid all lightness, jesting, and foolish talking.
3. Converse sparingly and cautiously with women. . . .
4. Do not affect the gentleman. You have no more to do with that character than a dancing master. A preacher of the gospel is the servant of all.[38]

The itinerant was urged to develop his capacities to the utmost; instructions were to spend five hours daily in study when "not traveling or engaged in public exercises." His reading, to be accompanied by much meditation and prayer, was to include the Scriptures, *Mr. Wesley's Rules, The Christian Library,* and "other pious books."[39] Men of Methodism, always on the move, were advised by their supervisors to maintain records so they could keep track of themselves. They customarily carried in their leather saddlebags journals or "notebooks," sermon notes, a plan of itinerary (to avoid repetition at appointments), and account ledgers of their book sales. Also crammed in their saddlebags were a change of clothing and shaving equipment. This habit produced efficient record-keepers, for which the western historian can be grateful; it also had the unfortunate effect of making the circuiteers fond of statistics. Many "notebooks," moreover, were the basis of autobiographies and biographies later published by the Methodist Book Concern. Such memoirs are a fruitful source for frontier mores and camp meeting history.[40]

To make sure that the church regulations were being carried out, stringent supervision was exercised through the clerical hierarchy all the way down to the veteran circuit rider who directed the first steps of the younger hand. Delinquency reports were filed on the preachers by their co-workers and presiding elders. The annual conferences acted as judicial bodies in bringing to task violators of the rules.

Ministers were removed from circuits for many reasons; personality clashes, argumentativeness, and "worldliness" are often mentioned. An example of the last was Benjamin Lakin's adverse report on his helper, Joseph Mains, for "inattention and light conduct" while traveling the White Oak, Ohio, Circuit in 1811. Mains' tour of duty in that year had been in the nature of a trial prescribed by the conference, for he had already been singled out as a person of questionable merit.[41] Alfred Brunson recalled being reprimanded by his presiding elder when the latter received a complaint from Brunson's riding companion, the senior preacher of the two, that Brunson had dared to say the blessing for several meals in visiting homes without waiting for his superior to arrive at the table. Two young exhorters, Thomas S. Hinde and James B. Finley, were tactfully disciplined in private by presiding elder John Collins when their overzealousness prompted them to start an unauthorized camp service of their own at a Deer Creek Circuit encampment in Ohio during 1809.[42] With such a system of close supervision it was possible to detect quickly and remove from the order that unusual character, the fraudulent circuiteer, who had joined up to further his own aims.

Absolute simplicity in dress and ornamentation was demanded by the Methodist church of its members and clergy to avoid pleasing personal vanity. Devout members did not wear rings or other ornaments, frills on clothes, or "artificials" (cosmetics). The "First Discipline" admonished the clergyman to give no encouragement to "superfluity of apparel," and this rule was strictly enforced.[43] When William Capers joined the preaching ranks in 1809 he ripped off his "deep frill of linen cambric and large breastpin," since in Methodist eyes these were disapproved decorations. He was but one of many who had to give up such evidences of "self-indulgence." The extremes to which plainness could reach are evident in the case of the unfortunate Reverend James Kelsey, a Georgia minister, who was brought up before the quarterly conference on the charge of ostentatious display in the wearing of "gold spectacles." The presiding elder upheld him over the objections of some of the members. One lady who sided with preacher Kelsey confided in her diary, "I am almost ashamed of it."[44]

Yet the circuit rider system was not all harsh discipline and rigid control from above. There was much camaraderie; many deep friendships were formed among the itinerants, and even between the presiding elder and his subordinates. Bishop Asbury showed the way by his socially democratic behavior. His ministerial friends were legion, and traveling companions who went along with him on his tours received nicknames. Thus he dubbed one preacher, Nicholas Snethen, "his silver trumpet."[45] Undoubtedly the criticism the leaders gave was constructive — an evidence of a desire to help the itinerant to be a better church spokesman.

The training programs that were developed for the preachers are still another instance of church discipline. In the earliest days of the traveling ministry, the only study edict was the *Discipline*. Yet even then there must have been others, besides Cartwright, whose supervisors gave them a study and reading course in literary and theological works and examined them quarterly. The *Discipline* of 1816 set forth a specific training plan. It was made the duty of the bishops or a committee appointed by the annual conferences to prescribe a course of study to be pursued by candidates for the itineracy. The presiding elder was to direct the trainees, and the latter were not to be admitted into full connection until they gave "satisfactory evidence respecting their knowledge of those particular subjects." Later, some of the conferences set up curricula. The Illinois Conference in 1825 established one which included "the principles of church government, especially your own, the philosophy or grammar of the English language, geography, ancient history, ecclesiastical history, moral and natural philosophy, and logic."[46] The General Conference of 1820 urged the annual conferences to establish literary institutions and authorized the bishops to appoint itinerants as officers and teachers in these colleges. Thereafter, schools and colleges were vigorously promoted among Methodists.[47]

But what educational opportunities existed for frontier preachers prior to the formation of these colleges? The early churchmen received their largest share of training through riding the circuit and preaching under the sage counsel of an older hand on their first round. It was often said among the Methodists that "the circuit is the true college of the young preacher." Peter Cartwright described the dearth of Methodist theological training facilities in the West in the first years of the nineteenth century, when he declared that the saddlebag preachers had "no Missionary Society; no Sunday school society; no church papers; no Bible or Tract Societies; no colleges, seminaries, academies, or universities; all the efforts to get up colleges under the patronage of the Methodist Episcopal Church in the United States and Territories were signal failures."[48] Thrown upon their own resources and spurred by the counsel of the *Discipline,* the itinerants educated themselves.

The journals and letters of such preachers as James B. Finley, Benjamin Lakin, William Colbert, Benjamin St. James Fry, and others reveal their remarkable zeal for knowledge. Self-education mainly in religious works was their leisure pursuit. The "Papers" of Benjamin Lakin include profuse notes on Bible readings and sermon briefs, as well as written exercises on such varied subjects as "Navigation by Dead Reckoning," "Problems in Mathematics and Geometry," "How to Write a Business Letter," and "Practice Notes from Books of Religious Experiences." Abel L. Williams, of the Illinois Conference, taught himself to "become proficient in ancient and modern history, and well acquainted with the literature of the Church."[49]

The principal textbooks of the pioneer preachers were the Bible, the *Discipline,* and the *Methodist Hymnal,* while the works of John Wesley, Fletcher's *Appeal,* and doctrinal tracts were also frequently carried in saddlebag libraries. These praying Bible students, according to one contemporary, read, studied, and marked the Scriptures "on their knees in the woods, in humble prayer to almighty God."[50] The well-worn copies of the Bible and hymnbook were the two arsenals from which they brought forth weapons to meet every emergency. They had a third aid "which they profoundly studied . . . the ever-open book of human nature."[51] This informal means of education was summed up by the itinerants in one of their favorite appellations for themselves, "Brush College Graduates."

Study opportunities were greatest in the intervals between tours. During this brief respite from circuit duties, the preacher would engage in prolonged gospel study, prepare new sermon outlines, and glance through the latest shipment of the Methodist Book Concern. By the 1820's religious newspapers, such as the *Zion's Herald,* the *Christian Advocate and Journal,* or the later *Western Christian Advocate* were added to his list of reading materials. Some men, like Michigan circuit rider James Gilruth, read a great deal while riding between appointments. Often the horse moved very slowly along the tortuous trail, and one could read while jerking along in the saddle. Then, too, the early morning and late evening hours on appointment days were available for Bible refreshment.[52] While the backwoods minister's studies were often too narrow in scope, what he read he learned well. Judged by results, the fairest of all measurements, the circuit rider educational plan had it points. It produced eloquent preachers, astute theological debaters, capable administrators, and efficient statisticians. It trained "Boanerges," "Sons of Consolation," and logical exponents of reason for the camp meeting rostrum.

The role of the circuit riders as cultural agents in the border regions has been largely overlooked or obscured. In spite of the vocal hostility to intellectualism expressed by some western preachers, they were a driving cultural force through their distribution of religious literature. After preaching time was over, they opened their saddlebags and assumed the role of book salesmen. Methodist, Baptist, Presbyterian, and Christian ministers alike sold Bibles, New Testaments, hymnbooks, and religious leaflets to those pioneers who could read. Many religious organizations of the East were contributing money and energy to the propagation of the gospel in the West, knowing the educational need was great. The literate pioneer had little leisure time and often less reading material. In a frontier cabin the Bible was usually the first piece of literature available. A single newspaper, whether denominational or secular, made the rounds of many a home in which reading had become almost a lost art. Thus the frontier ministers were also welcomed as subscription agents for their church's newspapers and magazines, such as the *Methodist Magazine* and the *Ladies' Repository,* which began publication in the third decade of the nineteenth century.

Methodist clergymen were among the first booksellers in the West as agents for the Methodist Book Concern, beginning in 1789. Later, the Methodist Western Book Concern was established at Cincinnati in 1828. Both the salesmen and the conference with which they were associated received a percentage of the sales. The volumes ranged over a wide field of subjects, including history, travel, philosophy, ethics, biography, and the Methodist perennials: the works of John Wesley, John Fletcher, Adams Clarke, Nathan Bangs, and Jesse Lee. Ranking above all others in sales volume, of course, were the Bible, the *Discipline,* and the *Methodist Hymnal.*[53] One can only speculate as to the educational advantages accruing to the ministers. Certainly having books in their possession was a strong inducement to read them prior to sale. Peter Cartwright raised the question whether he had done the most good in his many years in the ministry by preaching or by distributing religious works. He boasted with typical immodesty that he alone had sold some $10,000 worth of books.[54] In short, the Methodist clergy was an educating as well as a preaching ministry.

The "brush preachers" shouldered additional burdens which sometimes proved too much even for them. As previously pointed out, the circuit riders, their superiors, and the annual conference members were camp meeting planners. During the camp meeting season each year the presiding elder's labors were at their height. For several months the district superintendent lived in the tented grove, visiting all the quarterly gatherings of his district. James Quinn, a presiding elder of the Ohio Conference, attended "one hundred and five quarterly and camp meetings" from 1806 to 1809.[55]

It was the saddlebag preacher who led in the preparation of the encampment. If merely renovating an old campground, he brought the volunteers together to clear away the fallen branches, repair the plank seats after a winter's disuse, and remove the old straw from the preacher's tent to get rid of the fleas. Such a task might take a whole day. The construction job of carving a new open-air auditorium out of the wilderness, however, might take three or four times as long. For this duty the pioneer revivalist also was able to gather together a group of willing workers.

Like so many other forms of frontier labor, camp construction became a social occasion. Always, however, it was a religious affair. Work was preceded by prayer, after which the preacher labored alongside his parishioners. A picnic lunch prepared by the womenfolk was spread before the busy workers. Specified times were set aside for song and prayer. When the clearing was made and the seats and speaker's rostrum were put in readiness, a traditional ceremony took place. In a short religious service the clergyman dedicated the campgrounds and prayed that the forthcoming meeting might produce a rich harvest. On occasion, the campground was not prepared until the very day scheduled for the camp meeting to commence. Such was the case at an early encampment in Pennsylvania. There, one leader preached in the wet, dirty shirt he had worked in during the day. His comment was interesting: "It so chanced that this state of perspiration proved favorable to my voice, so that I made an unusual noise for a short time."[56]

The same men who advertised and helped prepare the campground prescribed the rules, arranged the program schedule, organized the camp guard, and led the camp meeting services. Undoubtedly, the circuit riders who doubled as camp meeting leaders were much overworked individuals. It is also accurate to say that not the least important source of the emotional excitement at the woodland revival was the hell-fire oratory of some of them — which was so fearful, yet so fascinating.

9

Frontier Evangelism

This audience was of men whose
physique had been cultivated at the
expense of much of their intellect; ...
whose knowledge had not come from
books, but from the hard necessities
and incessant exertions of a laborious
and perilous life. The speaker, then,
must use their vernacular ... and his
metaphors and similes, if he used them
at all, must be such as would readily
penetrate beneath their tangled hair
and find lodgment in their intellects.
And he must, at the same time, appeal
to their feelings; for the feelings exer-
cise a much quicker and surer power
over the intellect, than the intellect
over the feelings.[1]
— Circuit rider William H. Milburn,
  1860

THE WEST NEEDED
a doctrine that would relieve the element of danger
inherent in pioneer living and at the same time empha-
size the direct relationship between a loving God and
man.[2] To a fighting population in constant peril from
ruthless Nature, Indian attack, lawlessness, starvation, and
illness, there was a certain comfort in the thought that
the Creator was ever present, ever watchful over his flock,
and all-powerful in the face of adversity. The possibility
of sudden extinction made the question of one's eternal

170

destiny a matter of great concern. Methodism as portrayed by the frontier camp meeting preachers in the early nineteenth century was acutely attuned to these fears and hopes, and consequently was the source of inspiration to which many turned. Its pietistic theme of the salvation of man was as wide as all humanity in its appeal, and its emphasis on personalized religion met the needs of the individual rather than of society as a whole.

The age-old problem of man's relation to an unseen God and the hereafter was apparently resolved by the techniques of the backwoods evangelists. They extolled the beauty of the Supreme Being, but never ceased to stress his awesomeness, believing that fear would act as a flash of light to the indifferent. Bishop Asbury's sermon notes for a Zanesville, Ohio, camp meeting of 1815 underscored this theme: "Knowing the terror of the Lord, we persuade men." The pioneer preachers had not ventured far from the Colonial pattern displayed in Gilbert Tennent's literal warnings of "The Solemn Scene of the Last Judgment" and "From the God of Terrible Majesty, or the Presumptious Sinner Detected, his Pleas Considered, and his Doom Displayed."[3] Hades could be conjured up for the wicked so vividly by western orators that the strongest men would tremble and quake, "imagining a lake of fire and brimstone yawning to overwhelm them and the hand of the Almighty thrusting them down the horrible abyss."[4] To the unschooled backwoodsmen the invisible became absolutely credible; the Day of Judgment, the doom of the wicked, and the eternal blessedness of the righteous were as real as the harrowing events of their daily lives.

Supernatural forces were personalized in persuasive fashion. At an early nineteenth-century camp meeting, the imaginative Peter Akers prayed for divine help to combat the Prince of Darkness whose influence was all-pervasive. Kneeling, his head almost touching the platform floor, Akers cried: "O Lord, the devil is a roaring lion, is in the neighborhood, in our houses, in the church, in our hearts, and if thou come not to our help, we shall all be devoured." Again, Peter Cartwright pictured Satan's agents on earth, the "sickly little devils," as being driven out of man by the smell of brimstone as God took hold of the situation.[5] It was not strange that Benjamin Lakin's observation at an 1806 camp meeting evoked serious thoughts: "I feel an impression that there is some man or young woman here . . . who will be tramping in hell before this time next year." A youthful member of the audience recalled that many young people became deathly pale, and that "for several weeks, the attenuated thread of human life, and of my own life in particular, appeared ready to sunder almost every moment."[6]

Many frontier denominations held the view that any profound religious belief had its roots in the emotions as well as in the mind. Even a modern social scientist has expressed the opinion that the "more deeply religious a person is, the more his faith becomes felt and experienced rather than thought out."[7] The itinerants themselves believed that the pathway to the intellect was through the feelings, and they used every weapon at their disposal to insure that no hearer would be unmoved. As the outstanding eastern revivalist, Charles Grandison Finney, phrased it, "Mankind will not act until they are excited." "How many there are," he exclaimed, "who know they ought to be religious, but they are procrastinating repentance until they . . . have secured some favorite worldly interest."[8] Such persons never would relinquish their ambitious schemes until they were so excited that they could contain themselves no longer. Thus the frontier ministers as a whole

were earnest and forcible. They felt that great issues were at stake . . . that perhaps this was the last time they should ever have the opportunity of speaking to them. The weight of souls was on them . . . they felt it their immediate duty therefore, most earnestly, and even passionately, to warn, to counsel, to entreat, to admonish, to reprove, to win them by the Love of Christ to be reconciled to God — this was the burden of their preaching. They were men of quick, intense, and profound emotions, of lively fancy, and vivid imaginations.[9]

Peculiarly susceptible to crowd suggestion, the secluded frontiersman reacted violently to the vigorous preaching of the western evangelists. "Mild homilies," said one historian, "had no effect, but vivid pictures of hell-fire and damnation contrasted with the happiness and peace of salvation, if used with sufficient dramatic force, would bring the strong man to his knees."[10]

In every revival of religion, excesses have been present in varying degrees of intensity. While a public display of one's inner feelings is unthinkable by today's standards, it was regarded as merely the expression of convictions "very pungent and deep" in the harvest time of the camp meeting. This mode of behavior was common even in the populous East. The point at which tension, confusion, and strife between the old sinful ways and the new were overcome by the awesome sermons, prolonged prayers, and crowd pressures was often accompanied by strange bodily manifestations. Automatisms (bodily excitement, crying out, and hallucinations), while not considered positive evidence of conversion, were viewed as probable tokens of God's presence and attested to the power of preaching.[11] A religious participant declared:

Physical demonstrations are not infallible marks of a divine work; neither is religion so spiritual that it never demonstrates its presence by prostrating the body. Because there have been counterfeits, we must not reject the genuine.[12]

Very many of the camp leaders and participants believed that the Creator's power was thus being evidenced. "It was of God, because it was superhuman, and beyond the power and control of man, or any evil spirit." Yet others decried bodily excitements which

in a great majority of cases affect the ignorant, rather than the enlightened, those in whom the imagination predominates over the reason, and especially those who are of a nervous temperament, rather than those of an opposite character.[13]

Modern psychologists conclude that these extreme bodily agitations at revivals were not the fruits of true religion but the results of nervous instability, pathological emotionalism, and the deadening of rationality. The convert felt very close to heaven at the moment of "self surrender," when the feelings of joy, relief, and safety replaced that of tension. Here again the theologian believed that the Holy Spirit had entered in, while the psychologists have coldly termed it nervous exhaustion — the only recourse left.[14]

After the camp meeting had matured, the delicate balance between reason and emotion was less often upset by emotional excitement. Emotional appeals were used as a springboard, a preliminary to an appeal to reason. "The saving, elementary truths of the gospel" were constantly reiterated. One writer declared in 1852: "The lost condition of the soul by nature, repentance towards God, faith toward our Lord Jesus Christ, justification, sanctification, the witness of the Spirit — such truths seemed to make up the alphabet."[15] In his opinion, if such themes were given excessive use, the error was on the safe side. Doctrinal sermons reviewed the fall of man, general atonement, and the tenets of individual conversion and simultaneous regeneration.

Since the Methodists considered all men sinful before repentance and equal in the eyes of God, all were appealed to, believer and unbeliever alike. Their invitation to Christian fellowship was embodied in a denunciation of sin. To gain admittance to a Methodist society, one had merely to be a true seeker after the Christian experience, to desire to flee from the wrath to come. Adam's original sin weighed heavily on his posterity, although the Lord would not consider it a

responsible sin until sanctioned by actual sin. It would have resulted in the eternal death of Adam and all the race in him, but for the Redeemer. It results in the temporal death, (rendered just by compensation) of all. It results in eternal death upon all who, by unrepentent actual sin, accept its guilt and penalty.[16]

The Arminian doctrine of free will, free grace, and individual responsibility was most compatible with the desires of an extremely independent and individualistic backwoods people. Whereas the Calvinistic tenet of predestination held by the Presbyterians gave hope of salvation to the few, the Methodist view of full and free grace to all was the more hopeful because the sinner himself aided in the conversion process. If conversion did take place, it had to be the result of each individual's personal consciousness and should be visibly demonstrated.[17] The democratic nature of the dogma appealed to the frontiersman, who could understand an idea if he could feel it emotionally. At the mourner's bench he would experience complete repentance and thus at a definite time and place be cleansed of his taint of sin, "washed clean in the blood of the Lamb." While an integral component of this seeming miracle was the factor of man's active role of choice, "justification by faith" was considered an act of God, the sinner himself having no control over the process.[18] The emotional catharsis left the individual "born again," wholly acceptable unto Christ.

Ideally, the penitent should not be allowed to feel that his duty was over and done with now that he was reborn. Persistence in holiness was a condition of salvation. The circuit riders stressed that regeneration was but the beginning, the start of a new life of "expansive benevolence."[19] To Charles G. Finney, representative of many other evangelical Christian leaders, regeneration was a turning to God, "loving God with all our heart and our neighbor as ourselves."[20] Having been saved himself, the convert should energetically assume the task of saving others. By the 1830's tens of thousands had turned from selfishness. By being their brother's keepers these enthusiasts hoped "to save the American church and nation from the judgment of heaven."[21] The social implications of this revival gospel were reflected in almost all the reforms attracting the nation in that day of the common man — temperance, women's rights, and antislavery, to mention but a few. Thus the Methodist equalitarian theology, whether expounded from the camp rostrum or the church pulpit, helped lay the foundations for the reform crusade that aimed at the perfection of man and the moral state.

At the camp meeting, the preacher entreated his listeners to perform good works to the utmost, and to observe their moral responsibilities. Sermons were often based on the manifold duties of man to man and the spiritual lift granted the individual when he fulfilled those obligations. By "close preaching," taking a subject close to everyday living "and stressing it so all understood its import," they drove their points home. For example, William McKendree chose to expose profiteering ("extortion") in the summer of 1806 at a Limestone encampment in Ohio, a landing place for most migrants from upper Kentucky. Winding up his message, he reflected:

Yes, it frequently happens, that some take advantage of the poor emigrant too, that has removed to your fine country to become your neighbour and fellow-citizen; you sell him your corn or other produce at double price, . . . and receive it too from the poor man who has to grapple with misfortunes to support his family.

While he talked on, an elderly man was seen to become more and more agitated until he seemingly could restrain himself no longer. The old farmer rose from his seat and shrilly broke in, "If I did sell my corn for a dollar a bushel I gave them six months to pay it in." "Sit down my friend," calmly replied the bishop, "sit down sir, if you please, we are discussing a subject and delineating a character, we are not in the habit of making *personal* reflections."[22]

The itinerants were not socially myopic, as their sermon themes indicate. They considered it their spiritual obligation to strike out against all forms of sin. In pungent language the evils of the day were fearlessly denounced: immorality, intemperance, tobacco, blasphemy, dueling, card playing, horse racing, and gambling. Even such minute matters as false pride in dress and manners were objects of scorn. Circuit rider James Axley of eastern Tennessee insisted that "a preacher that was good and true had a trinity of devils to fight — superfluous dress, whiskey and slavery."[23]

Benjamin Lakin's sermon notes explored the theme of human vanity: "The eyes of other people are the eyes that ruin us — If all but myself were blind, I should want neither fine clothes, fine houses nor fine furniture."[24] James Axley belabored the same topic in a more flamboyant and hence more effective style. On one occasion he used a humorous approach, calling into play his abilities as a ventriloquist, to rebut those who insisted fashion decreed conformity in dress. His colloquy was with an imaginary apologist, seated at the rear of the congregation. The apologist was made to say that "some Methodist ministers dress in fashionable style and in air and manner enact the dandy." Axley vigorously denied this allegation, but the straw man said: "Well, sir, if you won't take my word for it, just look at those young preachers in the pulpit behind you." The preacher turned and gazed upon his fashionably dressed brethren. Turning back to the congregation he concluded in a subdued tone: *"If you please sir, we'll drop the subject!"*[25] Such speeches often produced positive results. At one Fleming Circuit camp meeting "many of the dressy ones" came down to the altar; and one in particular, "Brother Benecraft's daughter," who had been converted, upon returning home began "tearing off her ruffels." The preacher in charge concluded, "I have never known a greater change in dress than hath taken place in this neighborhood since the Lord began to revive his work in it."[26]

The effect of stringent rules preached and enforced by Methodist circuiteers concerning daily behavior is mirrored in Cartwright's recollection:

The Methodists in that early day dressed plain; attended their meetings faithfully . . . they wore no jewelry, no ruffles. . . . They could, nearly every soul of them, sing our hymns and spiritual songs. They religiously kept the Sabbath day: many of them abstained from dram-drinking. . . . Parents did not allow their children to go to balls or plays; they did not send them to dancing

Yours respectfully

Peter Cartwright

schools; they generally fasted once a week, and almost universally on the Friday before each quarterly meeting.[27]

A frequent target of many "Men of Zeal" was the prevailing whiskey habit. James B. Finley, ignoring the counsel to "preach the gospel and let people's private business alone," let no occasion go by without dwelling on the evils of drink. He would often "pledge whole congregations, standing on their feet, to the temperance cause." James Axley even devoted a sermon to the evil of making stills — an evil even though, he said, the cooper himself might not have tasted, bought, sold, or distilled a drop of brandy.[28]

Peter Cartwright's straightforward talk at a Tennessee camp meeting of 1815 was representative of the attitude of other roughhewn preachers toward adultery. The "Kentucky Boy" refused to accept on trial an apostate Baptist preacher who wanted to join the Methodist church. "Give up this course of living," the petitioner was advised, "put away the woman with whom you are now living, and go live with your lawful wife." The man burst into tears and said he couldn't comply but still wanted to be given a six-months' probationary period. Cartwright was adamant; "so we parted, and I feared he was eternally lost." From the pulpit, circuit rider William Colbert used the same theme, adultery, and found that his target was close at hand. As he confided in his *Journal:*

I preached [at] John Lords [in the Somerset Circuit, Maryland] on Matthew 5 27 to 32 and for preaching against whoredom was very severely tongue lashed by a woman of that stamp who has left her husband and children and taken up with another man who was present, and was offended likewise at my preaching so pointed.[29]

Another expert in driving home "practical truths" was

James Quinn. He demonstrated his talents in an admonition to delinquent parents who complained, "1 can not give my children religion."

To such we say, you can do more in this matter than you are aware of — perhaps more than you are willing to know. You can do as much toward giving your children religion, as you can toward raising a crop of corn. In the latter case you can clear the ground, break the soil, plant in due time, improve the season of culture; then look and pray for dew and the gentle rains of heaven. Now by education, an education favorable to moral as well as intellectual culture, clear and prepare the soil. Plant or sow the seed of pure evangelical truth in their hearts; then cultivate by precept and example. Teach them by theory and show them by practice, how to be religious; all the while offering up to God for them in their hearing, and out of their sight, the earnest, continued, and fervent prayer of faith, and leave the rest with God.[30]

However strict the teachings in matters moral and spiritual, liberty was a recurrent theme of camp sermons. Civil and religious liberty was treated in a high-flown address by the eccentric Lorenzo ("Crazy") Dow at a woodland revival in the early days of the Mississippi Territory. Arising from a sick bed to bring a disorderly crowd under control, Dow traced the ideology of individual freedom of expression since the American Revolution. He depicted the lives and sacrifices of Methodist preachers and concluded by saying that "any man who interrupted a Methodist preacher in the discharge of his high office, was a mean, low-bred scoundrel." One of the guilty parties was sufficiently ashamed to leave the audience, saying "I always was a fool."[31]

While none of the churches in the early days ever looked upon human slavery as a good, for all viewed the institution as evil in nature, few Methodist circuit riders in the southern regions preached against it because of the prevailing mores. Nevertheless, the mistreatment of slaves and even slavery itself did come in for censure. Hardy souls like James Axley of Tennessee, James Craven of Virginia, Peter Cartwright of Kentucky, and Jacob Gruber, veteran of Maryland circuits, sometimes found themselves in trouble when they treated any phase of this subject. After 1824 Cartwright transferred his activities to Illinois so that he could be free to criticize slavery at will. Once there he continued his campaign by giving stump speeches on the question of admitting slavery into the prairie states.[32] At that time the issue was agitating Illinois, and was sure to arouse interest.

Doctrinal sermons and "close, pungent, heart-searching" expositions on experiential religion crowded the practical subjects for pulpit time. Bishop Asbury recorded a synopsis of one of his doctrinal sermons, "His Voice," given at an Ohio camp meeting of 1815 based upon the text Heb. 3:7-8. He described the voice of the Almighty as the gospel of grace — "its blessing, promises, means, ordinances, doctrines, and precepts." Men hardened their hearts against that call by "open, notorious sinning; by secret wickedness; by sinful tempers indulged; by a wilful neglect of Gospel men and Gospel means." If God's voice was audible that day, concluded Asbury, "then speaker and hearer do all you can for God."[33] Taking as a text Christ's Sermon on the Mount, Benjamin Lakin elaborated in his sermon notes on the subject, "No man can serve two masters." In direct opposition were

God, the author of all good, and giver of all blessing, the source of purity, and center of perfection, and Mammon, which includes not only riches but also all the things of the world in which men seek happiness independent of God — Take a view of what is implied in serving God — the word Serve signifies to attend to a command. What is implied in serving of Mammon? Take a view of the impropibility [*sic*] of serving God and Mammon. Contrast the consequences of the service of God and Mammon.[34]

Lakin's talk on "Reward" had the theme that "God hath promised to reward every man according to his works." The picture would not be complete if it did not include such curious addresses as those presented at two Lawrenceburg Circuit encampments in Indiana during 1818 in which one preacher spoke against shouting at the services, while another preached in favor of the practice.[35]

Doctrinal heresy from without the Methodist ranks was treated no less keenly and pugnaciously than that from within. The beliefs of competing denominations on the frontier came in for acrimonious debate, and the Methodists gave battle to the Baptists, Presbyterians, Shakers, and Universalists. Much pulpit time on the campground was devoted to the cut-and-thrust of denominational argument. A Baptist missionary noted parallels between his church's preaching and the Methodists' in the trans-Allegheny West in 1813: "It much resembles the Baptists — is very controversial and most bitter against Calvinists. They rail very much against the practice of the Presbyterians receiving pay for preaching calling them hirelings."[36] At a Whitewater Circuit gathering in Indiana, Robert W. Finley devoted an entire sermon to the varying rites of baptism. "I will not say that any man who baptizes by immersion is an indecent man," he summarized, "but I will say, he has been guilty of an indecent act."[37]

On occasion, debates between two denominations were held, such as that between the Universalists and Methodists in the Wabash River Valley in Indiana. Below the Ohio River Baptists and Presbyterians would join forces to denounce the revivalistic tactics of Methodism. Their respective church publications carried on the attack.[38] The

Western Christian Advocate contained Peter Cartwright's report of an 1839 meeting at Salt Creek, Illinois, that was "infested by the Campbellites and Waterites," and the columns of the *Calvinistic Magazine* contained violent condemnation of emotional evangelism. Tracts and pamphlets distributed by the circuiteers at camp meetings were so scurrilous that one revival critic was led to condemn them as "most deceitful, unfair, and abusive attacks on the faiths of other denominations."[39]

Factions of most of the frontier churches at the same time were quarreling among themselves, and bitter partisanship resulted in the drawing of strange conclusions. Theodore Dwight Weld, famed antislavery apostle, declared that the Presbyterian revival preachers in New York

preach nothing but the loose, disconnected rhapsodies of Methodists in the main. Their preaching is exhortation and appeal, dwelling upon the love of Christ etc., and all addressed to mere "sympathy." They reason little and investigate less.[40]

Extemporaneous speaking was a dominant characteristic of the "primitive school" of Methodist preaching. As was true in the courtroom, in Congress, and on the hustings, that orator in the pulpit was most popular who did not have to rely on manuscript or notes. Since most of the preachers "came out from the people and knew how to address them," they used the local idiom to season their illustrations from everyday experience. Needless to say, this unpretentious approach was well adapted to the prevailing religious themes and the intellectual level of the audience. Impromptu address was calculated to produce an immediate effect — conversions. Men who were generally unlettered or, at best, lacking in literary polish won converts through the gift of "colloquial direct-

ness and force." Their mode of illustrating self-evident
truths was striking, and sometimes picturesque in the extreme. To one sputtering preacher, addressing an illiterate
audience, Heaven could only be described as a "Kaintuck
of a place."[41]

A reflection of the universal popularity of the spontaneous address was the frontiersman's disdain of college-
trained preachers who read high-toned discourses or used
voluminous notes in delivery. Congregational minister
Julian M. Sturtevant, a member of the Yale Band and
the first instructor at Illinois College, was made painfully aware of this attitude in 1829 when he delivered a
sermon from a prepared manuscript for the first and last
time. He later said, "I could see from their countenances
that many were thinking: 'I wonder if that young man
calls that preaching!' "[42] Failure to speak extemporane-
ously was an indication to some that the speaker had
never experienced the soul-cleansing event of spiritual
rebirth. In a Virginia town a Presbyterian elder actually
went up to a young man who had just read his sermon
from manuscript, and inquired whether he had ever been
converted![43]

Certainly, many backwoods preachers considered the
delivery of manuscript sermons a disgrace to the profession. The sight of an educated clergyman trying to read
a sermon reminded one brother cleric of "a gosling that
had got the straddles by wading in the dew." James B.
Finley, railing against book preaching in the columns of
the *Western Christian Advocate* in 1839, insisted it
"operates against the preaching of the Word." He aimed
his criticism specifically against a sketchbook of sermons,
counseling against its being used even as an outline for a
talk. No man could be an effective speaker, Finley con-

tinued, if he tried to memorize these sketches, "bones, as they are called."[44]

The Spirit within was guide enough. But this selfsame Spirit led some men to fantastic lengths. Some speakers drawled out their sermons in a singsong tone; others rose to a high pitch and stayed there.[45] In the best, stout lungs, vigorous gestures, copious tears, a flair for the dramatic, and a ready tongue were necessary attributes.

When the preacher arose to address the campers he usually "threw the reins upon the neck of feeling and let her run full speed."[46] As a result, some talks ran on for two or three hours, with the listeners becoming more and more enthusiastic in their fervor. On occasion it took another churchman to remind the speaker that the sermon or exhortation had accomplished its objective, and that further talk would be useless. James B. Finley was interrupted at an Ohio encampment by a cohort who said: "Now brother, stop; keep the rest for another time, and throw out the Gospel net; it is now wet and we shall have a good haul."[47] As Parson William G. Brownlow, pugnacious circuit rider of the southern highlands, phrased it, "Of all the deaths that ever any people died, there is none so distressing as that of being preached to death!" Since he was a long-winded speaker himself, he apparently did not heed his own advice.[48] By and large, however, brevity was not considered a virtue, nor was plain unadorned phraseology. The critical listener could quite correctly comment that at times

it was a matter of astonishment to what length they could spin out a sermon embracing only a few ideas. The merit of a sermon was measured somewhat by the length of it, by the flowery language of the speaker, by his vociferation and violent gestures.[49]

Spread-eagle oratory (a combination of much bombast,

mixed metaphors, and hyperbole) made some preachers' discourses colorful if not at the same time informative. Florid and overly sentimental narration was in vogue. Among the many strains evident in the circuiteers' style, as reflected in religious periodicals of the day, was that of poetic imagery. An almost overwhelming example of this profuse, flowery, exaggerated technique is contained in a churchman's report on an Ohio revival in 1845:

Now Bro Chambers the old ship Zion is under full sail. Last night she hove down upon the enimy [*sic*] and after firing round shot, grape, and canister, she poured in a broadside of chain and bar shot, which cut away the enimy's [*sic*] riging [*sic*] and down came her spars which gave us the opportunity of boarding, which we did with a mighty shout of victory on death, and succeeded in capturing and bringing off thirteen livis [*sic*], and we expect our Captain Jesus, will, in the morning's meeting, which is appointed for mourners, appear and knock off their shackles and put them to duty on board the old ship.[50]

In delivering his religious discourse the Methodist man of God often mispronounced words or gave them ludicrous meanings—and with good reason, for he lacked any prolonged acquaintance with the schoolroom. He was usually his own teacher. One itinerant learned "to preach at night the Scriptures that he had studied through the day." Another, riding circuits on the Ohio-Indiana frontier in 1819, centered his reading and studies on subjects "almost exclusively theological," as he "could not see the propriety of studying even the English grammar." After being rebuked for violating the rules of grammar fourteen times in one exhortation, he began to realize that the meaning of his messages was being obscured by his poor command of the English language.[51] As Peter Cartwright put it, "It is true we could not, many of us, conjugate a verb or parse a sentence, and murdered the king's English almost every lick." "But," he continued, "there was a divine unction [that] attended the word preached, and thousands fell under the mighty power of God, and thus the Methodist Episcopal Church was planted firmly in this Western wilderness."[52] A visitor, unfamiliar with the evangelical style, based his criticism of camp meeting sermons exclusively upon the errors in syntax. He called them "harangues . . . composed of medley, declamation, and the most disgusting tautology."[53] Yet in all fairness, the addresses heard at the camp services can be neither dismissed in this manner nor neatly catalogued.

It would be untrue to say that the woodland preachers gave no thought to the mechanics of their craft. Distinct articulation would enable even the people in the back rows of the encampment to understand every word spoken. Bishop McKendree thought that modulation was more important than mere volume, but probably many practitioners believed in cultivating a voice like a "mountain horn." According to one contemporary minister, "The appeals had all the freedom of the open air and the winds and the directness and speed of the lightning. . . . The converts in those days were born strong into the kingdom, and entered it shouting."[54] Even Francis Asbury, taking off his coat and neckcloth, preached to great throngs in the open, "arousing them to repentance by the awful peals of his voice."[55] A stentorian voice was indisputably an advantage to the circuiteer who had to project his voice above background noises of every description.

Perhaps the preaching style of the outdoor revival can best be described as loud, vigorous, crude — but effective. As one visitor put it, "If heaven is only to be taken by storm, he [the circuit rider] was a proper leader for his congregation." The stout heart of the frontiersman was conquered by the "Boanerges" who alarmed rather than consoled. Through him the "violated law spoke out its thunders."[56] At an Indiana camp meeting this type of attack caused an old Revolutionary War veteran to rush up from the rear of the encampment to proclaim:

Quarter! Quarter! Quarter! and falling upon his knees, said: "I am an old soldier. . . . I have heard the cannons' loud roar, and have seen blood and brains flying in every direction around me; but since God made me, I never heard such cannonading as this. I yield! I yield!"[57]

The successful circuit rider always observed the precept that

the awful importance of the theme should be fully reflected in the *manner* of the speaker. The fire of his soul should be revealed in the flash of his eye. The solemn notes of warning should be re-echoed as with the blast of a trumpet, and every gesture and movement should add impressive power to the words that proclaim the fearful destiny of the impenitent soul.[58]

Many a pioneer could agree with Abraham Lincoln that "when I see a man preach I like to see him act as if he were fighting bees."[59] To drive a point home a backwoods minister might bend his knees and body with a sudden downward jerk and then shoot up again with a start. Just as effective with these audiences would be the weeping-prophet technique demonstrated by Ralph Lotspiech, who "wept much" in his discourses. Another of this school, Bishop Enoch George, moved rather than instructed his audience, and kept one listener "bathed in tears from the beginning to the close of his sermon." Bishop George's way of removing the tears which blinded his small and deeply seated eyes, by running his finger behind his spectacles while he uttered in soft and subdued tones, "Glory," was "peculiar and impressive."[60]

There were the tragedians like the inimitable John Collins, whose impersonations caused him to be the "living embodiment of his theme, and with a soul on fire he poured out the living truth till every heart was moved."[61] When a different situation called for it, a touch of humor was deftly applied. Peter Cartwright seemed to be a master of the art of ridiculing by sarcasm either the tenets of an unbeliever or a preacher of a rival denomination.[62]

Successful camp leaders possessed a magnificent sense of timing and a profound knowledge of human nature. In their effort to generate a high charge of religious enthusiasm, they were aided by certain unwritten laws of evangelism that practically guaranteed successful meetings. A Baptist newspaper summarized a few guiding principles:

Let your time be fully occupied—multiply your meetings as much as is practicable; lest while you sleep, the enemy sows tares among the wheat.

Let not the dread of novelty deter you from the employment of any measures.

Bring into the field every instrumentality. Not only the heavy ordnance of the ministry, but also the small arms of tracts, etc. *"Whatsoever* the hand findeth to do, do it with thy might." For who knoweth which shall prosper, either this or that.[63]

The showmen's ingenious techniques were various. To arouse interest, ministers stood on stumps around one service area and alternately recited Bible verses. At an open-air revival in New Jersey, seven trumpeters added a dramatic touch by playing in unison to announce the next public meeting.[64] A startling technique used at a camp meeting of the West Union Circuit of Ohio in 1835 was the work of John Collins, John Baughman, and Maxwell P. Gaddis. They arranged an elaborate marching ceremony which preceded the midnight sermon. As the campers, three abreast, marched around the woodland auditorium seven times, they sang this spirited song:

> Blow ye the trumpet, blow
> The gladly-solemn sound,
> Let all the nations know,
> To earth's remotest bound,
> The year of jubilee is come;
> Return ye ransomed sinners home.

The message that followed devastated the aroused audience. Religious excitement lasted through the night; some fifty persons were converted by the time the sun rose over the campers' tents.[65]

At another encampment, an unusual stratagem was used to outwit "Beelzebub." The Reverend James Havens shifted the location of the altar, saying to his audience: "We have fought the Devil *there* til he understands that ground as well as we do; we will take him by surprise tonight." The move had the desired psychological effect, for with the aid of hymn singing, fervent exhortation, prayer meetings in the tents, and a "praying circle" out under the stars, some sixty to seventy were converted. At sundown the following evening, the preacher switched the service back to the old site, announcing, "The Devil expects us to fight him up yonder where we did last night but we will take him by surprise again."[66]

The camp meeting atmosphere frequently brought forth histrionic brilliance of which the itinerant had not realized he was capable. Exalted feelings increased the speaker's effectiveness, and the out-of-doors seemed to make communion with God easier. One observer noted that "if there is anything like eloquence in him it is sure to be aroused."[67] As a result, the westerners, who were as "inflammable as tow," were swept into some of their decisions by contagious excitement, reflecting the religious zeal of their preachers. In 1810 at one camp meeting in Ohio, noted Benjamin Lakin, his colleagues had preached such "pointed and alarming sermons" that he was convinced that if the worshipers never had another gospel sermon "the warning they have this day had is sufficient to leve [*sic*] them without excuse."[68] Evangelical Protestantism as preached by the old western ministers utilized the few positive truths of the future life to convince heretofore indifferent frontiersmen, and in many cases bore the fruit of transformed lives.[69]

10

Camp Meeting Hymns

I will sing with the Spirit, and I will
sing with the understanding also.[1]
I Cor. 14:15.

T HE REMARKABLE
growth of Methodism has been attributed as much to its
congregational singing as to its preaching, theology, and
flexible church policy. It has been aptly named the "singing church." On the American frontier, where people
were more apt to sing than read, the followers of John
Wesley not only lived the gospel, they sang it. Charles
Wesley's and Isaac Watts's hymns of inspiration re-
created the evangelical experience; they gave the Methodist movement "life and warmth and heart." Such songs
"provided the necessary emotional outlet of the people
through voicing those intimate devotional thoughts which
so many have had and so few possess the capacity to
express."[2] Thus song became a potent force in early
Methodism — and especially was this true at camp meetings. The early nineteenth century's record of conversions
bears a close kinship to the fervent singing of camp songs.

Unfortunately, many favorites were never recorded.
This lost body of revival song has been classified by
scholars as "unwritten music." The campers frequently
relied on the preachers to supply both the words and the
tune for group singing. Some encampment hymnody,

192

however, was compiled by itinerants and others, and published in camp meeting hymnbooks—one of the legacies of the outdoor revival in America.

These song manuals began to appear in print shortly after the Kentucky Revival. Between 1805 and 1843 there were at least seventeen such Methodist songbooks printed in the United States.[3] All but one were edited prior to 1840, the first appearing in 1805. The years preceding the "Roaring Forties" marked the high tide of the camp meeting hymnal. The Northeast was the principal generating center, although Stith Mead's *Hymns and Spiritual Songs,* published in Richmond, Virginia, in 1805; David B. Mintz's *Spiritual Song Book,* originating in Halifax, North Carolina, that same year; and Thomas S. Hinde's *The Pilgrim Songster,* first published in Cincinnati, Ohio, during 1810, are exceptions.

Popularity seemed assured for any such compilation.[4] The demand was so great for Orange Scott's camp songbook that the five thousand copies making up the initial edition (1829) were sold in eighteen months; three thousand of the second edition were bought quickly; and several months later when the third edition went to press, fifteen hundred were earmarked for paid subscribers. The preface of this publication contained the argument that its price, selection, and size made it preferable to some larger camp meeting hymnals, because they "are not of course so convenient for the pocket." "Pocket-size" editions varied in dimensions. The 1832 work of Scott's measured two and three-fourths inches by four and one-half inches; another songbook published four years later was two inches by three and one-half inches.[5]

In itself, the pocket-sized hymnbook was not an innovation caused by the advent of camp meetings. For example, the officially sanctioned Methodist hymnal of 1830, certainly intended for use at all types of religious gatherings, was also of that size. It bore the title, *The Methodist Pocket Hymn Book, revised and improved.* Because competition was great, a request appeared in the preface: "We most earnestly entreat you, if you have any respect for the authority of the Conferences, or of us, . . . to purchase no Hymn Books, but what are signed with the names of your Bishops."[6] Like many other songbooks used at encampments, this publication was not solely restricted to a pocket size. In 1831 it appeared in three forms, the smallest being the "Pearl" edition. This was advertised as the most diminutive of the "compact and portable little books," and it was urged that "every child that can read ought to be put in possession of one." While the sponsors of the official hymnal attempted to reduce the circulation of the camp song manuals, they were not entirely successful.[7]

Campers' hymnals when first published were similar to other church song collections of their day in that they contained only the texts of the songs without musical notation. Their indexes listed the selections, as many as 125, either by title, or, as was more frequently the case, by first line. John and Charles Wesley and Isaac Watts were favored composers. Revival tunes with scores appended first appeared in country-sing manuals, beginning with the *Christian Harmony,* printed in New Hampshire in 1805. Thus the tunes of the camp meetings were originally publicized by the country singing masters.[8]

One of the best-known camp songbooks was *The Pilgrim Songster.* Between 1810 and 1828 the combined circulation of its three western editions was not less than ten thousand, a large audience for that day.[9] The *Songster* also went through several editions in Philadelphia, Baltimore, and New York. Thomas S. Hinde, the original compiler, insisted in 1828 that other editors "neglected to give credit to the proper authors"; most of the songs were "mutilated."[10] This statement offers a valuable clue to the nebulous history of camp meeting hymnody. Variations in songs copied by various persons at different times meant transformation of many backwoods favorites. Outdoor revival hymns were seldom created in an immutable form. The number of hymnals patterned after Hinde's publication bears further testimony to the widespread appeal of revival psalmody.

Greatly contributing to the success of *The Pilgrim Songster* were the many selections written by the two "western poets," John A. Granade and Caleb Jarvis Taylor, both Great Revival alumni. In the third edition of the work one-third of all the spiritual tunes listed were produced by those two collaborators. Historian Bangs said Granade's compositions, the "Pilgrim's Songs," were "among the most popular hymns which were sung at those camp meetings, and perhaps became the fruitful source whence sprung the numerous ditties from which the Church was, for some time, almost deluged."[11]

In spite of the plethora of publications available, camp leaders were continually confronted with a shortage of songbooks. Undaunted, they cut up the hymnbooks and distributed the leaves so that all could learn some words by heart. The practice of "lining the hymn" also aided the worshipers in their memorizing task, a technique especially helpful to the many in the audience who were illiterate. In this procedure the preacher read two lines and then everyone sang them; he continued in this way until all the verses had been sung. If the selection was as popular as Isaac Watts's "Am I a Soldier of the Cross?" prompting was not necessary. Instrumental accompaniment was frowned on because "it detracted from the simplicity of the services."[12]

It has been truthfully said that in the early days of Methodism "congregational singing was worship and the beginning of prayers." Joyous songs as well as mournful dirges, inspirational hymns as well as martial airs were evoked by the mood and the occasion. The themes were predominantly versions of the doctrines and teachings of the word of God

> which have been recognized in all ages as the most ready to arouse the sinful heart: the agony and sufferings of Christ in Gethsemane, and on Calvary; the coming of the Saviour a second time to . . . claim his oppressed, tempted, and suffering followers; heaven . . . the evils of earth and a probationary condition, . . . hell . . . a place of actual increasing punishment, set forth in fearfully vivid language; death . . . to the wicked a foretaste of the consuming wrath of God that shall devour all his adversaries.[13]

The traditional hymns—the "allowed" hymns—were popular, but the folk products more nearly satisfied the new religious conditions of the camp meeting. These folk songs can be arbitrarily categorized into three mutually exclusive types: religious ballads, hymns of praise, and revival spirituals.[14] Worldly tunes were wedded to otherworldly texts, a practice engaged in years earlier by John Wesley in England. Any worshiper who had gone to a social affair and raised his voice in song could be equally exuberant at the camp meeting. His old favorites now carried a religious message, but the musical score remained the same.

The "religious ballads" probably did not spring from any particular religious movement, for they had long been in existence. They were of many subtypes. Composed for individual singing, those narrating biblical happenings were strong favorites. Scriptural giants were personalized in song, and the glories of Zion were made real. A not uncommon twist was the addition of one's own personal religious experiences after a narration from the Scriptures. The traditional beginning for one was:

> When Joseph his brethren beheld,
> Afflicted and trembling with fear,
> His heart with compassion was fill'd,
> From weeping he could not forbear.
> A while his behavior was rough,
> To bring their past sins to their mind:
> But when they were humbled enough,
> He hasten'd to show himself kind.

John Newton, the maker of the text, attached four more stanzas relating to his own trials.[15] This type was extremely popular during the early nineteenth century when camp meeting altar services were introduced, although by the 1850's it was not considered proper for public worship.

These experiential songs or mourner's songs always began with the traditional "Come all ye" and went on to explain how the subject who was born in sin experienced religion, was saved, and became a child of God. Such songs that stressed man's short temporal life and the imminence of the Judgment Day were effective in swaying the wavering sinner at the altar. For example, the words of the first of six verses of "Pray Cast a Look Upon That Bier" vividly described the tenor of the preacher's exhortation:

> Pray, cast a look upon that bier,
> A corpse must preach to-day,
> It tells the old, the young and fair,
> Their house is built of clay.

Another pointedly called the attention of the listener to the consequences of his actions:

> Stop poor sinners, stop and think,
> Before you further go;
> Will you sport upon the brink of everlasting wo!
> On the verge of ruin stop,
> Now the friendly warning take;
> Stay your footsteps, ere ye drop
> Into the burning lake.[16]

One can only speculate as to the effectiveness of the chanting of the following by bystanders as the penitents were being exhorted at the mourner's bench:

> Pray on, my brethren in the Lord;
> Pray 'til you feel the pow'r of God;
> Pray 'til he drives your doubts away,
> Pray 'til you see the gospel day.
>
> Pray for the mourners; see their grief;
> Pray 'til the mourners find relief;
> Pray for the wicked everywhere;
> Pray that your garments may be clear.[17]

In fact, every camp songbook offered a variety of mourner's songs to choose from. The following lines reveal their themes: "Hark my gay friend, that solemn toll," "Ye mourners who in silent gloom," "Farewell, dear friends, I must be gone," "When blooming youth is snatched away."[18]

In exhorting others to enjoy the advantages of a holy life, the campers often invoked a martial spirit. They viewed themselves as soldiers enlisted under the banner of Christ, pledged to wage "unceasing warfare against sin." At one encampment, preacher Granade led a part of the congregation in this stirring ballad:

Ye soldiers of Jesus, pray stand to your arms,
Prepare for the battle, the gospel alarms;
The trumpets are sounding, come, soldiers, and see
The standard and colours of sweet liberty.

At the same time Taylor led the other group in a similar song:

Hark! Brethren, don't you hear the sound!
The martial trumpets now are blowing; . . .

Bounty offered, joy and peace;
To every soldier this is given;
When from toils and war they cease,
A mansion bright, prepared in Heaven.[19]

The first lines of some selections indicated this warlike spirit: "The gospel calls for volunteers," "Am I a soldier of the Cross," "Hark, listen to the trumpeters!" and "A soldier, Lord, thou hast me made." An especially expressive hymn was included in *The Wesleyan Camp Meeting Hymn Book:*

I've listed in the Holy War,
To fight for life and endless joy;
And grace more boundless than the seas,
Is the rich wages I receive.

Under Captain, Jesus Christ,
I now am listed during life,
To fight against the powers of Hell,
In favour of Immanuel. . . .

I have a sword which, when I wield
The stoutest foes must quit the field;
The word of God must e'er prevail,
Eternal truth can never fail.

A final category included in the religious ballad grouping, the "farewell songs," dealt intimately with the backwoods revival institution. Here was voiced the worshiper's sadness in breaking up camp or leaving the meeting. Used in the parting handshake ceremony, they told a familiar story:

> Lord, when together here we meet,
> And taste thy heavenly grace,
> Thy smiles are so divinely sweet,
> We're loath to leave the place.
>
> Yet Father, since it is thy will
> That we must part again,
> O let thy precious presence still
> With everyone remain.[20]

The "hymns of praise," on the other hand, were joyous in spirit. Converts who were "washed white in the blood of the Lamb" were anxious to sing of it, and their songs were given forth in a wholehearted manner. The texts had been earlier superimposed on old folk melodies, in the evangelical fervor surrounding the Baptist and Methodist beginnings in England and later in America.[21] That the communicants experienced blissful joy was evident in "Almighty love inspire," "Hosannah to Jesus! I'm filled with his praise," "Hail the blest morn," "Come saints and sing to Christ our King," "O' how charming, O' how charming," and "How Happy, how loving, how joyful I feel." The words of a "Hymn of Rejoicing in Communion with God" embody the mood of the hymns of praise:

> Come, thou fount of every blessing,
> Tune my heart to sing thy grace;
> Streams of mercy never ceasing,
> Call for songs of loudest praise.
> Teach me some melodious sonnet
> Sung by flaming tongues above;
> Praise the mount! I'm fixed upon it,
> Mount of thy redeeming love.[22]

While some of the foregoing texts were undoubtedly composed on the grounds, it remained for the camp meet-

ing to sire a new brand of song, the "revival spiritual."
As an aftermath of the Kentucky Revival, the traditional
hymns and folk hymns were literally sung to pieces, and
a final advance of the song movement toward the folk
level was achieved. Text simplification during the encampment's heyday created this true camp meeting song.
Often spontaneous, it was an organically constructed tune
which refused to let formalism deter its impact. Words
that interfered with the meter were changed, sometimes
making little sense except to the camper. The old hymns
of Wesley and Watts were frequently too sober or too
complicated to express the aroused feelings of the preacher and his camp audience. In contrast, spiritual songs
combined the strongly marked rhythm and the graphic
narrative method of the folk ballad, and at the same time
used a combination of scriptural phrases and everyday
language. Repetition rendered them contagious and easily
remembered. English tunes which were put to use were
adapted with lyrics considerably altered. Textual simplification, their chief characteristic, was achieved in a
variety of ways.

Verses were shortened, refrains added, and expressions
and ejaculations interpolated. The revival spiritual that
represented the least change from the orthodox hymnody
of the eighteenth century was that in which each stanza
of text, usually four lines long, was followed by a chorus
of the same length.

> On Jordan's stormy banks I stand
> And cast a wishful eye,
> To Canaan's fair and happy land
> Where my possession lie.
>
> *Chorus*
> I'm bound for the promised land,
> I'm bound for the promised land,

Oh, who will come and go with me?
I'm bound for the promised land.[23]

While only a few might know the verse, all could join in the chorus. For that reason the infectious chorus and refrain of "Shout Old Satan's Kingdom Down" made it especially popular:

This day my soul has caught new fire
Halle, hallelujah!
I feel that heav'n is coming nigh'r
O glory hallelujah!

Chorus
Shout, shout, we're gaining ground,
Halle, hallelujah!
We'll shout old Satan's kingdom down,
O glory hallelujah![24]

Others went into a refrain after the first text couplet or one-line verse:

There is a school on earth begun,
Chorus: Halle, Hallelujah;
Supported by the holy one
Chorus: Glory O Hallelujah
He calls his pupils for to prove,
Chorus: Halle, Hallelujah
The greatness of redeeming love,
Chorus: Sing Glory O Hallelujah.[25]

An even simpler form, including much repetition, was one in which new poetic lines were not added in subsequent stanzas, but only one or two words were changed. Thus the name of the person appealed to—preacher, father, mother, and so on—was substituted in the original verse.[26] Simplicity itself was the song of one short phrase repeated three or four times, and then followed by a one-phrase refrain. A chorus could substitute one Bible hero after another in the stanzas of one ditty that began with Noah's exploits:

> Oh where is good old Noah?
> Oh where is good old Noah?
> Oh where is good old Noah?
> Safe in the promised Land.
>
> He went up through the flood of waters
> He went up through the flood of waters
> He went up through the flood of waters
> Safe in the promised Land.[27]

The apparent ultimate in text reduction was reached when one short phrase or sentence was repeated to fill out a tune frame and complete a stanza. For example:

> Come to Jesus,
> Come to Jesus,
> Come to Jesus just now,
> Just now come to Jesus,
> Come to Jesus just now.[28]

Preachers may have originated some of the last category, but the singers themselves probably started most of the ejaculatory hymns in their desire to convey a religious experience or emotion, and the throng spontaneously took the songs over.

Revival spirituals also included such arresting lines as "How precious is the name, brethren sing, brethren sing," "An early summons Jesus sends," and "How lost was my condition." The narrative of these songs was expressive and could have been sung on any frontier campground. Indeed, the nondenominational phraseology makes it difficult to discern to which branch of Protestantism the authors belonged. One explanation may be that the songs were used in the early "General Camp Meetings" of the Kentucky Revival in which the Methodists,

Baptists, and Presbyterians united in worship.[29] On the other hand, a definitely sectarian number, "The Methodist," was a perennial favorite among the evangels:

> The *world,* the *Devil* and *Tom Paine*
> Have try'd their force, but all in vain,
> They can't prevail, the reason is,
> The Lord Defends the Methodist.
>
> They pray, they sing, they preach the best,
> And do the Devil most molest,
> If Satan had his vicious way,
> He'd kill and damn them all today.
>
> They are despised by Satan's train,
> Because they shout and preach so plain,
> I'm bound to march in endless bliss,
> And die a shouting Methodist.[30]

Negro spirituals, sung by both the white and colored people, can be considered another subdivision of the revival spiritual. Although their themes are various, the emphasis on otherworldliness suggests that their primary value was in providing an escape from the cruel realities of bonded labor. Optimism is evident in lines such as "Look away in de heaven, Lord," "Heaven, heaven, everybody talkin' 'bout heaven ain't goin' there," and "Dere's a great camp meetin' in de promised land." One favorite had these oft-repeated words:

> Oh I'm going to glory — won't you
> Come along with me?
> Don't you see the angels beckoning
> And calling me away?
> Don't you see the golden city and the everlasting day?[31]

Among the present-day Negro spirituals that apparently had their beginnings in the early nineteenth century are "All My Sins Done Taken Away," "Dere's No One Lak Jesus," "Death Is in Dis Lawd," "Glad I Got Religion."[32]

Some writers have called the spirituals an "oral Bible," for they gave illiterates a chance to glimpse the Savior and His Kingdom. Song themes centered around the church, the Christian, and the world; the Scriptures themselves provided much material for the verses. "Jordan's Banks," "Canaan's Fields," and the "New Jerusalem" were mentioned frequently. The Judgment Day was most vividly described:

> My Lord what a morning when de stars begin to fall,
> You'll see de worl' on fire,
> You'll see de moon a bleedin' an'
> De moon will turn to blood.[33]

The Negro spiritual had a definitive quality setting it apart from the songs sung by the white campers, yet there are many similarities between the two. Contrariwise, the differences between them make uncertain the exact origin of the Negro spiritual. One church historian believed that "the camp songs of the Negroes, like the corn songs of that period, were rich, original and general African productions." A Negro folk singer has agreed with the theory that the religious songs had direct African roots. After studying the forms and sources of African songs and American folk hymnody, he characterized them as "Aframerican religious folk songs" rather than "Negro spirituals." An anthropologist has claimed that "Negro music to some extent reflects this African background," while at the same time it has been influenced by regional development in America.[34] It seems true that musical patterns, more than any other aspect of culture, tend to lodge on the unconscious level.

In comparing the spirituals of the Negroes with those of the whites, one finds that both the subject matter and the form are closely allied. One favorite white spiritual begins:

> They crucified my Savior
> And nailed him to the cross
> See Mary comes a-weeping
> To see where he was laid.
> He arose and ascended in a cloud.

This was changed by the Negroes to:

> Dey crucified my Savior
> And nailed him to de cross.
> Oh, Mary come a-runnin'
> Her Savior for to see
> He rose, he rose from de dead.[35]

More than eighty songs have been thus compared by one musical scholar, and were found to be adaptations of early religious compositions of the whites. Some of the songs sung on the plantation were the well-known church hymns, while others "of a wilder more indefinite character were picked up at camp meetings." The Negro in America probably created many songs by the same process as the whites, "by endless singing of heard tunes and by endless, inevitable and concomitant singing differentiation."[36]

When a multiplicity of hymns were sung at the same time with each group trying to "outsing" the other, din and disorder were created. An early nineteenth-century writer credited the "merry airs" adapted from old songs —"miserable as poetry and senseless as matter"—with contributing to the emotional excitement.[37] Climaxing hours of preaching and exhorting, these songs opened the way for a show of great feeling. When some people jumped and screamed, clapped their hands, thumped and patted the floor, and agitated their bodies while accompanying the songs, great excitement ensued. At times the whole congregation followed suit. One of John Wesley's rules for congregational singing was certainly carried out at camp meetings:

Sing lustily, and with a good courage. Beware of singing as if you were half dead, or half asleep; but lift up your voices with strength.[38]

Camp meeting hymnody neither began nor ended on the campground. The songs found their way into the cabins of the backwoodsmen and were not infrequently a part of the family prayer service. Insofar as song texts are concerned, camp meeting songs have left no visible imprint on present-day Methodist hymnody. But the music itself is quite another matter. Some of the tunes have reappeared in church hymnals, and it is the judgment of an outstanding musical scholar that there seems to be an increasing tendency to use more of them.[39] In the 1860's a number of Granade's and Taylor's spiritual songs were still included in various hymnals, but the authors' names appear to have been unknown to the editors. Then too, the hymn itself was either garbled or improved by the compilers. The Methodists for the past fifty years have progressively eliminated folk tunes from their authorized hymnals, but the 1935 edition showed a checking of this tendency. Seven tunes in that work have been identified as early folk melodies. After long study, numerous musical scholars have concluded that the country folk were not far wrong when they described folk music —which includes the camp meeting hymns—as "the most beautiful music on earth."[40]

II

Sociability in the Tented Grove

[Camp Meetings] tend to draw us off unwarily from our principal design of worship and to engage our affections to the novelties of the scenes, and the greetings of new faces, and the hospitality of reciprocal visits, the exemption from the usual labours and cares, the reports of the doings within and without the camp: ALL these things may give pleasing agitations to the mind, but are they certainly holy? ... Take away the worship, and there would remain sufficient gratifications to allure the most of young people, and thousands if equally fed and freed from labour would follow.[1]
— "Scrutator," 1822

THE "EVILS" OF camp meetings were summed up in the above manner by John Fanning Watson, a trenchant but nevertheless friendly Methodist critic.[2] In his condemnation the writer unwittingly underscored the very features of the revival which made it a vital socioreligious institution in the western backwoods. It was a holiday occasion as well as a time of devotion for the pioneer. In the almost barren life of the rural world that was America during the early nineteenth century, the frontier camp meeting was a significant social experience.

Loneliness and desolation were inevitable when settlement was sparse and widespread; they were the common laments of frontier women. When the head of the family was out trapping or shooting game for weeks at a time, the solitary life became almost unbearable. During the bear hunting season of 1816, one Indiana wife confided to Morris Birkbeck, the English traveler, that "she was quite overcome with lone," not having seen her husband or anyone else for several weeks.[3] Relief from isolation for the residents of the border regions consisted mainly in the visiting of neighbors, perhaps for a house-raising, a cornhusking, or a sewing or logging bee. Also refreshing was the two-day militia muster, held usually in the fall, which was three parts frolic and one part military drill. If a town were near by, then attending court, weddings, funerals, political barbecues, and church could be added to the limited social schedule. Generally, however, religion afforded the major outlet for the backwoodsman's pent-up emotions. Whether practiced in the Quaker or Methodist, Baptist or Presbyterian manner, the worship services might be held in a cabin home, a tiny log church, or the open clearing. The Methodist camp meeting was one among many means of ministering to the pioneer.

"Going to camp meeting" was a high point in the social routine of the farmer and his entire family. Supplying the need of group association to overcome the seclusion and monotony of frontier life, the woodland revival offered relief from farm drudgery and a chance for four whole days of preaching, praying, and singing together. It was an event which many had been anticipating for months. Here the settler had a chance to make new friends and to meet with old ones. Here frenzied courting went on among the younger folk. One old-time camper remarked that the encampments at Rock Spring in Lincoln

County, North Carolina, "had been mating grounds for that state for fifty years."[4] Within and without the campground, youths and grownups engaged in "sparking" as best they could when confronted with the event-packed schedule of the open-air revival. A young lady recorded in her diary after a Georgia camp meeting in 1846:

> I have attended the Houston camp meeting and enjoyed myself well in one respect. We had beaux in abundance, which always gratifies the vanity of girls — too much for their spiritual good. I made several new acquaintances among the gentlemen, Dr. Oliver Robinson, D. Lockett, with whom I was particularly pleased.[5]

At an Alabama encampment three years later, another girl wrote a friend that she had acquired "many boy friends," and that all the young women enjoyed themselves "more than they ever had before."[6] Mother Nature was also at work at an Indiana gathering of 1829. A visitor disgustedly reported the breakfast-time courting of the younger set: "I marked many a fair but pale face, that I recognized as a demoniac of the night, simpering beside a swain, to whom she carefully administered hot coffee and eggs."[7] Love found a way at the outdoor revival as elsewhere.

Camp meetings afforded the settler an opportunity to indulge in his love of camping out. Traveler-writers often commented upon the Americans' fondness for the great out-of-doors. Camping out was a pleasurable pastime of all, and particularly a passion of the residents of the rural regions. They looked forward to making a journey of sufficient distance from home to necessitate staying away overnight. This usually involved sleeping outside in some improvised shelter, a practice made possible by the long summers and mild autumns. The evangelistic device — the camp meeting — met that universal yearn-

A MASSACHUSETTS
camp meeting, *circa* 1856. The fancy pulpit, smooth wooden
benches, and permanent buildings in the background suggest the
maturer stage of the camp meeting. Courtesy of the Bettman
Archive.

ing and at the same time surmounted the obstacles of distance from a house of worship and lodging for the traveler, obstacles which previously had kept many from the observance of religion. No longer was there any excuse to stay away from preaching. The backwoodsman's enthusiasm was indicated in the distance of thirty, fifty, and even one hundred miles he traveled to attend. Thus the woodland gathering, an integral part of the culture pattern of young America, was also a great stimulus to religious activity. In 1846 a Prussian traveler commented that "it is asserted that not a few resort to camp meetings for the sake of camping and in order to relieve the uniform tedious observance of Sunday."[8]

"Camp meeting religion" had a contagious attraction for the westerner. Living dangerously and often at the animal level of existence, he wanted an optimistic, emotional type of salvation preached to him. Moreover, the camp services carried an equalitarian flavor — all men were equal and sinners in the eyes of a forgiving God. This leveling aspect was reflected in a popular camp meeting ditty:

> Come hungry, come thirsty, come ragged, come bare,
> Come filthy, come lousy, come just as you are.

The over-all lure of the woodland Bethel has been outlined by one contemporary as being composed of

the love of variety and novelty — the desire for excitements — romantic feelings — tedium of common everyday life — love of good fellowship — and even a willingness to obtain cheap religious character and a secret hope that they please God and merit Heaven for so exhalting and long continued devotion.[9]

To many, the attraction of the "tented grove" proved irresistible. The story is told of one shoe repairman whose business failed because of neglect while he visited camp meetings far and near, in Maryland, Virginia, Delaware, and Pennsylvania. The distinguished western writer, Baynard Rush Hall, wrote of how once or twice a year children were removed from school and whole families rushed to the camp meeting "under the belief that the Christian God is a God of the woods and not of the towns."[10]

Few events excelled the amusement and excitement of a trip to a backwoods encampment. When "camp meetin' time" arrived, empty clearings became crowded with people eager for the worship and companionship ahead. Long journeys over tortuous trails were undertaken uncomplainingly. Pioneers came in every possible means of conveyance — ox carts, sledges, hay wagons, covered wagons, chaises, coaches — and on horseback and on foot. Along with them came the inevitable provisions, tents, and makeshift shelter materials; a few worshipers even carried beds and cooking stoves. One Alabama camper described the elegant style in which some wealthy families traveled to a Sunday camp service in 1843. There was the special cushioned carriage, "delicately lined and trimmed within with linen, silk, and satin." This two-seated vehicle might contain the mother and daughters, with a waiting maid and well-dressed Negro slave perched in the high driver's seat. Following close behind would be the buggy drawn by a gelding, carrying the master and his Negro attendant. Then came the fancy saddle horses manned by the planter's sons, and pulling up the rear were possibly two mules bearing the oldest male and female slaves. In sharp contrast were the outfits of the poor who made a special trip to the campground on the Sabbath. Some came by oxcart, others by the one horse they owned, with that creature bearing up under the load of one in the saddle, one on the rider's lap, and one behind.[11]

A contemporary sketch gives a glimpse of campers going to a Bloomington, Indiana, revival in the 1840's. As the group wended their way, they were joined by others mounted and on foot. Young and old alike journeyed along singing snatches of their favorite religious songs, chanting enthusiastically the trumpet melodies suitable for marching such as "Glory! Glory! Glory!" "He's a coming, coming, coming," and "Come, let us march on, march on, march on!" They made a striking picture in their homespun clothes, the men in wool hats, breeches, and moccasins, and the women in similar footwear, scoop-shovel bonnets, and calico dresses. Encountering strangers, they would invite them "to go to camp meeting," promising that they would be rewarded, for many were "saved" there. If the offer were refused and one asked why they worshiped God in the woods, he was told: "Oh! come and see! Only come to camp and git your cold heart warmed — Come git religion — let it out with a shout — and you'll not axe that infidel sort of question no more."[12]

Because the Methodists were able to proselyte so effectively through their camp meetings, other denominations frequently sought to keep their own members from attending them. Despite such bans non-Methodist churchmen attended. For example, in 1809 Moravians came to the first Methodist encampments held in the Wills Creek Circuit of Ohio. Another forest revival six years later, the first of its kind in the Mechanicsburg, Ohio, area, attracted many "New Light" Presbyterians. In 1815, a rival North Carolina meeting attracted numerous members of the Moravian sect away from their own services, testifying to the strength of the camp meeting's initial appeal.[13]

Many other than the religious-minded attended the frontier encampments. The worst as well as the best people of the community were drawn there by the longing for a spectacle, and they brought their morals with them. Apparently, the immoral and irreligious were always in approximately equal numbers with the professing Christians and the serious-minded. A traveler of the forties estimated that one-fourth of all the persons present at one revival were not interested in the message delivered, but came only to be startled and amused. Yet many of the curious-minded who came to be entertained by this unusual religious drama "had an interest awakened in their hearts" under the spell of the revival preaching and the awesome night services.[14]

Politicians often visited, some to worship, others to make friends and influence voters. Campaigners, hungry for votes, shrewdly appraised the crowded encampments as worth-while stopping places. At the larger meetings territorial or state governors were present. Electioneering at the camp services was frowned on by the church authorities, and on at least one occasion public notice to this effect was made in the local newspapers.[15] Merchants of all types, selling gingerbread, lemonade, watermelon, corn, other edibles, and liquor, peddled their wares. Although liquor salesmen were forbidden entrance to the grounds, their products came in by devious means with frequently disturbing results. Horse thieves and women of easy virtue plied their respective trades. Others inviting patronage included book agents, dentists, doctors, daguerreotypists, barbers, and even bootblacks. One camper reminisced about this sad state of affairs:

We have even heard a venerable minister publicly announce the fact that a man was present at the meeting who desired to "pull teeth." We have heard in prayer meeting, upon a Sabbath morning, a painfully silly and flippant harangue from a pretended convert, prefaced by the declaration that the speaker was a vendor of shoe-blacking. . . . How many boxes of blacking his profession of piety enabled him to sell we are not prepared to state, but there is not a shadow of doubt that the rascal had expressly contrived the imprudent trick for the occasion. We have also seen a man bustling from tent to tent, thrusting into the faces of the occupants a printed notice promising speedy and gratuitous relief from the headache.[16]

On the Sabbath, when residents from the near-by towns journeyed out to the encampment, the attendance often swelled to double and triple its weekday size. No fewer than three complete services were scheduled for the benefit of the campers who knew the day would be event-packed. A southern camp meeting might have to compete against such attractions as the cock-fighting arena of New Orleans, which offered in 1822 not only front seats for fifty cents but two glasses of refreshment free. One proverb put it this way: "The good people go to camp meetings Friday, backsliders Saturday, rowdies Saturday night, and gentlemen and lady sinners Sunday."[17] But regardless of background or motive, all the spectators, including the most devout, expected the camp meeting to be entertaining.

The backwoods revival has been described as "the most mammoth picnic possible," where hospitality abounded, and where " 'tis no one's fault, saint or sinner if he gets not enough to eat, and that the best the land affords."[18] Cooking was usually done by groups of women, each of whom had saved her best pickles and preserves for the occasion. They evidently competed with each other in turning out banquet fare. At an Ohio meeting of 1818, a preacher waxed lyrical over the Saturday night dinner set before him: "This bounteous meal is of the flesh-pots of Egypt, being mainly composed of *hog-meat* — pardon the title; we see no vulgarity in it here — in all shapes of cookery, mutton, beef, and hecatombs of cold chickens." Indeed, a prime attraction to more than one visitor was the rare chance to get a piece of fresh meat. There was "no want of creature comforts" when a worshiper could look forward to an excellent dinner's being served as soon as the morning services were over.[19]

That some did overstress the nonspiritual feature of "good eats" at the summer revival meeting is evidenced by the fact that the editor of the *Western Christian Advocate* thought it necessary to advise his readers on the subject. He urged the "plainest fare" at camp meetings, and leaving nothing to chance, enumerated the items he had in mind. Approved were dried beef, boiled ham or pork, and bread, all to be prepared in advance. "Leave your veal and chickens at home" to eliminate "all the frying, and boiling and otherwise preparing of meat at the camp fire," he added. Tea, coffee, and water were acceptable beverages. No vegetables were to be brought except potatoes, indicating a definite lack of interest in balanced nutrition. The significance of this culinary advice is much broader than that of dietetics itself. Primarily, such simplicity in food preparation freed the woman of the family from the cooking chores, giving her more time to attend the services. Abstinence from feasts had a good effect on all, for the emphasis on purely sensual enjoyment would be lessened. Finally, simple menus would stress the equalitarian aspect of "camp meetin' time": "The poor and the rich would, as is very meet, be placed on such an equality as would have an excellent effect. The one class would be humbled, and the other exhalted."[20]

The spirit of friendliness and good fellowship that prevailed was always remarked on by both sympathetic and hostile observers. There was something cheery about clustering around an open fire to roast ears of corn or meat on forked sticks. As one traveler remarked, the western camp meeting was "the very heart and soul of hospitality and kindness." Reminiscing about his father's liberality, a veteran camper said it was his practice to announce at the end of an afternoon's service that if there were any unprovided for, "Come around to the . . .'s tent for supper." The Swedish traveler, Fredrika Bremer, recounted that she had accepted the invitation of a "red-hot Methodist" family at a Georgia camp meeting in 1850, and had all her wants provided.[21] Not infrequently large tents were erected on the grounds by the more affluent churchmen to accommodate strangers with free food and lodging. Meals at moderate prices were also served in boarding tents at encampments both north and south of the Ohio.[22]

Unfortunately, the camper's hospitality was often sorely imposed upon. "Spongers" appeared to be a perennial problem of the revival's sponsors in the sparsely settled communities. Too often, campers expected to live off the land and their tent neighbors, without contributing anything in return. Especially unenthusiastic about this practice were the churchmen who had allowed the encampments to be set up on their land, even setting aside pasturage for the horses. Because of the spoilage of crops, the consumption of fodder, the stealing of "the hay in the shock in the field," and the "borrowing" of feed troughs, water buckets, and the like, a few donors withdrew their offers. If one newspaper correspondent is to be believed, many women became so discouraged from overwork and inability to participate in the religious worship because of slaving to feed and house these uninvited guests that they discontinued the yearly camp meeting habit.[23]

The evil grew to such huge proportions that the individual preachers resolved to end it once and for all. Each camper must be prepared to provision himself. The sponsors of a Whitewater Circuit camp meeting in Indiana announced that they did not intend to feed "man, woman, or child, horse, ox or ass." This strategy worked, for although some young men "in the habit of going to camp meetings, far and near, to sponge" attended, they went away empty handed.[24] Parallel situations were similarly handled at a Chillicothe campground in 1814, at London, Ohio, in 1825, and at Charlestown, Indiana, in the same year. Yet even fourteen years later the *Western Christian Advocate* still carried admonitions to "spongers."[25]

Other problems beset these worshipers in the woods. They were at the mercy of the elements, and not infrequently violent storms struck the encampments. While there are no recorded fatalities, at an Elyria meeting in northern Ohio in 1834 one man was nearly killed by a falling tree. "Powerful rains" drove the people from their seats at a Tennessee gathering led by James Axley in 1815, and "the work of God prospered in the tents." At another encampment, however, at Chillicothe, Ohio, in May, 1809, a minor hurricane did not even interrupt the services.[26] The prayers by camp sponsors for good weather were obviously not always answered.

Fire hazards were among the dangers of life in tent

city, All the lanterns, candlestands, pine-cone torches, "fire altars," and cooking fires in use were potential sources of conflagrations, but only one instance has been found of a frontier campground's being devastated by fire. This occurred in a Carter's Valley Circuit, Tennessee, encampment in 1833.[27] Perhaps a partial explanation for the campers' phenomenal success in controlling the danger lay in the careful regulations. According to eastern camp rules, a bucket of water was to be placed outside each tent at night and smoking was prohibited "in the society tents or within the circle of tents."[28]

No precautions, however, could prevent the spread of contagious diseases that appeared among the tent occupants. Epidemics had ideal conditions in which to thrive. Measles, no discriminator of age, took hold of circuit rider John Scripps at an Illinois encampment where it was "very prevalent in the congregation." Itinerant Henry Smith got the "bilious fever" so badly at a Winchester Circuit encampment in Virginia during the year 1805 that he had to leave on the fifth meeting day. He added that no one died of the fever there but that this sickness "became very prevalent throughout the country about this time; and some were foolish enough to lay it to the camp meeting."[29] Yet even those who were aware of the risks they were taking in mingling in large crowds retained their admiration for the outdoor meeting. One Alabama woman related in 1849:

Our camp meeting [Indian Creek] is over. . . . Olivia and myself tented together. . . . Olivia was up yesterday. . . . they expect to attend Pike Creek camp meeting the last of the week if her children do not take hooping cough. . . . Our next door neighbor at camp meeting had it in his family.[30]

Then there were other health hazards. The cumulative

effect of a prolonged outdoor revival upon the nervous system and physical well-being of the worshiper was, and is, a matter of some conjecture. If the word of the eccentric Lorenzo Dow is accepted, a stay at a camp meeting had solely a beneficial effect: "Many go home better than they came, even delicate women, who rarely step off a carpet for twelve months, grow more healthy from that time." One other camp meeting alumnus, however, recalled that the over-all physical impact was a "constant ringing in the ears of all varied sounds lasting usually forty-eight hours."[31] Certainly four to six days spent in the open would not in itself be harmful. What was possibly injurious to health was the penitent's practice of lying on the ground or the straw floor of the altar during his religious ordeal. More serious consequences of these frenzied services (particularly during the Kentucky Revival) were the resultant fainting spells, nervous collapses, and hallucinations. To Samuel K. Jennings, a Methodist minister who attempted a "Defense of Camp Meetings" in 1805, it was immaterial whether the worshiper's mental health was endangered by anxiety at the altar:

If the exercise preparatory to a gracious state be a deep sense of sin and its awful consequences followed by a humble acceptance of mercy on terms of the gospel; then it must follow that whatever effects it may produce it will be prudent to submit to the operation.[32]

As far as the children were concerned, the novelty and fun of an encampment far offset any possible dangers involved. In a frontier region where playmates were few, the camp meeting crowds and excitement must have been eagerly awaited by the young folk. When a tent city sprang up in a forest clearing as if by magic, many teenage boys came to see this spectacle which had all the glamour, excitement, and pageantry of the later-day circus. The woodland meeting with its row on row of tents surrounding the speaker's platform, its banners, and its campfires was something amazing to behold. Games could be played by children during the day, sometimes in a recreation area designated by the camp regulations. But always there were baby brothers and sisters to be watched or the family belongings to be guarded while the parents were engrossed with the saving of their souls. Boys were also used as "runners . . . who whipped away dogs and hogs etc." from the outdoor auditorium during church sessions.[33]

Yet the supervisors had the thought of religious instruction always uppermost in their minds. Youthfulness did not spell escape from long-winded services. Older children sat through the worship period under the watchful eyes of their parents; it was not unusual for converted "sinners" of ten years of age to be the "instruments through which the Lord wrought."[34] More than one curious youth who wandered about the encampment ended up as a penitent in the "circle of brotherly love." Some of the greats of the early circuit riding days traced their religious awakening to a Methodist outdoor revival they attended while of an impressionable age.[35]

Ample opportunity was afforded the gregarious settler to "git acquainted." Even when specific "visiting times" were not set aside by the camp planners, there was enough time between the various service routines to meet one's neighbors. Mealtime around the cooking fires was a popular period of companionship. Then campers talked of crops, of their children's latest exploits, and of the political situation. Here the married women had a chance to exchange gossip, while the girls might tell of their latest boy friends. A favorite topic, however, that rivaled all others in that day of personal religion was the church and its activities. Worshipers were eager to inform companions of their spiritual experience or the circumstances surrounding the recent salvation of some close friend. Serious conversation, especially at the dinner table, was enjoined upon prospective campers. Those planning to attend an annual conference camp meeting in 1839 were advised that the emphasis should not be on this world, but on the world beyond.

Should we at table spend twenty minutes in discussing the merits of Van Buren, Clay, and Harrison, and their claims to the presidency, or in debating the comparative viciousness of "Whiggism" or "Loco Focoism" would any good result from it? For Christ's sake let us avoid these themes, and not introduce them among people who seek our society, not to reform their politics, but to save their souls.[86]

Here again can be discerned the hand of the local church leaders seeking to lead the people along religious paths.

Many spectators were not content to entertain themselves only in the intervals between the services. To the ultimate discomfort of the more serious-minded and the speakers themselves, they sought amusement during the religious proceedings. Exposing their souls to salvation appeared to be the farthest thought from their minds. It seemed that the nonreligious

only attend for amusement of which there is no lack. While the devotees were rolling on the ground in agonizing fervor to behold, the others were enjoying themselves comfortably with smoking, chewing tobacco, drinking, chatting with the women or talking politics with the men.[87]

This was a dilemma faced by all camp meeting governors. The regulations drawn up by them in the interest of maintaining proper religious decorum specifically forbade persons from "walking to and fro, talking, smoking, or otherwise disturbing the solemnities of the meeting." Yet, in the eyes of many, these laws were simply rules made to be broken. The problem was publicly aired in the press in 1822. A letter writer complained that camp ordinances in central Ohio were being ignored on the basis that they were drafted without the consent of the participants, and therefore were not applicable. Further, "the worshipers are not in a house." Confusion and disorder were the result. He lamented: "Hence they walk about the camp ground, their hats on, talk, laugh, smoke cigars, get on seats prepared for the ladies and transgress the rules of the meeting in various other ways."[38]

On the lighter side were the practical jokes perpetrated by members of the audience and the backwoods preachers in this age of giant hoaxes and uninhibited jesters. At a Tennessee outdoor revival in 1815, Peter Cartwright arranged a plot to embarrass one offensive member of the congregation who not only took every chance he could get to interrupt, but who proudly exhibited "a mighty bushy roached head of hair." Two members of the camp guard got the offender alone by urging him to follow them to the woods for a drink, and then proceeded to shear his locks. Later Cartwright had a hard time keeping down his "risibilities" as he threatened more violent deeds. At this same meeting, one tough failed in his plot to lasso Cartwright's neck with frogs "strung on a hickory bark" while the minister was stooping and praying for the mourners.[39]

Some sought amusement of a less innocent form during the services, bringing their own "brown betty" jugs and playing cards. Worshipers often had to listen to drunks carouse through the night. Mock sacraments in the woods would be held with whiskey as the lubricating agent, and tipsy "mourners" acting their parts at make-believe altars.[40] To the temperance advocates the sight of revelers on their way to an encampment presented "a spectacle to the sober mind of a disgusting character."

A few states, in part because of church pressure, passed laws prohibiting the sale of intoxicating beverages within a radius of one and sometimes two miles of a campground.[41] But this was not a foolproof measure. The local justice of the peace or constable might choose to ignore the statute, for some states — Indiana, for example — neglected to include a penalty for violations. While certainly not in the majority, a number of early campers themselves were vocal in their denunciation of restrictive legislation. Were not beer, liquor, and cider "very necessary for the comforts of the attendants?"[42] One had only to look just beyond the specified zone to find a beverage salesman, or he might possibly locate a wagoner legally operating within the encampment whose food staples hid the jugs and cups. A Methodist newspaper editor even suggested that all "victualers" should be sent packing, for it was the merchants who were the main sources for "beer, whiskey, profanity, and quarrels."[43] When the huckster wagons began to compete with the altar area as the center of attraction, it seemed to Allen Wiley, seasoned Indiana camp leader of the 1840's, that one or the other had to go:

Since the country has become more densely populated, there are more persons who go to such meetings merely for recreation, than in former days; in consequence of which, hucksters find it a more profitable business to attend these meetings than formerly. I have myself seen as many as fourteen huckster wagons at one camp meeting, and perhaps one-fourth as many boys, and lads, and young men, and even middle-aged, and old men about them, as were on the camp ground to attend religious service. Many of these young, and even middle-aged persons never came on the camp ground, unless it was to interrupt the quiet of the meeting. While they were about these wagons, they learn to run, jump, wrestle, play, yell, swear, talk vulgar, and in some instances, there is more mischief done to the morals of the youth of the land about these wagons, than there is religious good effected on the camp ground. Now, although the preachers and their people are not to blame for the evil done, in consequence of the coming together of such crowds of heedless sinners, we and other denominations will have to give up our popular meetings in the woods.[44]

Toughs and "jugs of inspiration" frequently added up to camp meeting proceedings that could scarcely be dignified by the term "religious." When horses and wagons were stolen, or acts of vandalism committed, there would be a hue and cry which rivaled that of the most strenuous altar service. On Saturdays and Sundays in particular every camp leader had to be prepared to match wits or fists with the disturbing elements. As one circuit rider related,

We were much annoyed by the rabble, who were set upon us by men professing to wear the garb of Christian ministers, but more frequently by the whisky-makers and venders themselves. Few men, in their sober senses, could be induced to disgrace themselves by interrupting the worship of God, and those few must be besotted and imbruted to a degree beyond recovery, who would cut to pieces the harness, saddles, bridles, tents, etc. of the worshipers and howl around the encampment like sulking wolves. Such creatures were sometimes handled pretty roughly by the conservators of the peace, [camp guard] and they learned often, by sad experience, that the way of the transgressor was hard.[45]

It might have helped to discontinue Saturday and Sunday meetings, but that would have been admitting defeat. One Ohio sponsor in announcing two forthcoming encampments on the Columbus Circuit in 1822 took the occasion to declare: "Such has been the conduct of the rowdies that many serious persons have become entirely opposed to the institution. But we do not feel disposed to give up a privilege, because of its abuse!"[46]

The camp meetings had as their leaders men who were not averse to using a frontier weapon — physical force — to carry on God's work. Like his pioneer audience, the itinerant did not seriously consider the biblical counsel to "turn the other cheek." For example, there was Peter Cartwright who interrupted his Sunday morning service at Marietta, Ohio, in 1806 to knock down singlehandedly three drunks, two of whom attempted to beat him with a horsewhip. The third inebriate was the local constable. A riot ensued, but the campers emerged victorious over the "Sons of Belial."[47] Another itinerant lost his temper and nearly killed a tough by striking him on the head with a cane at a Pennsylvania camp meeting in 1813. When officers came to investigate, the minister's associates hid him in their tent, disguising him with different clothes. Fortunately the victim recovered, and no charges were pressed. Circuit rider Brunson had the law on his side when he secured the arrest of a rowdy who just missed hitting him in the face with a firebrand at an Erie County encampment in western Pennsylvania in 1833. The famous Ohio and Michigan circuiteer, James Gilruth, a giant of a man, taught a lesson to one roughneck leader who put out the lights of a woodland gathering held near Columbus, Ohio, in 1838. Gilruth leaped from the platform, knocked the man down three times, and dragged him across near-by Alum Creek to the doorstep of the justice of the peace. Gilruth's so-called "sermon of strength" and a short jail term were equally effective in showing the miscreant the error of his ways.[48]

Notwithstanding all the prior planning and regulations, the success or failure of a camp meeting was often solely dependent upon the ingenuity of the saddlebag preacher. Often an application of human psychology did more to curb the excesses than did direct force. This was certainly true at two separate camp meetings when circuit riders Cartwright and Brunson independently honored the chief troublemakers by making each a "Captain of the Guard." The drunk whose canteen of whiskey was hung upon a sapling for all to see, plainly labeled with his name, was also a little nonplused.[49] Again, an outspoken scoffer, with too many drinks under his belt, might find himself tied hand and foot to a tree to listen to the preaching.[50] Many times the very men who plotted to disrupt a meeting stayed too long to listen to the revival preaching and were converted before they could carry out their intentions.

Most often the worshipers co-operated wholeheartedly with the preacher in charge. Over two hundred young men went along with the camp leader at a Marietta encampment to rout a whiskey seller who had started to market his product a short distance from the grounds in violation of the state law.[51] At another camp meeting near Mantua, Ohio, in 1824, Alfred Brunson caught wind of a scheme to break up his services that was being planned by "certain lewd fellows of the baser sort." Thinking quickly, he mounted the rostrum and requested "all Christians, all gentlemen and ladies, to take their seats, leaving the rowdies on their feet that we may know whom to take hold of." His second appeal succeeded in getting everyone seated, possibly because he added that the guards were ready for action, and he himself, who had taken part "in the second war of Independence and helped defend this very ground," would not be driven off. Bishop Asbury likewise received the support of an audience when on one occasion he stopped preaching because of whiskey sales going on at the same time. "The people soon knew how deeply we felt the insult, and they were driven away."[52]

The salient fact has been too often ignored that the backwoods camp meeting was a time of social companionship for the settler; a time of release from arduous labor and physical insecurity; a period of fun and frolic which was an effective antidote to "lone" sickness. Here was a unique chance for "pleasurin' in the backwoods." To lay stress on the many instances of ludicrousness and emotional extravagance of the religious services while ignoring the revival's significance as a social medium is to misinterpret the camp meeting's role in the cultural pattern of frontier life. If many proponents came to oppose the frontier revival as a social evil, more remained enthusiastic adherents of "camp meetin' time." The parting ceremonies of a Portsmouth, Ohio, camp meeting of 1818 revealed something of the pioneer's love for this social institution:

The thoughts of parting to meet no more, or of meeting to part no more, produced the melody of those groans and shouts which far exceed all description. When we for the last time marched in order around the camp and sung our parting hymn, the scene was truly solemn and impressive. The tents struck; the waggons in readiness; weeping circles of young converts folded in each other's arms; ministers surrounded with weeping hundreds, crying out as they presented the parting hand, "pray for me and mine!"[53]

12

Contemporary Appraisals

Much may be said about camp meetings, but, take them all in all, for practical exhibition of religion, for unbounded hospitality to strangers, for unfeigned and fervent spirituality, give me a country camp meeting against the world.[1]
— *Circuit rider James B. Finley, 1853*

MANY CALUMNIES were uttered against the frontier camp meeting in its heyday as well as during the period of its growing obsolescence. Its merit seemed to be, like beauty, "altogether in the eye of the beholder." In truth, "much may be said about camp meetings," as Finley so aptly put it. But in the comments, the commentators revealed themselves and their backgrounds much more clearly than they did the new and unfamiliar scene spread out before them. Those who wrote about the backwoods revival during its flowering time, the visiting foreign travelers, the fiction writers, the disgruntled observers from nonrevivalistic churches, and the participants of all denominations provide a window on the frontier camp meeting the view from which constantly changes as the angle of vision is shifted.

It has often been stated that there is nothing more misleading than the superficial observations of travelers.[2] Unacquainted with the western patterns of life, the visitors from foreign lands, particularly the British, constantly interpreted the camp meeting as an evidence of license that naturally flowed from the system of democracy. Because of her freedom, the United States seemed to them to be poised on the verge of dissolution and barbarity. Both James Flint and Frances Trollope found that the Indiana encampments they attended in 1818 and 1829 substantiated their preconceived notions that American disorder and lack of taste were all too prevalent. To understand the sounds pouring from a "multitude of bellowing mouths," wrote Flint, "would require the ear of Jove." And to note the preacher's "insidious lips approach the cheeks of the unhappy girls" at an altar service made the daughter of an Anglican clergyman, Madame Frances Trollope, turn away shuddering. "It was too dreadful to look upon long."[3] Scotch Presbyterian John Duncan didn't even bother to visit a camp meeting when he came to America, for hearsay had convinced him that the services were detrimental to true religion. Thus he could not write about the revivals "except with strong disproval."[4]

Visiting the rampaging frontier of 1831-32, Captain Thomas Hamilton remarked upon the prevalence of camp meetings and other revivals cast in the design of "ignorant fanaticism." The Englishman listed, wth tongue in cheek, the surface changes in personal habits that resulted:

Young ladies chant hymns, instead of Irish melodies; and the profane chorus gives place to rhythmal doxologies. Grog parties commence with prayer, and terminate with benediction. Devout smokers say grace over a cigar, and chewers of the NICOTIAN weed insert a fresh quid with an expression of pious gratitude.

This may appear ludicrous in description; yet it ought not to be so. The sentiment of devotion — the love — the hope — the gratitude — the strong and religious desire to conform our conduct to the Divine will . . . even in our most trifling enjoyments are among the most valuable fruits of true religion.

Conceding that it was easy to ridicule the extravagant emotionalism and ignorance exhibited in revivalistic services, he went on to stress that any religious process was a positive good in the western woods where "the restraints of public opinion and penal legislation are little felt."[5]

But there were Britishers who recognized that measures impractical in their own country were called for when preachers were scarce and settlement farflung. Captain Frederick Marryat declared in 1839 that the purpose of camp meetings was laudable, but that they "are now too often sullied by fanaticism on the one hand, and on the other by the levity and infidelity of those who go not to pray but to scoff; or to indulge in the licentiousness, which it is said, but too often follows, when night has thrown her veil over the scene." This same emotional excitement, so common among the women that he observed at Virginia encampments, was commented on by a representative from the Congregational Union of England and Wales, the Reverend Andrew Reed. Such a detriment, however, did not negate the usefulness of the forest revival on a new frontier, for "it interests a careless people in their own moral and religious wants; and is the natural and general forerunner, as the population thickens, of the school-house, the church, and all the appliances of civil life."[6]

As is to be expected, a Frenchman, unhampered by Calvinistic prejudices, would be tolerance itself to any deviation from the social norm. Alexis de Tocqueville was especially sympathetic to the efforts of the circuit riders in bringing religion to the "half-peopled country of the Far West." When he inquired from a Detroit settler whether the voice of religion had ever reached that outpost of civilization in 1831, he was told that

almost every summer, it is true, some Methodist preachers come
to make a tour of the new settlements. The noise of their arrival
spreads with unbelievable rapidity from cabin to cabin: it's the
great news of the day. At the date set, the immigrant, his wife and
children set out by scarcely cleared forest trails toward the indicated meeting place. They come from fifty miles around. It's not in
a church that the faithful gather, but in the open air under the
forest foliage. A pulpit of badly squared logs, great trees felled
for seats, such are the ornaments of this rustic temple. The
pioneers and their families camp in the surrounding woods. It's
there that, during three days and three nights, the crowd gives
itself over to almost uninterrupted religious exercises. You must
see with what ardor these men surrender themselves to prayer,
with what attention they listen to the solemn voice of the preacher.
It's in the wilderness that people show themselves almost starved
for religion.[7]

Like the travelers, the fiction writers as a general rule
tended to fill their accounts with gorgeously dressed half-
truths and explosive epigrams. A western fiction writer,
Baynard Rush Hall, poked fun at the backwoods revival
and at the same time made some incisive observations.
Before attending an 1843 encampment, he appraised it
as a doubtful means "of *little* permanent good." Any
camp meeting of more than a day's duration forced the
introduction of "novelties . . . which are invariably exciting and entertaining, but *never* spiritual and instructive."
After a one-day visit to an Indiana campground near
Bloomington, the author's previous skepticism was lessened to a slight degree. A camp meeting was, all things
considered, a remarkable contrivance for gaining converts
in a short time. Nor could Hall easily forget the experience; for a day and a half after his stay there the cries of
the worshipers continued to ring in his ears.[8]

Those churchmen who saw their members being
proselyted away to a revivalistic church could be expected
to rail against the institution. Consider, for example, the

assertion of a Unitarian visitor to an 1836 encampment in Ohio that the open-air revival was "about as much out of date in these days as would be the chivalry of the middle ages in our sober modern society." The partisan temper of church leader Alexander Campbell is indicated by his charge that the Methodist church could not live without her *"glory! glory! glory! . . .* her periodical *Amens* dispossess demons — storm heaven — shut the gates of Hell — and drive Satan from the camp."[9] The whole camp meeting plan was considered dishonest because its sponsors urged folk to come to camp meetings "to git religion," when what they really wanted was a new crop of Methodists. In fact, the task of nonrevivalistic denominations was made all the harder, said one critic, for if men did not succumb to the lure of the encampment that the Methodists provided, they would frequently decry all religion under the misapprehension that "camp meeting religion" was the norm. They could find all the excuses they desired for neglecting, despising, and ridiculing religion. "Thus these poor souls became more and more prejudiced and hardened than they were before."[10]

Occasionally churchmen of other persuasions carefully evaluated the camp meeting, pinpointing its basic weaknesses. Some of their arguments were buttressed by the Methodist leaders themselves, who frequently brought the same charges against that socioreligious institution.

To the fundamentalists, the forest revival was suspect because there was no biblical authority for the practice. Camping out in thin cloth tents was injurious to health, and hence contrary to the Bible's strictures; likewise the praying, exhorting, and singing by individuals in camp services were forbidden by "the order prescribed in the gospel." To the rational revivalists, an otherworldly atmosphere of quietude and introspection, an atmosphere scarcely attainable when hordes of fun-loving pioneers were gathered together in the open, was essential to genuine religious feeling. Only in a church building where noise and confusion was avoidable could the Lord be worshiped. A Presbyterian, opposed to the resumption of the forest revival in his own denomination, declared in 1832 that such outdoor gatherings

have always appeared to me adopted to make religion more an affair of display, of impulse, of noise, and of animal sympathy, than of understanding, the conscience, and the heart. In short, they have always struck me as adopted, in their ordinary form, to produce effects on our intellectual and moral nature analogous to strong drink.[11]

The matter of appealing to the emotions to attain conversions seems to be at the heart of the disputation concerning the camp meeting. "Merely animal or mechanical conversion" was neither preferred nor lasting to many a denominational critic. It was almost as if conversion were an endurance contest; if the applicant could pass through the prescribed course of excitement, fear, distress, falling down, and then could compose himself, he considered himself converted. A German Reformed Church theologian in 1844 dwelt upon the unsatisfactory effect of all revivals which utilized the "pressure of artificial excitement." Of all the hundreds that were reported as converts to the Methodists, United Brethren, and Winebrennarians, he continued, "how small a proportion give evidence subsequently that they have been truly regenerated." Among other Methodists, circuit rider Allen Wiley was beginning to be skeptical about encampment conversions. When he found that some who had joined the society at the final outdoor gathering of 1822 had become backsliders by the time his successor arrived the following spring, he was convinced that he should wait until their names were entered upon the "class papers" of a local organization before reporting them as converts. This awareness of an inevitable percentage of defections was apparently shared by his fellow Indiana itinerants, for by the mid-forties Wiley noted that they were following his practice. John Mason Peck, Baptist missionary and educator, went even farther to say that because of these impermanent conversions the churches themselves fell into a state of collapse shortly after the revival tide had passed.[12]

Because of its freedom and emotional appeal, the camp meeting attracted too many of the settlers intent only upon a good time unrestricted by conventions. Here the critics unconsciously underscored a hallmark of the revival, its universal appeal. It furnished the occasion for the "high gratification of the wicked." Immorality was thus encouraged, and the day of God profaned. If mere sensuality were stressed the mourners would have no idea of proper theology. At the mourner's bench, continued one non-Methodist critic,

very little or nothing is said to them upon the pure motive . . . and their firm obligations to *the law* of God. They are taught that misery is the great evil to be dreaded and happiness the great object to be sought; and not that the supreme concern is to submit to God and obey him.[13]

Still another argument was offered against the woodland meeting: it was frequently staged in settled regions where adequate church facilities made it unnecessary. This was a frequent theme of eastern writers. Writing a parody on "Camp-Meetings and Agricultural Fairs," John Fanning Watson cited many of the evils already enumerated.

One soul might be saved, while many more might be lost if an encampment near a large town should create conditions under which the visitors would be tempted to sin.[14]

Since camp meeting religion has been such a subject of disputation, it seems only fair to look at that instrument from the viewpoint of those closest to it — the saddlebag preachers who led the meetings. To many, the camp meeting was not a name but an emotion. Their high regard for it unmistakably colors the pages of their diaries and journals. One minister informed the editor of the *Western Christian Monitor* in 1816 that he doubted the propriety of the occasions, but "still loved them, because at well conducted meetings of this kind, the power of God has been so universally manifested in awakenings, conversions, sanctifications and powerful revivals of religion." These manifestations, he concluded, "are the strongest evidences that the institution is owned and blessed of heaven." When Thomas S. Hinde's heart trouble became so bad that he was informed by the doctor that he had not long to live, he immediately visited all the encampments within his reach so that he could take his "flight" from one of those beloved spots "if it pleased that Almighty Being, the disposer of all things, to permit it."[15]

The unqualified endorsements of such veteran circuiteers as James B. Finley, Benjamin Lakin, Peter Cartwright, and William C. Smith, to cite but a few, point up the popularity of this extra-device. The "Kentucky Boy" flatly declared, "I am certain that the most successful part of my ministry has been on the camp-grounds." Benjamin Lakin stressed the liberalizing influence of camp sermons which were given often where "they had not heard a sermon perhaps for five years." According to the pithy estimate of William C. Smith, Indiana circuit rider, "No instrumentalities have ever been used by the church which accomplished so much good in the same length of time and at the same cost."[16]

Many of the shortcomings of the camp meeting depicted in articles and books by non-Methodist churchmen stung the revival's advocates into action. Aware that the defects laid bare by partisans contributed to the disenchantment of numerous visitors and participants alike, they engaged in a vigorous rebuttal. Many refused to apologize for the weapon of emotional excitement that they used. It was the very element of power by which most people were "thoroughly and speedily affected." The Reverend M. Emory Wright in 1861 insisted that these emotional appeals had accomplished the one and only purpose of the open-air revival:

It never attempts the mature development of a Christian character, and never professes any such intention. This is hopelessly forbidden by the brevity of its sessions. It is able only to arouse the spiritual slumberer to his danger, and to give him a vigorous and seasonable start in the path of safety.[17]

He concluded that spiritual apostasies were apt to follow all religious reform efforts, yet the "particular agencies whereby such reforms are promoted are not responsible for these subsequent defections." The important thing was that men were made aware of the consequences of their sins in an emphatic way.

It was only natural that religion should excite the worshiper, said one defendant of "mourner's bench revivalism," for

man is a complex being consisting of soul and body. And these two are so interwoven with each other, that you cannot touch the one without affecting the other. When religious truth is to be communicated to the soul, it must be done through the channel of the body. . . . Another self-evident truth is, that any kind of mental emotion will affect the body . . . but what is religion metaphysically considered? Is it not an emotion? Take for instance one part of religion, say repentance, what is this? It is sorrow for sin, and remorse excited in the mind of an awakened sinner. . . . Sorrow is a mental emotion, remorse is the same, only in a higher degree. *When we remember that man has but one set of outward FEELINGS which governs his inward EMOTIONS should it be thought strange that men should become excited under the influence of religion?*[18]

Tumult was to be expected. A camp meeting was no place to go with high looks, retorted one eastern minister in 1824; one had to be willing to be wrought upon by the Spirit in any fashion He so desired. "When the arrows of conviction are flying, and many are mortally wounded, a sigh or a groan is neither unfrequent nor untimely," the apologist went on.[19] Thus those who championed the woodland revival's emotionalism could not be expected to apologize for the disorder there, for was not the whole matter in the hands of the Lord? Since justification by faith was considered an act of God, the sinner had no control over the process. The evangelists did not consider the use of public affirmation a false issue, in contrast to those who claimed that the mourner's bench was too exciting and too far removed from cool reflection to be a true testing ground for religious conversion. A defendant of the "Religion of the Bench" heatedly declared that

pardon of sin, and our knowledge of that occurrence, is far beyond the reach of reason, or metaphysical research; it is a doctrine of Revelation, and a matter of experience. And the individual who has been converted at the Mourner's Bench, and has there felt the atoning blood of Jesus Christ applied to his guilty and troubled soul, can never be convinced by all the D.D.'s in the Universe, that the Mourner's Bench, "creates a false issue."[20]

Just as there were many kinds of camp meetings,

ranging from the tumultuous to the sedate, there were many varieties of camp meeting protagonists. Not all the leaders discarded appeals to man's reason, nor did all excuse the excesses of emotionalism that were evoked. The soberer individuals did not count the success of the revivals in the numbers of converts at the altar, but in the quickening of religious life and the raising of the moral tone of a community after the outdoor revival season was over. Writing in 1861, one spokesman summarized the spiritual fruits of the camp meeting as principally the admission of new church members, the increase in spiritual strength of the professing Christians who attended, the doubts placed in the minds of non-Christians paving the way for later conversions, and the frequent awakening of a community from a state of religious apathy to one of religious and humanitarian fervor.[21] Allen Wiley asserted in the 1840's that "no human being can correctly estimate the amount of good which this country has realized from camp meetings. Perhaps nearly one-half the members of the Methodist Episcopal church are the fruits of camp meetings, directly or remotely."[22] Similarly, many of the great names in Methodism could date the beginning of their religious awareness from a camp meeting they had visited early in life. The roster would include Peter Cartwright, James B. Finley, Stephen Beggs, Maxwell Gaddis, William Capers, John A. Granade, John Collins, William Brownlow, Allen Wiley, John Stewart, and John Dempster.[23]

The fact seems indisputable that the camp meeting caused many to lead a more socially desirable existence, even conceding that for a great number its regenerating effect was short-lived. The skeptics of the woodland revival frequently overlooked another truth which its

sponsors recognized: many of those "saved" at the altar
were not sinners in the ordinary sense of the word, but
were professing Christians and young children of Christian parents. Having been freed from the burden their
exaggerated sense of sin had laid upon them, they went
on to purer and more useful lives. Henry Boehm happily
noted in 1808 that "from the aged Father to the child of
seven years of age, the prospects are blooming." The
youthfulness of many of the converts was a striking
feature of camp meeting religion.[24]

Much of the criticism leveled against the frontier
camp meeting was undoubtedly warranted, but was certainly not sufficient to condemn it as a religious device.
Eastern encampments, moreover, with their huge crowds
and frequent disorder, seem to have furnished much of
the grounds for criticism. In the religious press of that
region some of the most savage indictments as well as
the most vigorous defenses are found. When any institution becomes great enough to excite public comment,
evaluations both favorable and adverse are likely to be
exaggerated. In spite of the camp meeting's basic weaknesses—noisy unchurchlike atmosphere, spurious and
short-lived conversions, excessively emotional services,
contribution to the spirit of religious intolerance, and
apparent prolongation beyond a point of usefulness in
the populous regions — the fact still remains that it was
a vital socioreligious institution in backwoods America.

Although it was rough, crude, and imperfect, the camp
meeting was an expression of the times. Clearly it arose
in response to a need: the spiritual poverty of the isolated
frontiersman. Men in the privations of pioneer life reverted to primitive traits in habits and customs of daily
living. The backwoods revival tamed those anarchistic

tendencies of the unchurched settler at the same time that it furnished him with an avenue of social expression. Hundreds visited Methodist encampments who seldom or never attended other religious meetings. In the absence of an established church the word of God was brought to many who might otherwise have remained untouched. Measured by the over-all results it achieved, the camp meeting was a wholesome weapon of the church in the trans-Allegheny West.

The tempo of the defense of the forest revival mounted as it passed into a final stage of slow disintegration. Yet, like all social institutions, the camp meeting still inspired blind faith in itself long after the conditions that had called it into being had passed away.

13

Decline of the Backwoods Revival

Must I say to our beloved camp
meetings, where thousands have been
saved and where thousands more might
be saved, farewell, a long farewell to
the delightful scenes of my best days,
because statesmen wish to banish you
[by failing to pass liquor control laws]
that they may secure the votes of the
drunken rabble? . . . Many a godly
father and mother have died with cheer-
fulness, believing that the wonderful
camp meeting influence would yet be
the means of saving their children, who
were unconverted at the time of their
death. Shall they be disappointed? I
fear they will.[1]
— Circuit rider Allen Wiley, 1846

THE CAMP MEETING'S
rise and fall in popularity followed the advance and retreat
of the frontier. In the trans-Allegheny West the harvest
time of the backwoods revival was apparently over by
the 1840's. The once-great institution had reached the
final stage of gradual but inevitable decline. Its reason
for being rapidly disappeared as border areas became
settled communities, as an expanding transportation net-
work drew them closer together, as towns and church
buildings multiplied, and as social life grew more varied
and more refined. The circuit riders, especially, were not

242

oblivious to the physical transformation that had occurred in the West in what had amounted to a relatively short time:

Great changes have appeared in our western field of labor . . . as have some bearing in our work as travelling preachers. Among these changes none are more palpable, than such as relate to the facilities for travelling. Where we used to convey our salt, venison and bear meat on pack horses, one now sees canal boats gliding along with flour and all the essentials of good life. Where we once followed the *dim* path guided by the blazes on the saplings made with the wooden axe, we now hear the coach wheels gently rumbling on the smooth M'Adamized turnpike. In the same place where we formerly swam our horses, beside the little canoe, plies the steam ferryboat, crossing and recrossing every five minutes, crowded with passengers; and where we used to plunge in on horseback at a venture, through flood and bog, current and quicksand, now rests the arched bridge on piers of granite.[2]

Operating alongside these underlying causes were the immediate and more obvious reasons for the decline of the frontier camp meeting. The holding of too frequent encampments in contiguous areas resulted in sparse attendance and few converts. Better results would have been attained, one preacher suggested, if the encampments had been more widely spaced in time and place. Experience taught "that Christians enjoy those meetings most which cost them the greatest sacrifice, and exclude them from the world." A fifty-mile journey was "a pretty sure pledge of a profitable meeting."[3]

Still another handicap to the forest revival was the fact that its bad reputation had grown rather than diminished through the years. This was particularly true of encampments staged near a large city or town. Opponents charged that the drunkenness and immorality that occurred there far outweighed any religious benefit that accrued from the services. Nathan Bangs, speaking out of a knowledge gained from his eastern experiences, warned in 1838 that a greater danger to camp meetings arose "from them degenerating into seasons of idle recreation, than of their being abused by ranting fanaticism." Some camp sponsors in the trans-Allegheny West wondered if it had not become an anachronism, or even worse, an influence for evil in the more densely populated regions. Allen Wiley reported that the numbers who came "merely for recreation" were on the increase. As a consequence, "hucksters find it a more profitable business to attend than formerly."[4]

The exact time of disintegration of the frontier camp meeting is difficult to establish. As every region differed in the degree to which it had passed through the settlement process, so the popularity of the outdoor meeting varied from place to place. The "annual camp meeting" continued in many circuits in the forties and fifties. In some regions encampments were so successful that several were held in a single season.[5] They were popular in the southern Appalachia, for example, even at the dawn of the twentieth century. One scholar set the first four decades of the nineteenth century as the day of the camp meeting; another concluded that for at least three generations the practice remained a vital force in the expansion of Methodism.[6] In 1859 an eastern chronicler exuberantly boasted that "annual camp meetings" were flourishing "from Martha's Vineyard to the Valley's of Oregon and California." Wherever new frontiers were opened to settlement, backwoods revivals were soon held. By the early 1830's, even though Protestant activity was illegal under Mexican rule, the Texas province had its campgrounds. On the west coast, traveling evangelist Orceneth Fisher of the Methodist Episcopal Church, South, staged a nineteen-day encampment near Stockton, California, in 1856.[7]

If the charting of the collapse of the frontier camp meeting produces a hazy picture, it is at least clear that by the decades of the thirties and forties the institution was outgrowing its frontier heritage in the Midwest. By that period the "New-Fashioned Camp Meeting" had replaced the "Old-Fashioned" one in many areas. Elaborate physical appointments were now a distinguishing feature. The makeup of the backwoods camp meeting had been simplicity itself; the later revival was noted for its comforts. A large wooden auditorium had replaced the natural amphitheater with its makeshift log seats and preacher's stands on stilts. Wooden cottages, some two stories high, substituted for the simple cloth tents. The freezing of camp site locations into permanent campgrounds encouraged this trend north as well as south of the Ohio. Thus Captain Frederick Marryat found a campground near Cincinnati in 1838, comprising about

an acre and a half [which] was surrounded on the four sides by cabins built up of rough boards; the whole area in the centre was fitten up with planks, laid about a foot from the ground, as seats. At one end, but not close to the cabins, was a raised stand, which served as a pulpit for the preachers, one of them praying, while five or six others sat down behind him in benches. There was ingress to the area by the four corners; the whole of it was shaded by vast forest trees, which ran up to the height of fifty or sixty feet without throwing out a branch; and to the trunks of these trees were fixed lamps in every direction, for the continuance of service by night. Outside the area, which may be designated as the church, were hundreds of tents pitched in every quarter, their snowy whiteness contrasting beautifully with the deep verdure and gloom of the forest. These were the temporary habitations of those who had come many miles to attend the meeting, and who remained there from the commencement until it concluded — usually a period of from ten to twelve days, but often much longer. The tents were furnished with every article necessary for cooking;

mattresses to sleep upon, etc.; some of them even had bedsteads and chests of drawers, which had been brought in the waggons in which the people in this country usually travel. At a farther distance were all the waggons and other vehicles which had conveyed the people to the meeting, whilst hundreds of horses were tethered under the trees, and plentifully provided with forage. . . .

In one quarter the coloured population had collected themselves; their tents appeared to be better furnished and better supplied with comforts than most of those belonging to the whites.[8]

In 1840 a strikingly similar picture was given in the *Western Christian Advocate* of a Cincinnati encampment that was "a village in the woods" with frame buildings two stories high. The lower story was used for dining and prayer meetings, the upper for lodging and private devotions. In Georgia, the mild weather did not necessitate a formal building, but an 1850 variation was the erection of a roofed shed large enough to shelter four thousand people. "Hundreds of tents and booths of all imaginable forms and colors" circled this wooden structure which had the altar at its center.[9]

Some contemporaries of the forties and fifties not only noted the change in physical appearance, but commented on the altered character of the services in "our fashionable camp meeting picnics of the present day."[10] The unemotional proceedings seen in the new-fashioned camp meeting were in sharp contrast to the fire and brimstone speeches of the speakers and the loud enthusiasm of the aroused worshipers of the frontier revival. More and more it took on the aspects of a social outing rather than a spiritual awakening. One writer even asked in an 1861 publication, "Is the Modern Camp-Meeting a Failure?" Another preacher, an Indiana circuiteer, listed the distinguishing characteristics of the new camp meeting as including not only fancy tents and log structures, but also "this order," "calm preaching," and the disappearance of the tradition of camper hospitality. Writing in 1873, he declared:

Except here and there an occasional fruitless effort to revive old-fashioned camp-meetings, which have rarely been repeated the second time on the same ground, there have been none for twenty-five years; and though we old people may occasionally sigh for their return, they are gone forever. The conditions which give them their special characteristics are gone. . . . However possible and desirable such meetings may yet be on the frontiers, if there be any such places anymore, they inevitably die out as the country improves. No camp-meeting can be a success now but the new-fashioned, the better its success.[11]

Further debilitating the camp meeting institution, an effective substitute appeared in the settled areas. This was the indoor "protracted meeting," itself as much a product of an urban environment as the open-air revival had been of the frontier. The indoor revival was made possible by population growth and by the construction of more and larger church buildings. Held in a house of God, the religious services were freed from the contamination of the whiskey sellers, the tradesmen, the gamblers, the loose-minded, and the scoffers. The orthodox setting also had a somewhat sobering effect upon the worshipers themselves, although protracted meetings still contained the familiar evangelistic touches — tearful testimonials, fervent prayers, shouting, and powerful exhortations. To the sophisticated townspeople, the more decorous protracted meeting had great appeal; these same folk considered the turbulent camp services outmoded.

In the Old Northwest, the drift toward the indoor revival was strongly marked in the 1830's and 1840's. Conditions had changed so in northwestern Pennsylvania by 1833 that saddlebag preacher Alfred Brunson expressed doubt as to the camp meeting's further usefulness there.

Brunson noted that the strongest argument in favor of camp meetings was the lack of churches. "But now we had churches enough for each circuit for *Winter* meetings, and for neighborhoods without churches the barns in the summer before harvest made good temporary places of worship." Protracted meetings in church or barn, he concluded, required little guarding against rowdies, were less expensive, and called for a smaller ministerial force. In 1838 some Baptist churches in Indiana began holding protracted meetings as a "yearly practice" and oftener, when interest warranted it.[12]

Camp veteran Maxwell P. Gaddis made no mention of camp meetings occurring in neighboring Ohio after 1836, but did report that many indoor protracted meetings were taking place. By 1840 presiding elder James Quinn of the Ohio Conference sadly observed that "an opinion prevails, to some extent, that these [camp] meetings should be discontinued and their place supplied with what are 'protracted meetings.' " Quinn felt, however, that this change was not satisfactory. Yet eleven years later, another backwoods preacher announced that encampments had indeed been replaced in these settled areas by the indoor services.[13]

The change of emphasis in Methodist newspapers, magazines, and other contemporary publications provides further evidence that the camp meeting had become less popular. Beginning in April, 1838, the Methodist *Western Christian Advocate* discontinued editorializing on the camp meeting and instead stressed protracted meetings in its news columns.[14] An encampment that was noted, such as that held in the Missouri Conference near St. Louis, in 1839, might be typically described as having "done much to revive the spirit of camp meetings in this region where it had well nigh died away." The authoritative church quarterly, the *Methodist Magazine,* and its successors generally ceased describing outdoor revival activity after 1822.[15]

Other published works tell much the same story. Nathan Bangs, whose history of Methodism included a chronicle of the camp meeting down to 1816, is notably deficient on that score in his later pages, for meticulous as he was, there just weren't the revivals to report as in former years. Southern as well as northern newspapers carried far less camp meeting copy; in North Carolina, for example, issues of the 1840's started the trend toward the omission of revival news. At about the same time the eastern press told of the camp meeting's loss of popularity.[16]

Also indicative of the disintegration of the camp meeting was the publication of camp meeting manuals in the forties and fifties. Their initial appearance coincided with a period in which the open-air revival's "showers of divine grace" diminished, and even some of its earlier advocates were questioning its usefulness. The manuals, apparently published only in the East, were called into being by this very situation. Their preacher-authors constituted a rear-guard action, a conservative phalanx battling to preserve the old. They insisted upon the continuance of the institution for its own sake, forgetting that it existed solely to serve the cause of winning people to a Christian way of life.

Although the manuals were not adopted by any official body, they had the blessing of some church groups. B. W. Gorham's *Camp Meeting Manual, A Practical Book for the Camp Ground,* was published in 1854 for the Ministerial Association of the Binghampton District of New York.[17] There was a striking similarity in organization and content among these manuals. The pattern of one seemed the pattern of all. One preacher-apologist of 1859 went so far as to confess that he copied large portions of an earlier treatment because it so ably presented the case for the outdoor revival. In the words of the borrower, his predecessor's work had "a nervously written value of 168 pages."[18] Approaching pocket size, the books measured 4 by 6½ inches and averaged 90 to 175 pages.

Granting the biased views of the authors, the contents of the camp meeting manuals are valuable because of the light they throw upon the camp meeting. They contain much campground data and many historical glimpses of the forest revival. Illustrations and camp layout charts added much to the narrative. The most preferred service plans, rules of order, favorite hymns with musical scores, and texts of sermons were outlined. Biblical quotations and revival testimonials were arrayed in profusion to confound the doubters; objections to the woodland meeting device were overwhelmed, one by one. Even more significant, the fundamental reasons for the decline of this evangelistic method are implicit in the preachers' refutations of contemporary criticisms. In their able apologies they admitted that many church leaders were disposed to abandon the camp meeting on the ground that its day of utility had passed. All attempted to explain away the contention of their opponents that "large towns and cities are regarded as taking the lead in that sort of refinement"; "that the necessity for Camp Meetings is passed away in consequence of the ample supply of church edifices, which the church is come of late to possess."[19]

The laments of the circuit riders themselves, like the

vigorous defense presented by the writers of the camp meeting manuals, bear testimony to the pioneer revival's loss of stature. Indiana saddlebag preacher William C. Smith argued that a maturing community, wealth, refinement, and the increase in church facilities were not sufficient reasons to justify the abandonment of the institution. Presiding Elder James Quinn pointed out that "well-protected, well-directed camp-meetings" could still serve a useful purpose in the 1840's, especially since the more newly favored protracted meeting could not solve the problem of lodging for those who had to travel a great distance. Peter Cartwright also lived long enough to bemoan the demise of his beloved camp meeting. On the final pages of his *Autobiography* he sorrowfully noted in 1856 that "The Methodist Episcopal Church of late years, since they have become numerous and wealthy, have almost let camp-meetings die out." Recollecting its effectiveness, he stubbornly refused to concede that times had changed, and urged the reinstatement of the summer revival. One week each year should be set aside "in each circuit, or station, on the tented field." He exhorted: "May the day be eternally distant, when camp-meetings, class-meetings, prayer-meetings and love-feasts shall be laid aside in the Methodist Episcopal Church."[20]

After the Civil War, encampments still dotted the landscape across the nation, but these modern vestiges bore only faint resemblance to their frontier predecessors. In Illinois, for example, the Des Plaines, Lake Bluff, Franklin Grove, Lena, Berger, and Centenary campgrounds, mostly instituted in the ante-bellum period, had continuous summer meetings through the 1930's. Occasionally, Methodist conferences united to hold summer sessions, while youth camps utilized numerous former campgrounds. When Camp Meeting Associations were chartered to administrate the sites through a president, trustees, and directors a commercial flavor was added. Many other encampments were transformed into middle-class summer resorts. Among the most profitable of these have been Ocean Grove and Atlantic Highland, New Jersey.[21]

Twentieth-century evangelical churches have banded together in many instances to rent or buy encampment grounds. The meetings held in Wisconsin during the present decade, for example, by the "Assembly of God" Church at Bryan and the "Church of the Brethren" in Waupaca have regularly commanded good crowds.[22] As recently as June, 1949, the Seventh Day Adventist Church sponsored a ten-day annual camp meeting at Takoma Park, Maryland, replete with seventy family tents. At the opening session, the president of the Potomac Conference, Howard J. Detwiler, addressed a crowd of two thousand people. He spoke of seeing signs of the "Last Days" of the world, a theme highly favored in millennial circles.[23]

Other encampments remained deserted, until the Chautauqua movement was organized through the joint efforts of Lewis Miller, an Ohio manufacturer and Sunday school teacher, and Bishop Vincent of the Methodist church. In 1874 they set up the "Chautauqua Assembly" which held summer sessions on the camp site at Lake Chautauqua, New York, for the purpose of providing Bible and management training for Sunday school teachers. Shortly, the courses were expanded in scope and length to include secular subjects as well. Lewis Miller affirmed the religious-democratic faith in the popularization of knowledge, holding that all knowledge was derived from God, and therefore all men should share in its enrichment. Independently founded traveling Chautauquas later took lecturers on cultural subjects and musical and dramatic artists over the countryside. Further urbanization after World War I, with the attendant radio, movie, and automobile, removed the primary reason for the Chautauqua's existence, but not before it had brought to the common people the same pleasures of participation and diversion its forerunner, the camp meeting, had previously afforded.

The revival impulse was carried on in the city gospel tabernacles of the evangelical churches and by the professional evangelists who hit the later "sawdust trail" in going from one summer tent service to another. Thus the frontier camp meeting left its successors, changed in many ways, but still following in the roughhewn tradition. The word "camp meeting" through the years has come to have many connotations. The phrase has found its way into modern political parlance and has even been used to denote the fervor and high-voltage excitement of national party conventions.[24] On the positive side of the forest revival's legacy is the spirit of the "Old-Time Religion," as preserved in the camp songbooks, the "unwritten music," the camp meeting manuals, and modern evangelical oratory. The mark of the frontier camp meeting is upon us to this day.

Appendix

A Traveler's Account of an Indiana Camp Meeting, 1829*

"The pen" was the space immediately below the preachers' stand; we were therefore placed on the edge of it, and were enabled to see and hear all that took place in the very center of this extraordinary exhibition.

The crowd fell back at the mention of the *pen,* and for some minutes there was a vacant space before us. The preachers came down from their stand and placed themselves in the midst of it, beginning to sing a hymn, calling upon the penitents to come forth. As they sang, they kept turning themselves round to every part of the crowd and, by degrees, the voices of the whole multitude joined in chorus. This was the only moment at which I perceived anything like the solemn and beautiful effect which I had heard ascribed to this woodland worship. It is certain that the combined voices of such a multitude heard at dead of night, from the depths of their eternal forests, the many fair young faces turned upward, and looking paler and lovelier as they met the moon beams, the dark figures of the officials in the middle of the circle, the lurid glare thrown by the altar-fires on the woods beyond, did altogether produce a fine and solemn effect, that I shall not easily forget; but ere I had well enjoyed it, the scene changed, and sublimity gave place to horror and disgust.

The exhortation nearly resembled that which I had heard at the Revival, but the result was very different; for, instead of the few hysterical women who had distinguished themselves on that occasion, above a hundred persons, nearly all females, came forward, uttering howlings and groans, so terrible that I shall never cease to shudder when I recall them. They appeared to drag each other forward, and on the word being given, "Let us pray," they all fell on their knees; but this posture was soon changed for others that permitted greater scope for the convulsive movements of their limbs; and they were soon all lying on the ground in an indescribable confusion of heads and legs. They threw about their limbs with such incessant and violent motion, that I was every instant expecting some serious accident to occur.

*Frances Trollope, *Domestic Manners of the American* (London, 1832), I, 240-45.

255

But how am I to describe the sounds that proceeded from this strange mass of human beings? I know no words which can convey an idea of it. Hysterical sobbings, convulsive groans, shrieks and screams the most appalling, burst forth on all sides. I felt sick with horror. As if their hoarse and overstrained voices failed to make noise enough, they soon began to clap their hands violently. . . .

Many of these wretched creatures were beautiful young females. The preachers moved about among them, at once exciting and soothing their agonies. I heard the muttered "Sister! dear sister!" I saw the insidious lips approach the cheeks of the unhappy girls; I heard the murmured confessions of the poor victims, and I watched their tormentors, breathing into their ears consolations that tinged the pale cheek with red. Had I been a man, I am sure I should have been guilty of some rash act of interference; nor do I believe that such a scene could have been acted in the presence of Englishmen without instant punishment being inflicted; not to mention the salutary discipline of the treadmill, which, beyond all question, would, in England, have been applied to check so turbulent and so vicious a scene.

After the first wild burst that followed their prostration, the moanings, in many instances, became loudly articulate; and I then experienced a strange vibration between tragic and comic feeling.

A very pretty girl, who was kneeling in the attitude of Canova's Magdalene immediately before us, amongst an immense quantity of jargon, broke out thus: "Woe! woe to the backsliders! hear it, hear it, Jesus! when I was fifteen my mother died, and I backslided, oh Jesus, I backslided! take me home to my mother, Jesus! take me home to her, for I am weary! Oh John Mitchel! John Mitchel!" and after sobbing piteously behind her raised hands, she lifted her sweet face again, which was as pale as death, and said, "Shall I sit on the sunny bank of salvation with my mother? my own dear mother? oh Jesus, take me home, take me home!"

Who could refuse a tear to this earnest wish for death in one so young and so lovely? But I saw her, ere I left the ground, with her hand fast locked, and her head supported by a man who looked very much as Don Juan might, when sent back to earth as too bad for the regions below.

One woman near us continued to "call on the Lord," as it is termed, in the loudest possible tone, and without a moment's interval, for the two hours that we kept our dreadful station. She became frightfully hoarse, and her face so red as to make me expect she would burst a blood-vessel. Among the rest of her rant, she said "I will hold fast to Jesus, I never will let him go; if they take me to hell, I will still hold him fast, fast, fast!"

The stunning noise was sometimes varied by the preachers beginning to sing; but the convulsive movements of the poor maniacs only became more violent. At length the atrocious wickedness of this horrible scene increased to a degree of grossness, that drove us from our station; we returned to the carriage at about three o'clock in the morning, and passed the remainder of the night in listening to the ever increasing tumult at the pen. To sleep was impossible.

APPENDIX II — A

A Report of the Cane Ridge Camp Meeting, Kentucky, August 6, 1801: The Falling Exercise*

Thoughtless infidels have fallen as suddenly as if struck by lightning . . . sometimes at the very moment they are uttering blasphemies against the work. Immediately after they become totally powerless, they are seized with a general tremor, and sometimes, though not often, they utter one or two piercing shrieks in the moment of falling. Persons in this situation are affected in different degrees; . . . sometimes when unable to stand or sit, they have the use of their hands and can converse with perfect composure. In other cases, they are unable to speak, the pulse becomes weak, and they draw a difficult breath about once a minute, in some instances their extremities become cold, and pulsation, breathing, and all the signs of life, forsake them for nearly an hour. Persons who have been in this situation have uniformly avowed that they felt no bodily pain; that they had the entire use of their reason and reflection, and when recovered they could relate everything that had been said or done near them. From this it appears, that their falling is neither common fainting, nor a nervous reflection. Indeed this strange phenomenon appears to have taken every possible turn, to baffle the conjectures of those who are not willing to consider it as a supernatural work. Persons have sometimes fallen on their way from public worship, and sometimes after they had arrived at home,

*George Baxter, Principal of Washington Academy, to A. Alexander, Washington Academy, January 1, 1802, printed in the *Methodist Magazine* (London), XXVI (February, 1803), 90-91.

and in some cases, when they were pursuing their common business on the farms or when retired for secret devotion. . . . I have conversed with many who fell under the influence of comfortable feelings and the account they gave of their exercises [was remarkable].

APPENDIX II — B

A Report of a Long-Calm Camp Meeting, Baltimore Circuit, Maryland, October 8th to 14th, 1806*

I was at a happy campmeeting in the first of October, the greatest I ever was at. Such an one I never saw before. Our Tents were pitched in form round the Stand—behind the stand were the coulered peoples tents—Three rows of tents faceing the stand—All the camp ground hedged in by a brush fence—Two gates for the Waggons to come in at—Plank seats, to seat three or four thousand people, or perhaps five thousand—Our stand was covered with a good shingle roof, and nicely plained—before it there was another stand for the Ministers and Majestrates to sit in—Round the stand we had a pen post and rail, with three gates, or gaps, and benches inside to bring the Mourners in after preaching. We had three guards, 1. the outer guard, 2. the iner guard, 3. the official guard. The outer guard was to guard the gates, and prevent disorder in the extremities of the Camp—The iner guard were to stand in the Iles and seat the people and prevent disorder there—The official guard were to bring forward the Mourners and admit them into the pen—where active persons ready to receive them and help them on to Jesus. And then we had what we called runners—Composed of lads and Boys who whipped away dogs and hogs &c—The order of every day was as follows—At day break the Trumpets were blown round the Camp for the people to rise 20 minutes afterwards for family prayer at the dore of every tent—if fair weather—at sunrise they blew at the stand for public prayer, and then brakefasted. At 10 ocloc they blew for preaching—by 2 ocl. Dinner was to be over in every tent. At 3 ocl. preaching again, and again at night— on the left side of the stand the preachers had a large tent consisting of two rooms, a dineing room, and a bed room—in our dineing room we had a large table (where for the preachers)

*Transcribed from Benjamin Lakin's handwritten extract from itinerant Henry Smith's letter, November 11, 1806, contained in the "Papers of Benjamin Lakin," MSS. (handwritten), repository at the Divinity Library, University of Chicago.

The Lord owned our labours and smiled upon us in a wonderfull manner 579 professed converting grace and 118 Sanctification —The glorious flame is spreading—Now I will tell you how we parted—On the last day after brakefast the tents were struck and the people made ready to move on towards home—They were requested to stand in a circular form at the doors of the first row of tents, and when the preachers fell upon their knees at the stand to give thanks to God in silent prayer they were to do likewise, Oh! what a power while hundreds were prostrate upon the earth before the Lord. The preachers then went round the Camp ground singing a parting Hymn, the people standing in form almost drowned in tears when we got round the stand 5 or 6. Trumpets were blown at or from the stand which made a tremendious roar, and the people invited to come round the stand—Oh! Solemn seen! will I ever see anything more like the day of Judgment on this side of eternity— To see the people runing, yes runing, from every direction to the stand weeping, Shouting, and shouting for joy pray was then made —and every Brother fell upon the neck of his brother and wept and the Sisters did likewise & then we parted. O! glorious day they went home singing and Shouting—

Baltimore Ct. November 11 . . 1806—H.S.

APPENDIX II — C

Circuit Rider James Gwin's Account of the Second Camp Meeting Staged in the Illinois Circuit, at Three Springs, Illinois, 1807*

We arrived on Friday morning on the camp-ground, which was situated in a beautiful grove surrounded by a prairie. A considerable congregation had collected, for the news of the other meeting [Edwardsville camp meeting of April] had gone abroad and produced much excitement. Some were in favor of the work and others were opposed to it. A certain major had raised a company of lewd fellows of the baser sort to drive us from the ground. On Saturday, while I was preaching, the major and his company rode into the congregation and halted, which produced considerable confusion and alarm. I stopped preaching for a moment and quite calmly invited them to be off with themselves, and they re-

*Recorded by James Leaton, conference historian for the Illinois Conference, in *History of Methodism in Illinois, From 1793 to 1832* (Cincinnati, 1883), pp. 52-53.

tired to the spring for a fresh drink of brandy. The major said he had heard of these Methodists before; that they always broke up the peace of the people wherever they went; that they preached against horse-racing, card-playing and every other kind of amusement. However, they used no violence against us, but determined to camp on the ground and prevent us doing harm. But at three o'clock, when Brother Goddard and I were singing a hymn, an awful sense of Divine Power fell on the congregation, when a man, with a terrified look, ran to me and said, "Are you the man that keeps the roll?" I asked "What roll?" "That roll," he replied, "that people put their names to when they are going to heaven." I supposed he meant the class-paper, and sent him to Brother Walker. Turning to Brother Walker he said, "Put my name down, if you please," and then fell to the ground. Others started to run off, and fell; some escaped. We were busy in getting the fallen to one place, which we effected about sunset. . . . Looking around upon the scene, and listening to the sobs, groans, and cries of the penitents, reminded me of a battle-field after a heavy battle. All night the struggle went on. Victory was on the Lord's side; many were converted, and by sunrise next morning there was the shout of a King in the camp.

APPENDIX II — D

Circuit Rider James Gwin's Account of the Third Camp Meeting Staged in the Illinois Circuit at Goshen, Illinois, 1807*

On Friday and Saturday, the Word preached seemed to do little good. An awful cloud seemed to rest upon us. In passing the preachers' tent I saw Brother McKendree alone, bathed in tears. I stepped in, and he said to me, "Brother, we have been preaching for ourselves, and not for the Lord. Go, brother, and preach Christ crucified to the people!" My heart was deeply affected. We fell upon our knees, and implored the help of God. This was about sunset. I preached at candle-lighting. My text was, "Behold the Man!" It commenced raining shortly after I began to preach, and as the audience was under shelter, I did not stop, although exposed to the rain. My heart was fired and my tongue loosened in an unusual manner. For a few moments nothing but sobs and sighs were heard . . . at length the whole congregation seemed suddenly smitten with the power of God. Many fell as in battle, and were

*Recorded by James Leaton, in *History of Methodism in Illinois, From 1793 to 1832* (Cincinnati, 1883), pp. 54-56.

presently raised to tell of pardoning mercy and encourage others to seek the Lord. We continued all night in the work. On the next day, Sunday, at nine o'clock in the morning, the Lord's-supper was administered.

It was a memorable day.... one conversation deserves particular notice. An Indian, of the Chickamauga tribe, on a hunting-trip, fell in with us at our camp-meeting. I will give his own account of his conversion. He said: "When I saw so many people, I thought I would stop and get some whiskey; and while you were talking in the rain, I was standing by a sapling, and there came on me a mighty weight, too heavy for me to stand under. I caught the sapling, but my hands would not hold it, and I fell to the ground. While there, blackness came over me. I tried to get away, but could not until about daylight. I thought surely I had been drunk; but then I remembered I had nothing to drink. Although I concluded not to go back, yet, when they began to sing, something drew me back, and before I knew it I was among them again, and then the same weight came upon me, and the darkness. I fell to the ground, and thought I was about to die.... At last a white man came and talked over me, and while he was talking I got lighter and lighter, and everything looked whiter than the sun could make it look. The heavy load and blackness left me. I felt glad in my heart, and jumped up and felt light." Arrangements were made to send this Indian to school. He soon learned to read and write, and at the last account of him he was trying to walk in the light. On Monday, the last day of the meeting, one hundred joined the Church.

Appendix III

Camp Meeting Songs

A. "Young People, All Attention Give"*

> Young people, all attention give,
>   While I address you in God's name;
> You who in sin and folly live,
>   Come hear the counsel of a friend.

*Anonymous, *The Camp-Meeting Hymn Book: Containing the Most Approved Hymns and Spiritual Songs Used by the Methodist Connexion in the United States* (Ithaca, 1836, 6th ed.), pp. 108-10. Five of the twelve verses are quoted.

I've sought for bliss in glittering togs
    And ranged the luring scenes of vice,
But never knew substantial joys,
    Until I heard my Savior's voice. . . .

Your sparkling eyes and blooming cheeks
    Must wither like the blasted rose,
The coffin, earth and winding sheet,
    Will soon your active lives enclose. . . .

Your souls will land in darker realms
    Where vengeance reigns and bellows roar,
And roll amid the burning flames,
    When the many thousand years are o'er.

Ye blooming youth, this is the state
    Of all who do free grace refuse;
And soon with you 'twill be too late,
    The way of life in Christ to choose.

B. Dialogue Song, "Methodist and Formalist"*

Methodist

Good morning, brother Pilgrim! What, trav'ling to Zion?
What doubts and what dangers have you met to-day?
Have you gain'd a blessing, then pray without ceasing,
Press forward, my brother and make no delay;
Is your heart now glowing, your comforts now flowing,
And have you an evidence now bright and clear?
Have you a desire that burns like a fire,
And longs for the hour when Christ shall appear?

Formalist

I came out this morning, and now I'm returning,
Perhaps little better than when I first came,
Such groaning and shouting, it sets me to doubting,
I fear such religion is only a dream.
The preachers were stamping, the people were jumping,

*From *The Hesperian Harp,* compiled by William Hauser, printed in Philadelphia, 1848, and reprinted in George P. Jackson (collector and editor), *Down-East Spirituals and Others* (New York, 1939), pp. 13-15.
Two sections of the camp meeting audience sang these verses alternately. The practice of seating the women on one side and the men on the other seemed to have furthered the use of this dramatic type of song.

And screaming so loud that I nothing could hear,
Either praying or preaching—such horrible shrieking!
I was truly offended at all that was there.

Methodist

Perhaps, my dear brother, while they prayed together
You sat and considered, but prayed not at all:
Would you find a blessing, then pray without ceasing,
Obey the advice that was given by Paul.
For if you should reason at any such season,
No wonder if Satan should tell in your ear,
That preachers and people are only a rabble,
And this is no place for reflection and prayer.

Formalist

No place for reflection—I'm filled with distraction,
I wonder that people could bear for to stay,
The men they were bawling, the women were squalling,
I know not for my part how any could pray.
Such horrid confusion—if this be religion
I'm sure that it's something that never was seen,
For the sacred pages that speak of all ages,
Do nowhere declare that such ever has been.

Methodist

Don't be so soon shaken—if I'm not mistaken
Such things were perform'd by believers of old;
When the ark was coming, King David came running,
And dancing before it, in Scripture we're told.
When the Jewish nation had laid the foundation,
To rebuild the temple at Ezra's command,
Some wept and some praised, such noise there was raised,
'Twas heard afar off and perhaps through the land.
And as for the preacher, Ezekiel the teacher,
God taught him to stamp and to smite with the hand,
To show the transgressions of that wicked nation
To bid them repent and obey the command.
For Scripture collation in this dispensation,
The blessed Redeemer has handed it out—
"If these cease from praising," we hear him there saying,
"The stones to reprove them would quickly cry out."

Formalist

Then Scripture's contrasted, for Paul has protested
That order should reign in the house of the Lord—

Amid such a clatter who knows what's the matter?
Or who can attend unto what is declared?
To see them behaving like drunkards, all raving,
And lying and rolling prostrate on the ground,
I really felt awful, and sometimes felt fearful
That I'd be the next that would come tumbling down.

Methodist

You say you felt awful—you ought to be careful
Lest you grieve the Spirit, and so he depart,
By your own confession you've felt some impression,
The sweet melting showers have soften'd your heart.
You fear persecution, and that's a delusion
Brought in by the devil to stop up your way.
Be careful, my brother, for blest are no other
Than persons that "are not offended in Me."
As Peter was preaching, and bold in his teaching,
The plan of salvation in Jesus'es name,
The Spirit descended and some were offended,
And said of these men, "They're filled with new wine."
I never yet doubted that some of them shouted,
While others lay prostrate, by power struck down;
Some weeping, some praising, while others were saying:
"They're drunkards or fools, or in falsehood abound."
As time is now flying and moments are dying,
We're call'd to improve them, and quickly prepare
For that awful hour when Jesus, in power
And glory is coming—'tis now drawing near.
Methinks there'll be shouting, and I'm not a-doubting,
But crying and screaming for mercy in vain;
Therefore, my dear brother, let us pray together,
That your precious soul may be fill'd with the flame.

Formalist

I own prayer's now needful, I really feel awful
That I've grieved the Spirit in time that is past;
But I'll look to my Savior, and hope to find favor,
The storms of temptation will not always last.
I'll strive for the blessing, and pray without ceasing,
His mercy is sure unto all that believe.
My heart is now glowing! I feel his love flowing!
Peace, pardon, and comfort I now do receive!

APPENDIX IV — A

John Waller's Baptist Camp Meeting Rules (Circa 1775-76)*

1st. No female, on any account whatever, shall be permitted to appear in the camp, until an hour after sunrise in the morning, nor stay there later than an hour before sunset at night.

2d. The persons in the comp shall depend for sustenance, during the camp-meeting, on the friendly hospitality of the neighborhood.

3d. Any person in camp, waking at any period of the night, may pray or sing, without disturbing the slumber of others.

APPENDIX IV — B

Camp Meeting Rules of the Granville Circuit, Ohio Conference, 1831†

1. The people will be notefied of the commencement of Publick Worship from time to time by the sound of the trumpet; when all persons within the space formed by the tents, are requested to take their seats in the congregation and conform to the order [of] Meeting.

2. The seats, and the grove of timber on the right hand of the stand are for the use, and retirement of the females; and the seats and grove of timber on the left hand are for the use and retirement of the men.

3. The trumpet will sound in the morning at 5 as a signal to rise and have prayer in the tents.

4. At the close of worship in the evening, the trumpet will sound as a signal of rest: when all are requested to go to their beds and be quiet; so as not to disturb others. And all persons not having tents to sleep in are required to leave the encampment till morning.

*David Benedict, *A General History of the Baptist Denomination in America, and Other Parts of the World* (Boston, 1813 ed.), II, 397.

†Adopted Sept. 2, 1831, for a camp meeting in Granville Circuit, Ohio Conference. From the "Journal" of James Gilruth (1831-32), cited in William W. Sweet, *Religion on the American Frontier. 1783-1840. Vol. IV. The Methodists. A Collection of Source Materials* (Chicago, 1946), pp. 720-21.

5. The hours for eating will be as follows: vis, breakfast at 7, dinner at 12, and supper at 5.
6. All person commiting any acts, or making any disturbence in, or about this meting, such as are prohibited by the state laws of Ohio, will be delt with according to law.

Signed

Benjn Pratt. Peter Thurston,
Alexander Devilbess,
Samuel Carpenter, Jacob Marten,
John Jaffield,

Committy.

Notes

Prologue

1. "Aspects of Methodism," *Millennial Harbinger* (Bethany, Virginia), VII (October, 1843), 463.
2. For these views in the order quoted, see Van Wyck Brooks, *The World of Washington Irving* (New York, 1944), p. 99; Herbert Asbury, "The Palmy Days of Methodism," *American Mercury*, IX (December, 1926), 439; Letter, Mr. C. Washburn, former agent of the American Home Missionary Society, Benton, Arkansas, September 6, 1846, printed in William W. Sweet, *Religion on the American Frontier. Vol. II. The Presbyterians: 1783-1840. A Collection of Source Materials* (New York and London, 1936), p. 695 [hereafter cited as *The Presbyterians*]; and Charles Giles, *Pioneer: A Narrative of the Nativity, Experience, Travels, and Ministerial Labours of Rev. Charles Giles* (New York, 1844), pp. 234-35.
3. In the order quoted, Alice F. Tyler, *Freedom's Ferment: Phases of American Social History to 1860* (Minneapolis, 1944), p. 35; Ralph H. Gabriel, *The Course of American Democratic Thought: An Intellectual History Since 1815* (New York, 1940), p. 32.
4. In the order quoted, Clement Eaton, *Freedom of Thought in the Old South* (Durham, 1940), p. 282; James G. Leyburn, *Frontier Folkways* (New Haven, 1935), p. 197.
5. John P. MacLean, "The Kentucky Revival and Its Influence on the Miami Valley," *Ohio Archaeological and Historical Quarterly*, XII (July, 1903), 246. Yet a twentieth-century historian of frontier Christianity concluded that the Methodists developed it "into the most important social institution of the frontier." See William W. Sweet, *Religion on the American Frontier: 1783-1840. Vol. IV. The Methodists: A Collection of Source Materials* (Chicago, 1946), p. 68. [Hereafter cited as *The Methodists*.]
6. The pungent exhortation technique of one Alabama camp leader directed at Captain Simon Suggs, denizen of the Old Southwest, was effective: " 'Breethring,' he exclaimed, 'I see yonder a man that's a sinner! I know he's a sinner! Thar he stands,' pointing at Simon, 'a missuble old crittur, with his head a-blossomin' for the grave! A few more short years, and d-o-w-n he'll go to perdition, lessen the Lord have mer-cy on him! Come up here, you old hoary-headed sinner, a-n-d git down upon your knees, a-n-d put up your cry for the Lord to snatch you from the bottomless pit! You're ripe for the devil; you're b-o-u-n-d for hell, and the Lord knows what'll become on you!' " For the entire story see Johnson J. Hooper, "The Captain Attends a Camp-Meeting," printed in Henry Watterson (ed.), *Oddities in Southern Life and Character* (Boston, 1883), pp. 55-69.
7. See for example Gilbert Seldes, *The Stammering Century* (New York, 1928), pp. 3, 36, 51-67, and Asbury, "The Palmy Days of Methodism," pp. 439-42. Herbert Asbury claims Francis Asbury as his great-great uncle.
8. For four sketchy studies of the later camp meetings in North Carolina, Missouri, and the Ohio Valley, see Guion G. Johnson, "Revival Move-

ments in Ante-Bellum North Carolina," *North Carolina Historical Review,* X (January, 1933), 21-43, and "The Camp Meeting in Ante Bellum North Carolina," *ibid.,* X (April, 1933), 95-110; Marie G. Windell, "The Camp Meeting in Missouri," *Missouri Historical Review,* XXXVII (April, 1943), 253-70; Ernest L. Carter, "The Early Camp-Meeting Movement in the Ohio Valley" (Master's thesis, Ohio Wesleyan University, 1922).

9. Editorial of Thomas A. Morris, editor, *Western Christian Advocate* (Cincinnati), August 15, 1834.

10. Bishop Francis Asbury to the Reverend T. L. Douglass, Richmond, Virginia, 1812, quoted in William W. Bennett, *Memorials of Methodism in Virginia, From its Introduction into the State, in the Year 1782, to the Year 1829* (Richmond, 1871), p. 566.

11. Itinerant James Gwin quoted in James Leaton, *History of Methodism in Illinois, From 1793 to 1832* (Cincinnati, 1883), p. 54.

1. *The Frontier's Religious Challenge*

1. Gabriel, *op. cit.,* p. 33.

2. Between 1790 and 1800 settlements west of the Alleghenies had grown rapidly and the United States Census Report for 1800 revealed that Kentucky had a population of 220,955; Tennessee, 105,602; The Ohio Territory, 45,365; while the Indiana and Mississippi territories (the latter including the future states of Alabama and Mississippi) contained more than 5,000 and 8,000 respectively. Statistics quoted in Catharine C. Cleveland, *The Great Revival in the West 1797-1805* (Chicago, 1916), pp. 1-2.

3. See C. R. Johnson, "Early History," *Badger State Banner* (Black River Falls, Wisconsin), April 17, and Lieutenant Colonel J. A. Watrous, *Milwaukee Morning Sentinel,* November 28, 1910, quoted in Horace S. Merrill, "An Early History of the Black River Falls Region" (Master's thesis, University of Wisconsin, 1933), pp. 75, 80.

4. Robert Davidson, *History of the Presbyterian Church in the State of Kentucky* (New York, 1847), p. 131. For similar views on the religious destitution of the West see Everett Dick, *The Dixie Frontier: A Social History of the Southern Frontier from the First Transmontane Beginnings to the Civil War* (New York, 1948), pp. 180-83.

5. See John F. Schermerhorn and Samuel J. Mills, *A Correct View of That Part of the United States Which Lies West of the Alleghany Mountains, with Regard to Religion and Morals* (Hartford, 1814), pp. 7, 15; and John M. Ellis, Kaskaskia, Illinois, December 29, 1828, Letters of Agents to the American Home Missionary Society (MSS [handwritten], Hammond Library, Chicago Theological Seminary, Chicago).

6. See James B. Pratt, *The Religious Consciousness; A Psychological Study* (New York, 1920), pp. 165-66.

7. James Gallaher, *The Western Sketch Book* (Boston, 1852 ed.), pp. 32-33. Benjamin Franklin wrote a cogent reply in 1785 to Thomas Paine after reading the latter's manuscript which attacked religion: "You yourself may find it easy to live a virtuous life, without the assistance afforded by religion; you having a clear perception of the advantages of virtue, and the disadvantages of vice. . . . But think how great a portion of mankind consists of weak and ignorant men and women, and of inexperienced incon-

siderate youth of both sexes who have need of the motives of religion to restrain them from vice, to support their virtue, and retain them in the practice of it till it becomes habitual, which is the great point of its security." Quoted in Paul L. Ford, *The Many-Sided Franklin* (New York, 1899), pp. 166-67.

8. "Quinze Jours au Desert," printed in George W. Pierson, *Tocqueville and Beaumont in America* (New York, 1938), p. 249.

9. William Colbert, "A Journal of the Travels of William Colbert, Methodist Preacher Thro' Parts of Maryland, Pennsylvania, New York, Delaware, and Virginia in 1790 to 1838" (MS [typewritten], Garrett Biblical Institute, Evanston, Illinois, III, 92.

10. Economic crises with accompanying mental strain often contributed to religious revivals, as witness the Fulton Street Revival of 1857. See Pratt, *op. cit.,* p. 173, and Frederick M. Davenport, *Primitive Traits in Religious Revivals* (New York, 1905), pp. 8-9, for the influence of the wilderness environment.

11. Peter Cartwright, *Autobiography of Peter Cartwright, the Backwoods Preacher,* ed. W. P. Strickland (New York, 1857), pp. 25-26.

12. Badgered by ceaseless labor, pioneers joyfully observed all neighborhood weddings, for, as one of their spokesmen observed, "a wedding was almost the only gathering which was not accompanied with the labor of reaping, log rolling, etc." Mann Butler, "Manners and Habits of the Western Pioneers" (MS [handwritten], Durrett Collection, University of Chicago), pp. 34-35.

13. Robert Boyd, *Personal Memoirs: Together with a Discussion Upon the Hardships and Sufferings of Itinerant Life* (Cincinnati, 1866), pp. 21-26.

14. See Cartwright, *op. cit.,* pp. 212-13. For similar statements see also Henry Smith, *Recollections and Reflections of an Old Itinerant,* ed. George Peck (New York, 1848), p. 62, and Finley, *op. cit.,* pp. 248-52.

15. Consult, for example, the observations of the Englishman William Brown in his *America: A Four Years Residence in the United States and Canada . . .* (Leeds, 1849), pp. 26-28.

16. Fortescue Cuming, *Sketches of a Tour to the Western Country Through the States of Ohio and Kentucky . . . . Winter of 1807 and Concluded in 1809* (Pittsburgh, 1810), pp.118-19.

17. Horace Bushnell, *Barbarism the First Danger: A Discourse for Home Missions* (New York, 1847), *passim.*

18. Albert J. Beveridge, *Abraham Lincoln, 1809-1858* (Boston and New York, 1928), I, 53-56. On the inadequacy of Ohio schools of 1813 see, for example, Schermerhorn and Mills, *op cit.,* p. 17.

19. "The most prominent of these habits is the propensity, with which, like the sons of Ishmael, they seem to have been gifted by Heaven, and which continually goads them on, to shift their residence from place to place, so that a Yankee farmer is in a constant state of migration; tarrying occasionally here and there, clearing land for other people to enjoy, building houses for others to inhabit. . . ." *Knickerbocker Magazine,* I, quoted in Lieutenant Francis Hall, *Travels in Canada and the United States in 1816 and 1817* (2nd ed.; London, 1819), pp. 46-47.

20. James Hall, *Letters from the West; Containing Sketches of Scenery,*

Manners, and Customs . . . . (London, 1828), p. 263. On western manners and characteristics see pp. 113-14, 118-20, 173, 238-40, 248-64.

21. *Ibid.,* p. 271. See also Davenport, *op. cit.,* pp. 63-65, and William W. Sweet, *The American Churches: An Interpretation* (London, 1947), pp. 34-37.

22. Quoted by James Flint, *Flint's Letters From America, 1818-1820,* Vol. IX of *Early Western Travels, 1748-1846.* Ed. Reuben G. Thwaites (Cleveland, 1904-7), p. 263.

23. Butler, *op. cit.,* pp. 56-57; James Hall, *op. cit.,* pp. 326-45.

24. George Shelton, New York, May 14, 1825, Letters of Agents to the American Home Missionary Society.

25. Frederick J. Turner, "The Ohio Valley in American History," *The Frontier in American History* (New York, 1920), pp. 164-65.

26. Davenport, *op. cit.,* pp. 63-64.

27. View of H. Richard Niebuhr, *The Social Sources of Denomination-alism* (New York, 1929), ch. vi, quoted in Sweet, *The American Churches,* pp. 68-69.

28. As an American Home Missionary pointed out in 1848, if their members were too disparaging, "the ministers reports will be filled with dark accounts of the deep ignorance and degradation of the people; and the people will be laughing among themselves about the minister for his want of common sense." Cited in C. P. Kofoid, "Puritan Influences of the Forma-tive Years of Illinois History, *Publications of the Illinois State Historical Society,* No. 10 (1905).

29. Sweet, *The Presbyterians,* p. 82.

30. The role of the frontier church as a disciplining agency is too little known. Drunkenness and adultery were the most common causes for cen-sure of church members whether by the Presbyterian session, the Baptist monthly meeting, or the Methodist weekly class meeting. See William W. Sweet, "The Churches as Moral Courts of the Frontier," *Church History,* II (March, 1933), 3-21.

31. Albert H. Redford, *The History of Methodism in Kentucky* (Nash-ville, 1868-76), III, 530.

32. Schermerhorn and Mills, *op. cit.,* p. 41.

33. The ideas expressed here are based upon Wesley M. Gewehr, "Some Factors in the Expansion of Frontier Methodism, 1800-1811," *Journal of Religion,* VIII (January, 1928), 101-6. See also Jesse Lee, *A Short History of the Methodists in the United States of America Beginning in 1766, and Continued till 1809* (Baltimore, 1810), p. 52, and Sweet, *The Methodists,* pp. 42-45.

34. The "quarterly conference" consisted of all the traveling and located preachers, the exhorters, class leaders, and stewards (class treasurers) of a circuit. Supervisor of this group was the overworked presiding elder who was obliged to attend every quarterly meeting in his district. At this conference, church business was discussed, the "quarterage" apportioned, and the sacrament administered. See Sweet, *The Methodists,* ch. iii, "The Methodist System," for a comprehensive treatment of this subject. See also James B. Finley, *Sketches of Western Methodism: Biographical, Historical, and Miscellaneous. Illustrative of Pioneer Life,* ed. W. P. Strickland (Cin-cinnati, 1854), p. 188 [hereafter referred to as *Sketches*]; and Robert

Emory, *History of the Discipline of the Methodist Episcopal Church* (New York, 1844), pp. 132-33, 135.

35. Only an elder could administer the sacrament, and that is why the presiding elder had to attend every quarterly meeting in his district. See Schermerhorn and Mills, *op. cit.*, pp. 40-41.

36. Ernest Sutherland Bates, "Peter Cartwright," *Dictionary of American Biography*, ed. Allen Johnson (New York, 1929-44), III, 547 [hereafter cited as *D.A.B.*].

37. William W. Sweet, *The Rise of Methodism in the West: Being the Journal of the Western Conference 1800-1811* (New York and Cincinnati, 1920), pp. 46-47.

38. Entry of July 24, 1812, Benjamin Lakin, "Journal of Rev. Benjamin Lakin (1794-1820)," (MSS [handwritten], Divinity School, University of Chicago), No. II; and William P. Strickland, *The Pioneers of the West, or Life in the Woods* (New York, 1856), p. 162.

39. Henry Smith, *op. cit.*, p. 166, and Francis Asbury to Henry Smith, Wasaws, [?] October 10, 1806, "Letters of Bishop Francis Asbury" (MSS [handwritten], Methodist Historical Society of the Baltimore Conference, First Methodist Church, Baltimore, Maryland).

40. Gewehr, "Some Factors in the Expansion of Frontier Methodism, 1800-1811," pp. 101-2.

41. Henry Smith, *op. cit.*, p. 352, and Sweet, *Rise of Methodism*, p. 41.

42. Finley, *Sketches*, pp. 178-84. Route fully described in James B. Finley, *Autobiography of Rev. James B. Finley; or, Pioneer Life in the West*, ed. W. P. Strickland (Cincinnati, 1853), pp. 193-94.

43. *Ibid.*, p. 268

44. James Gilruth, "The Journal of James Gilruth 1793-1873" (MSS [typewritten], Vol. I [April 4 to August 31, 1831]; Divinity School, University of Chicago), and Henry Smith, *op. cit.*, p. 173.

45. Henry Smith, *op. cit.*, p. 173.

46. "Autobiography of Rev. William Burke," quoted in Finley, *Sketches*, p. 87.

47. The Congregationalists and the Presbyterians had this same problem on the frontier. The Reverend Henry Ruud, a home missionary, traveling eight miles to preside at a "Sugar Tree Grove" sacramental service in Indiana in 1824, reported that "Some of the Communicants had rode a full day's ride and some near two days ride to attend the meeting; several now had [communion] for the first time in the state, some who had been six and others three and four years [in that state] . . . ." Indiana, August 6, 1824, Letters of Agents to the American Home Missionary Society.

2. Seed Time

1. Giles, *op. cit.*, pp. 234-35.

2. Quoted in Holland N. McTyeire, *A History of Methodism* (Nashville, 1924), p. 154.

3. *Ibid.*, pp. 154, 157.

4. "Sunday 20 [May] . . . Perhaps it [these strange physical phenomena] might be because of the hardness of our hearts, unready to receive anything unless we see it with our eyes and hear it with our ears, that God, in tender condescension to our weakness, suffered so many outward signs

of the very time He wrought this inward change to be continually seen and heard among us. . . . Yet many would not believe. They could not *deny* facts; but they could *explain* them away. . . . Today Monday the 21st, our Lord answered for himself. For while I was enforcing these words 'Be still and know that I am God,' He began to make bare His own, not in a close room . . . but in the open air, and before more than two thousand witnesses. One and another was struck to the earth, exceedingly trembling at the presence of His power. Others cried with a loud and bitter cry 'What must we do to be saved?' " Nehemiah Curnock (ed.), *The Journal of the Rev. John Wesley, A. M.* (London, 1909-16), II, 202-3; see also 186-87, 203-4.

5. George B. Griffith, "Camp Meetings," *Ladies' Repository: A Monthly Periodical Devoted to Literature and Religion* (Cincinnati, Ohio), XXXV (January-June, 1876), 114.

6. Cuming, *op. cit.,* p. 69. In the East, as well as on the frontier, the absence of churches and poverty of transportation facilities led to the development of camp meetings. Concerning the Eastern Shore of Maryland, for example, see William H. Wroten, Jr., "A Chronicle of the Religious Beginning of Dorchester County, Maryland" (Master's thesis, University of Maryland, 1948), p. 137.

7. The year 1769 is the date such meetings were begun by the Separate Baptist preachers, according to Robert Semple, *A History of the Rise and Progress of the Baptists in Virginia,* ed. G. B. Beale (Richmond, 1810), p. 13. On the Separate Baptist movement see William W. Sweet, *Religion in Colonial America* (New York, 1942), pp. 300-306, and Wesley M. Gewehr, *The Great Awakening in Virginia, 1740-1790* (Durham, 1930), chs. v and vii.

8. The most factual description is found in David Benedict, *A General History of the Baptist Denomination in America and Other Parts of the World* (Boston, 1813), II, 396-97. Outdoor revivals of the 1770's in the Virginia Colony led by preachers Harriss and Read were described by one contemporary: "It was not uncommon at one of their great meetings for many hundreds to camp on the ground, in order to be present the next day. . . . There were instances of persons travelling more than one hundred miles to one of these meetings; to go forty or fifty was not uncommon." Quoted in Sweet, *The Story of Religion in America,* p. 220. See also Gewehr, *op. cit.,* p. 118.

9. Thomas Ware, *Sketches of the Life and Travels of Rev. Thomas Ware* (New York, 1842), p. 235.

10. *Ibid.,* p. 237.

11. Paul H. Eller, "Revivalism and the German Churches in Pennsylvania, 1783-1816" (Ph.D. dissertation, Divinity School, University of Chicago, 1933), pp. 191-94.

12. The year 1799 is listed as the date of origin of the camp meeting by Redford, *op. cit.,* pp. 265-66, and by John F. Wright, *Sketches of the Life and Labors of James Quinn* (Cincinnati, 1851), p. 105. Minton Thrift, *Memoir of the Rev. Jesse Lee with Extracts from his Journals* (New York, 1823), p. 288, however, says 1803 was the originating date.

13. The Rehoboth Church was the earliest Methodist church west of the Catawba River. Albert M. Shipp, *The History of Methodism in South Carolina* (Nashville, 1884), p. 271.

14. Nicholas Watters, James Fulwood, and Dr. James Hall, a Presbyterian pioneer minister from the neighboring Iredell County, were the other leaders. *Ibid.,* p. 271.

15. John Atkinson, *Centennial History of Methodism* (New York, 1844), pp. 489-90.

16. Shipp, *op. cit.,* p. 272.

17. Henry Boehm, *Reminiscences, Historical and Biographical of Sixtyfour Years in the Ministry,* ed. Joseph B. Wakely (New York, 1865), pp. 128, 408. John McGee is also named as the originator by another contemporary. See *Camp-Meetings Described and Exposed and "Strange Things" Stated* (n.p., n.d., *ca.* 1826), p. 7.

18. Cleveland, *op. cit.,* p. 53.

19. Jesse Lee, *op. cit.,* p. 279.

20. See *The Biography of Eld. Barton Warren Stone, Written by Himself: With Additions and Reflections by Elder John Rogers Written in Part by John Rogers* (Cincinnati, 1847), pp. 6-7.

21. See, for example, sermon extracts in James McGready, *The Posthumous Works of James McGready,* ed. James Smith (Louisville, 1831), I, 228-29.

22. George P. Jackson (coll. and ed.), *White and Negro Spirituals: Their Life Span and Kinship* (New York, 1943), pp. 79-80. The law of "sympathetic like-mindedness," necessary for a revivalistic rebirth, was in operation. Davenport, *op. cit.,* pp. 1-2, defines like-minded people as those "whose mental and nervous organizations respond in like ways to the same stimuli."

23. The prayer covenant is printed in James Smith, *History of the Christian Church, From Its Origins to the Present Time; Compiled From Various Authors. Including a History of the Cumberland Presbyterian Church, Drawn From Authentic Documents* (Nashville, 1835), pp. 565-66. Every great revival has been preceded by such a period of expectancy, emotional strain, and prayer for divine outpouring. Psychologists have termed the stimuli McGready used in generating an atmosphere of mutual sympathy for the movement a facet of the "law of expectancy." Davenport, *op. cit.,* pp. 9-10.

24. James McGready to Thomas Coke, Logan County, Kentucky, Summer, 1801, printed in the *Methodist Magazine* (London), XXVI (May, 1803), 181.

25. Few historians consider this "indoor service" a true camp meeting. One who did place it in this category added that the Gasper River meeting the month following was the "first camp-meeting in Christendom that was appointed and intended for a camp-meeting." See B. W. McDonnald, *The History of the Cumberland Presbyterian Church* (Nashville, 1888), pp. 12-13.

26. In one letter, McGee, writing twenty years after the event, inaccurately lists it as a 1799 meeting. Letter, John McGee to Thomas L. Douglass, June 23, 1820, Nashville District, entitled "Commencement of the Great Revival of Religion in Kentucky and Tennessee in 1799" printed in the *Methodist Magazine* (New York), IV (May, 1821), 189-91. In another letter he described this Red River meeting as an 1800 event. See John McGee to Bishop Asbury, Cumberland, Tennessee, June 10, 1801, printed in William W. Bennett, *op. cit.,* pp. 419-20.

27. John McGee, letter, *Methodist Magazine* (New York), IV (May, 1821), 192. It is strange that in contrast to McGee's account, McGready reported only "about" ten converts at that indoor meeting. See James McGready to Thomas Coke, Logan County, Kentucky, Summer, 1801, *op. cit.,* p. 182.

28. James McGready, "A Short Narrative of the Revival of Religion in Logan County, in the State of Kentucky, and the adjacent settlements in the State of Tennessee from May, 1797, until September, 1800," printed in the *New York Missionary Magazine and Repository of Religious Intelligence,* IV (1803), 154.

29. Cartwright, *op. cit.,* pp. 36-37.

30. McGready, "A Short Narrative of the Revival of Religion," p. 192. Not until he describes the later Muddy River Sacrament does McGready talk of camping out. Many "provided for encamping at the meeting-house" while others slept outside. *Ibid.,* p. 196.

31. It is a curious fact that McGready himself appeared unaware that he was instituting any radical departure in religious technique. His biographer in the *Dictionary of American Biography* makes no allusion to his contribution to the camp meeting, nor is any specific mention made of either the Red River or Gasper River services of 1800. See Oswald L. Brown, "James McGready," *D.A.B.,* pp. 56-57.

32. Consult Franceway R. Cossitt, *The Life and Times of Rev. Finis Ewing, One of the Fathers and Founders of the Cumberland Presbyterian Church* (Louisville, 1853), p. 66; Davidson, *op. cit.,* p. 134; and Sweet, *The Presbyterians,* p. 85.

33. McGready, "A Short Narrative of the Revival of Religion," p. 194; Cartwright, *op. cit.,* p. 37; and Nathan Bangs, *A History of the Methodist Episcopal Church* (New York, 1838-41), II, 102-3.

34. "Red River Revival," printed in the *Western Christian Advocate* (Cincinnati), April 16, 1902.

35. McGready, "A Short Narrative of the Revival of Religion," pp. 193-95. Printed also in Cleveland, *op. cit.,* pp. 56-57.

36. James McGready to Thomas Coke, Logan County, Kentucky, Summer, 1801, p. 182, and McGready, "A Short Narrative of the Revival of Religion," p. 196. Twenty-two wagonloads of campers came to the Muddy River meeting. In western Kentucky alone ten Presbyterian camp meetings were held during the last half of the year 1800. Sweet, *The Presbyterians,* p. 86.

37. Gallaher, *op. cit.,* p. 359.

38. Henry Smith, *op. cit.,* pp. 54-55. Another participant, Colonel Robert Patterson, seemed to be of like mind. "Partly by necessity and partly by inclination" the practice of encamping developed. There was a force impelling the audience to remain on the meeting grounds; they disliked interrupting the services and had formed an attachment to the arena in which sinners had grappled with their consciences. This feeling was summed up in the cry, "Surely, the Lord is in this place." See letter to John King, Lexington, Kentucky, September 25, 1801, printed in the *Methodist Magazine* (London), XXVI (February, 1803), 86.

39. Jesse Lee, *op. cit.,* pp. 279-80. Methodist historian Bangs acknowledged grudgingly that the camp meeting "did not originate with the Methodists, but upon a sacramental occasion among the Presbyterians, at which

time there was such a remarkable outpouring of the Divine Spirit in the people as inclined them to protract their exercises to an unusual period . . . and finally so many [came] that no house could hold them; this induced them to go into the field and erect temporary shelters for themselves." Yet he confuses the issue by using John McGee's report of the occasion as that of an 1799 Red River sacramental meeting of James McGready. See Bangs, *op. cit.*, II, 112.

3. *Campfires in the Wilderness*

1. Letter from the Principal of Washington Academy to A. Alexander, Washington Academy, January 1, 1802, printed in the *Methodist Magazine* (London), XXVI (February, 1803), 93.

2. Peter G. Mode, *The Frontier Spirit in American Christianity* (New York, 1923), p. 152.

3. See editorials, *Western Christian Advocate* (Cincinnati), August 15, 1834, and July 28, 1837.

4. Jesse Lee, *op. cit.*, p. 360. Writing in the 1840's, historian Bangs described the encampments of 1809 on the more populous Atlantic seaboard as having rows of tents, three to six columns in depth, "arranged on several streets, numbered and labelled, so that they may be distinguished one from another, and passed between." The cooking fires were usually located behind the tents "so that the people may not be discommoded with the smoke." See Bangs, *op. cit.*, II, 266.

5. For a thorough description of an encampment, with diagrams, consult B. W. Gorham, *Camp Meeting Manual, A Practical Book for the Camp Ground* (Boston, 1854), pp. 125-44.

6. Banks, *op. cit.*, II, 265-66. Similar improvised shelters were set up at the first island camp meetings on Maryland's Eastern Shore. See "Duncan Noble Collection" cited in Wroten, *op. cit.*, pp. 137-38.

7. McKendree MSS, quoted in Robert Paine, *Life and Times of William McKendree* (Nashville, 1922), p. 127, and Edward Eggleston, *The Circuit Rider: A Tale of the Heroic Age* (New York, 1905), p. 253.

8. Consult Chapter VII below for details on the altar, an enclosed area set up directly in front of the pulpit. Like so many other features of camp meeting religion, this subject is a shadowy affair. The Reverend James Quinn, writing in 1840, was emphatic in his insistence that the altar was not a part of the Great Revival.

9. Finley, *Autobiography*, p. 318.

10. Italics his. William P. Strickland, *Genius and Mission of Methodism: Embracing What is Peculiar in Doctrine, Government, Modes of Worship* (Boston, 1851), pp. 111, 113.

11. On illumination, see Bangs, *op. cit.*, II, 266, and Alfred Brunson, *A Western Pioneer* (Cincinnati, 1872-79), I, 284.

12. Report of John Scripps cited in Leaton, *op. cit.*, p. 62.

13. See account of James Gwin, *ibid.*, p. 54.

14. James McGready to Thomas Coke, Logan County, Kentucky, Summer, 1801, *op. cit.*, p. 184. See also Benedict, *op. cit.*, pp. 108-9.

15. Davidson, *op. cit.*, p. 138.

16. "Autobiography of Rev. William Burke," quoted in Finley, *Sketches,*

p. 79. William McKendree "saw to it that the union was dissolved amicably," according to Henry Smith, *op. cit.*, pp. 59-60.

17. Finley, *Autobiography*, p. 165.

18. Davidson, *op. cit.*, pp. 136-37.

19. In the order given, Bangs, *op. cit.*, II, 107; George Baxter, Principal of Washington Academy, to A. Alexander, Washington Academy, January 1, 1802, pp. 88-89; also see estimates of Presbyterian minister John Lyle, "Diary of John Lyle (1801-1803)" (MSS [typewritten], Durrett Collection, University of Chicago), *passim.*

20. Cartwright, *op. cit.*, p. 31.

21. Richard McNemar, *The Kentucky Revival; or A Short History of the Late Extraordinary Outpouring of the Spirit of God in the Western States of America* (New York, 1846), p. 23. Exponents of "crowd psychology" have offered the explanation that suggestibility is enhanced by the presence of a mass. Inhibitions were weakened because the individual's sense of responsibility was lessened, and similar responses were induced in those viewing the uninhibited. "Personal will" was lost in the will of the crowd. See Pratt, *op. cit.*, pp. 179-80, and Gustave Le Bon, *The Crowd: A Study of the Popular Mind* (London, 1900), p. 55.

22. Lyle, Diary MSS, p. 22.

23. James Quinn quoted in Wright, *op. cit.*, p. 120.

24. Bangs, *op. cit.*, II, 113.

25. Lyle, Diary MSS, pp. 47-48. Lyle tells of two watchers who "were peeping about the meeting house thinking they had found a lewd couple, but when they got a candle and rushed in they found only two men who had lain down to sleep." See *ibid.*, p. 40.

26. A Gentleman to his sister in Philadelphia, Lexington, Kentucky, August 10, 1801 (Durrett Collection, University of Chicago).

27. McGready, *op. cit.*, I, 228-29. Compare this technique to that of the Connecticut revivalist of the Colonial Great Awakening of the 1740's, the Reverend James Davenport: "You poor unconverted sinners in the pews, I wonder you do not drop into hell . . . now, now, now you are sinking into the pit." Cited in Ross Cannon, "The American Revival 1800-1840" (Ph.D. dissertation, Department of Theology, Chicago Theological Seminary, 1937), p. 5.

28. Printed in the *Methodist Quarterly Review* (New York), XLI (1859), 411-12.

29. Based in part upon Cartwright, *op. cit.*, p. 46; Colonel Robert Patterson to John King, Lexington, Kentucky, September 25, 1801, *op. cit.*, pp. 82-86; and John Lyle, Diary MSS, p. 102.

30. John McGee to Thomas L. Douglass, June 23, 1820, p. 190.

31. Letter, John Evans Finley, Mason County, Kentucky, undated [1803], printed in the *Methodist Magazine* (London), XXVI (March, 1803), 126.

32. George Baxter, Principal of Washington Academy, to A. Alexander, Washington Academy, January 1, 1802, *op. cit.*, pp. 89-91. James B. Finley, in his *Autobiography*, pp. 367-68, gives an almost identical description of the falling exercise.

33. See letter of Colonel Robert Patterson to John King, Lexington, Kentucky, September 25, 1801, pp. 82-83.

34. Bangs, *op cit.*, II, 108. This was the Cabin Creek Revival of May,

1801. The same procedure was practiced at Cane Ridge; see John Lyle, Diary MSS, 21-35.

35. McDonald, *op. cit.*, p. 47.

36. Colonel Robert Patterson to John King, Lexington, Kentucky, September 25, 1801, *op. cit.*, p. 86.

37. Stone, *op. cit.*, p. 39. Some of the bodily exercises could have existed only among the New Lights, according to Franceway R. Cossitt, *The Life and Times of Rev. Finis Ewing, One of the Fathers and Founders of the Cumberland Presbyterian Church* (Louisville, 1853), p. 417.

38. Cartwright, *op. cit.*, pp. 48-49, and Lorenzo Dow, *History of Cosmopolite, or the Writings of Rev. Lorenzo Dow* (Cincinnati, 1858), p. 184.

39. The accounts of bodily exercises are based upon the following sources: "rolling," McNemar, *op. cit.*, p. 64; "dancing," Stone, *op. cit.*, p. 39; "running," Cartwright, *op. cit.*, pp. 50-51; "singing," Stone, *op. cit.*, p. 39; "laughing," *ibid.*, and John B. McMaster, *A History of the People of the United States, from the Revolution to the Civil War* (New York, 1883-1913), II, 581.

40. McMaster, *ibid.*

41. Also known as the "Cain Ridge" or "Kain Ridge" revival. See George Baxter, Principal of Washington Academy, to A. Alexander, Washington Academy, January 1, 1802, *op. cit.*, p. 86.

42. Letter, John Evans Finley, September 20, 1801, printed in the *New York Missionary Magazine, and Repository of Religious Intelligence*, III (1802), 342. Also reprinted in Cleveland, *op. cit.*, pp. 79-80; the appendixes to that volume contain invaluable contemporary reports on the various camp meetings.

43. Stone, *op. cit.*, p. 38. For the varying estimates of the audience, see Cartwright, *op. cit.*, p. 30; McNemar, *op. cit.*, pp. 26-27; and Finley, *Autobiography*, p. 364.

44. Cartwright, *op. cit.*, p. 31. William H. Milburn, itinerant preacher, termed Cane Ridge the "first camp-meeting ever seen." See *The Pioneers, Preachers and People of the Mississippi Valley* (New York, 1860), p. 361. Lending support to Burke's view that Cane Ridge lacked a "tent city" is the absence of any mention of tents in Cartwright's and James B. Finley's accounts. See "Autobiography of Rev. William Burke" printed in Finley, *Sketches*, pp. 77-78; Cartwright, *op. cit.*, pp. 30-37, and Finley, *Autobiography*, pp. 166-68, 364-65. Yet Lyle spoke of "sleeping in a Mr. Venable's tent" and of walking around "the camp." See John Lyle, Diary MSS, p. 23.

45. A Gentleman to his sister in Philadelphia, Lexington, Kentucky, August 10, 1801 (Durrett Collection, University of Chicago).

46. "Autobiography of Rev. William Burke," printed in Finley, *Sketches*, p. 78.

47. Finley, *Autobiography*, pp. 166-67.

48. Lyle, Diary MSS, p. 23; Letter, John Evans Finley, September 20, 1801, 340-41; McNemar, *op. cit.*, pp. 26-27.

49. Finley, *Autobiography*, p. 364, and John Lyle, Diary MSS, pp. 22-24.

50. David Ramsey, *The History of South Carolina, 1670-1808* (Charleston, 1809), II, 36. In 1803 the General Assembly of the Presbyterian church had made a similar appraisal: "The Assembly cannot believe that a dispensation, by means of which, the ignorant are enlightened, the vicious

reclaimed, the erroneous made to acknowledge and obey the truth as it is in Jesus, the haughty infidel humbled . . . and the general aspects of society, changed from dissoluteness and profanity, to sobriety, order and comparative purity, can be any other, than a dispensation of the grace of God." See "Minutes" printed in the *New York Missionary Magazine, and Repository of Religious Intelligence,* IV (July, 1803), 265-66.

51. William W. Sweet, *Men of Zeal: The Romance of American Methodist Beginnings* (New York, 1935), pp. 200-201, and *The Story of Religion in America* (New York, 1939), pp. 334-35. In one year alone, 1802, 13,860 persons joined the Methodist church. See Jesse Lee, *op. cit.,* p. 283.

52. McNemar, *op. cit.,* p. 26.

53. Henry Smith, *op. cit.,* p. 105.

54. Henry Ryan and William Case introduced camp meetings into Canada in 1805, according to Bangs, *op. cit.,* II, 98-101.

4. *Camp Meetings Gain New Sponsors*

1. McNemar, *op. cit.,* p. 27.

2. Based upon accounts in Sweet, *The Presbyterians,* pp. 89-98, and William W. Sweet, *Revivalism in America: Its Origin, Growth, and Decline* (New York, 1944).

3. On Presbyterian camp meeting activity see *Alton Observer,* July 27 and October 27, 1836; *Western Christian Advocate* (Cincinnati), September 29, 1837, and 1832 letter of Dr. Samuel Miller, exact date not cited, *Lectures in Revivals of Religion,* Appendix X, quoted in Lewis B. Schenck, *The Presbyterian Doctrine of the Children in the Covenant* ("Yale Studies in Religious Education," ed. Luther A. Weigle and Robert S. Smith [New Haven, 1924-1947]), p. 78.

4. For documentary accounts of the Cumberland and New Light Presbyterian schisms, including "The Minutes of the Synod of Kentucky, 1802-1811" and "The Minutes of the Cumberland Presbytery, 1803-1806," see Sweet, *The Presbyterians,* pp. 282-392.

5. Cartwright, *op. cit.,* pp. 31-32.

6. MacLean, "The Kentucky Revival and Its Influence on the Miami Valley," pp. 246-59.

7. McNemar, *op. cit.,* p. 73.

8. Stone, *op. cit.,* pp. 61-84.

9. David Turpie, *Sketches of My Own Times* (Indianapolis, 1903), pp. 311-12.

10. Two Shaker societies were in New York, four in Massachusetts, one in Connecticut, two in New Hampshire, and two in Maine. See Sweet, *The Presbyterians,* pp. 96-98.

11. Consult Calvin Green and Seth Wells, *A Summary View of the Millennial Church, or United Society of Believers, Commonly Called Shakers* (Albany, 1848), pp. 79-82.

12. "MS Autobiography of Issachar Bates" (page not cited) printed in MacLean, "The Kentucky Revival and Its Influence on the Miami Valley," pp. 264-67.

13. Green and Wells, *op. cit.,* pp. 79-80.

14. Barton W. Stone's Introduction to his "Letters on Atonement," cited in McNemar, *op. cit.,* p. 102.

15. Levi Purviance, *The Biography of Elder David Purviance, With His Memoirs* (Dayton, Ohio, 1848), p. 287.

16. "MS Autobiography of Issachar Bates" (page not cited), printed in MacLean, "The Kentucky Revival and Its Influence on the Miami Valley," pp. 269-70.

17. Six Shaker communities in all were established in the western region, including three in Ohio, two in Kentucky, and one in Indiana. For exact locations, see Green and Wells, *op. cit.,* pp. 75-76.

18. McDonnald, *op. cit.,* p. 171.

19. *Ibid.,* pp. 279-82.

20. Quoted in Richard Beard, *Brief Biographical Sketches of Some of the Early Ministers of the Cumberland Presbyterian Church* (Nashville, 1867), p. 14.

21. Letter, Finis Ewing, Kentucky, June 27, 1818, cited in Cossitt, *op. cit.,* pp. 245-47, 263.

22. *Revivalist* (Nashville), September 18, 1823.

23. In Arkansas, however, the Presbyterians still considered the Cumberland group to be their strongest competitors in 1846. The latter used the camp meeting, for "they could hardly believe it possible for a revival of religion to exist where there was not such noise and confusion, or that a sinner could be converted but at a campmeeting. . . . Religion is made to consist almost entirely in the strong excitement of feeling, and of course is periodical and spasmodic. . . . They depend entirely upon the contributions taken at their campmeetings to sustain the ministry and all Christian institutions." See letter, Mr. C. Washburn, former agent of the American Home Missionary Society, dated September 8, 1846, in Sweet, *The Presbyterians,* p. 696.

24. George H. Genzmer, "John Winebrenner," *D.A.B.,* XX, 284-85.

25. John W. Nevin, *The Anxious Bench* (Chambersburg, Pennsylvania, 1844), pp. 80-81.

26. *Second Advent Hymns: Designed to be Used in Prayer and Camp Meetings* (3rd ed.; Concord, 1843). Their melodies, especially those for the millennial march, were often borrowed from the Methodists. See Grover C. Loud, *Evangelized America* (New York, 1928), p. 120.

27. For examples of Association camp meetings, see Cleveland, *op. cit.,* Appendix VI, and Miles M. Fisher, *Short History of the Baptists* (Nashville, 1933), p. 43. On indoor meetings of the annual sessions of local Baptist Associations in Kentucky and Illinois see *Baptist Banner and Western Pioneer* (Louisville), July 16 and August 20, 1840.

28. *Camp-Meetings Described and Exposed,* p. 5.

5. *The Camp Meeting Matures*

1. Francis Asbury to Thomas Sargent, Camden, South Carolina, December 28, 1805, Asbury MSS.

2. For example, there is no mention of the camp meeting in the Journals of the Western Conference (1801-1811) when the revival was still a startling innovation. There is but one reference in the Journals of the Ohio Con-

ference (1812-1826). See Sweet, *The Rise of Methodism in the West, passim,* and by the same author, *Circuit-Rider Days in Indiana, the Ohio Conference from Its Organization in 1812 to 1826. Edited with Introduction and Notes* (New York and Cincinnati, 1923), p. 181.

3. Jesse Lee, *op. cit.,* p. 362.

4. Editorial, *Western Christian Advocate* (Cincinnati), August 15, 1834.

5. Entry of October 21, 1810, Francis Asbury, *Journal of Rev. Francis Asbury* (New York, 1852 ed.), III, 349.

6. See entries of Asbury, *Journal,* II, 476-77, and III, 86; and letter of Bishop Asbury, dated 1802, quoted in Atkinson, *op. cit.,* p. 490.

7. Letter of Bishop Asbury, dated 1802, quoted in Atkinson, *op. cit.,* p. 491.

8. Entry of December 12, 1805, Asbury, *Journal,* III, 210-11.

9. Letter, Rembert Hall, South Carolina, December 14, 1807, Asbury MSS.

10. Entry of August 13, 1809, Asbury, *Journal,* III, 317.

11. Entry of September 3, 1809, *ibid.,* p. 319; and Henry Boehm to the Reverend Jacob Gruber, Granger County, Tennessee, October 22, 1809, Asbury MSS.

12. Letter to Jacob Gruber, Bedford, Pennsylvania, August 6, 1809, Asbury MSS.

13. Francis Asbury to the Reverend Jacob Gruber, Greene County, Tennessee, November 22, 1809, *ibid.,* and Letter to Thomas Coke, Pittsburgh, September 2, 1811, printed in the *Methodist Magazine* (London), XXXV (1812), 316.

14. Atkinson, *op. cit.,* p. 492. In the Western Conference membership had doubled between 1805 and 1811, with nearly twelve thousand reported in 1805. See "Minutes, 1805," *Minutes of the Annual Conferences of the Methodist Episcopal Church* (New York, 1855), I.

15. Francis Asbury to Dr. Thomas Coke, November 27, 1811, p. 316; and letter to Jacob Gruber, Pittsburgh, September, 1811, Asbury MSS.

16. Sweet, *The Methodists,* pp. 68-69, and *The American Churches,* p. 23.

17. Francis Asbury to Daniel Hitt, presiding elder of the Alexandria District, Virginia, from Shephards Town, Pennsylvania, August 22-23, printed in *Quarterly Review of the Methodist Episcopal Church, South,* XV (1861), 158-59.

18. Elizabeth K. Nottingham, *Methodism and the Frontier: Indiana Proving Ground* (New York, 1941), pp. 121, 165, 206.

19. By 1809-10 both circuit riders Benjamin Lakin and Peter Cartwright talked of their "yearly camp meetings." Journal entry of August 31, 1810, Lakin MSS, No. 9, and Cartwright, *op. cit.,* pp. 45, 90. James B. Finley, presiding elder of the Ohio District in 1816, stated that "the last round of quarterly meetings for the year were camp meetings, with few exceptions." Finley, *Autobiography,* p. 289. See also Sweet, *The Methodists,* p. 159.

20. See entry of October 1, 1808, Asbury, *Journal,* III, 290.

21. One such Illinois camp meeting in 1838, however, occasioned a dissent from a delegate which may have been representative of the opinion of a considerable group. The Reverend Alfred Brunson complained that the two activities conflicted with each other; men needed at the business sessions were away at the campground, and many preachers essential to a successful revival were unavailable because of conference duties. Only in

the evening and on Sunday, he declared, was "good work done." He thus doubted the propriety of camp meetings staged concurrently with the sessions of the conference. Brunson, *op. cit.,* II, 124-25.

22. See issue of July 23, 1823.

23. Wiley, "Methodism in Southeastern Indiana," *op. cit.* (March, 1927), 40-41.

24. In the Scioto Circuit of Ohio, land was donated as early as 1809. See Finley, *Autobiography,* p. 191. For a listing of the names of camp-grounds founded in central Illinois up to 1845 see John H. Ryan, "Old Time Camp Meetings in Central Illinois," *Transactions of the Illinois State Historical Society for the Year 1924,* pp. 64-69. For Old Southwest camp-grounds see Anson West, *A History of Methodism in Alabama* (Nashville, 1893), pp. 181, 230, 231, and John B. Cain, *Methodism in the Mississippi Conference, 1846-1870* (Jackson, 1939), pp. 26-28.

25. Giles, *op. cit.,* p. 367.

26. A *Western Christian Advocate* editorial of July 28, 1837, urged cir-cuit leaders to secure campgrounds "by a written lease for years or by deeds forever." See also Sweet, *The American Churches,* p. 56.

27. This schedule was patterned after the quarterly meeting routine. Jesse Lee, *op. cit.,* pp. 361-62, and Finley, *Autobiography,* p. 317.

28. Bangs, *op. cit.,* II, 131-32.

29. In the eastern camp meetings separate standing committees of preach-ers and laymen were sometimes established to superintend lights and fires, regulate use of the water springs, arrange for religious services, and preserve order. See Andrew Reed and James Matheson, *A Narrative of the Visit of the American Churches by the Deputation from the Congregational Union of England and Wales* (New York, 1835), I, 295.

30. William C. Smith, *Indiana Miscellany* (Cincinnati, 1867), p. 72.

31. Finley, *Autobiography,* p. 317.

32. See Appendix for the Camp Meeting Rules and Order of Service of a Baltimore Circuit camp meeting in October, 1806. See also Jesse Lee, *op. cit.,* pp. 361-62.

33. Henry Smith, *op. cit.,* p. 166.

34. See Appendix, and "Diary of John Early," *Virginia Magazine of History and Biography,* XXXVI (1928), 328.

35. Letter, T. L. Douglass, dated Nashville District, October 15, 1820, printed in the *Methodist Magazine* (New York), IV (1821), 191-95.

36. Francis Asbury to Daniel Hitt, undated, printed in *Quarterly Review of the Methodist Episcopal Church, South,* XV (1861), 330.

37. Bangs, *op. cit.,* II, 266-68.

38. Jacob Young, *Autobiography of a Pioneer* (Cincinnati, 1857), p. 169. See also *Camp-Meetings Described and Exposed,* p. 3.

39. Campbell, "Aspects of Methodism," p. 463.

40. Provision of the Granville Circuit Camp Meeting Rules of September 2, 1831, in Appendix. See also Bangs, *op. cit.,* II, 266.

41. Frederick Von Raumer, *America and the American People* (New York, 1846), pp. 342-43.

42. Herbert Asbury in his "Palmy Days of Methodism," p. 442, is pos-sibly responsible for this canard, for he wrote: "Then as now [1926] camp meetings were followed by a great increase in the number of illegitimate births." The idea is paraphrased in Leyburn, *op. cit.,* p. 197: "It has been

suggested that at the camp meeting more souls were begotten than saved."

43. See editorial, *Western Christian Advocate* (Cincinnati), August 15, 1834, urging discontinuance of martial practices. See also Thrift, *op. cit.,* pp. 288-89, and *Zion's Herald* (Boston), August 23, 1826.

44. John M. Duncan, *Travels Through Part of the United States and Canada in 1818 and 1819* (Glasgow, 1823), II, 37. Writing about unrestrained emotionalism in the Methodist churches in the East, John Fanning Watson inveighed against the excitable women who assumed "most indelicate female attitudes even in the house of the Lord," exciting at least one minister to fall "into sin." See John Fanning Watson ("By a Wesleyan Methodist"), *Methodist Error: or Friendly, Christian Advice, to Those Methodists Who Indulge in Extravagant Emotions and Bodily Exercises* (Trenton, New Jersey, 1819), p. 25. The distinguished historian of church history, Professor William W. Sweet, established the identity of the author of the work in question through a study of the MS at the Huntington Library in 1948.

45. Letter, John Humphrey Noyes, dated 1867, quoted in Tyler, *op. cit.,* pp. 193-94.

46. Cartwright, *op. cit.,* p. 51.

47. Bishop William Capers, MS Autobiography, quoted in William M. Wightman, *Life of William Capers, D.D.* (Nashville, 1902), pp. 51-52.

48. *Wesleyan Repository, and Religious Intelligencer,* I (1821-22), pp. 141-42; and Enoch George to Daniel Hitt, Frederick Circuit, Virginia, December 19, 1804, printed in *Quarterly Review of the Methodist Episcopal Church, South,* XV (1861), 630.

49. Statement of Cornelius Springer, July 4, 1873, reported in *Magazine of Western History,* II, pp. 139-40, quoted in Carter, *op. cit.,* p. 62.

50. Howells, "Camp Meetings in the West Fifty Years Ago," p. 204.

51. Letter of "An Observer," *Wesleyan Repository, and Religious Intelligencer,* II (1822-23), 360. A Long Island, New York, camp meeting conducted an all night session in 1818 without any muscular Christianity appearing. Bangs, *op. cit.,* II, 270.

52. John Meacham, Issachar Bates, and Benjamin Youngs, from Tribblecreek, Warren County, Ohio, April 27, 1805, "Letters of the Shakers" (MSS in the Western Reserve Historical Society Collection, Cleveland, Ohio).

53. Henry Boehm to Jacob Gruber, Granger County, Tennessee, October 22, 1809, Asbury MSS.

54. Italics his. Letter, T. L. Douglass, dated Nashville District, October 15, 1820, printed in the *Methodist Magazine* (New York), IV (1821), 195.

55. Wiley, "Methodism in Southeastern Indiana" (December, 1927), pp. 423-24.

56. "A Camp Meeting," *Western Messenger Devoted to Religion and Literature,* II (November, 1836), 234-35; and Davidson, *op. cit.,* p. 155.

6. Methodist Harvest Time

1. Letter to Jacob Gruber, Pittsburgh, Pennsylvania, Asbury MSS.

2. Theophilus Arminius, "Short Sketches of Revivals of Religion Among the Methodists in the Western Country," *Methodist Magazine* (New York), X (May, 1827), 225.

3. Journal entry of 1819 (exact date not cited), Lakin MSS, No. 13.

4. Italics his. Theophilus Arminius, "Short Sketches of Revivals of Religion," *op. cit.,* X (May, 1827), 226.

5. At Russellville, Kentucky, Cartwright, *op. cit.,* p. 234.

6. On rare instances of falling at a Marietta campground on the Hockhocking Circuit in 1808, and at an 1810 encampment on the same circuit, see respectively *ibid.,* pp. 92-93, and journal entry of September 14, 1810, Lakin MSS, No. 9.

7. See Hosea Rigg's and James Gwin's reports in Leaton, *op. cit.,* pp. 50-53.

8. The camp site was thirty miles south of Pittsburgh, on the Monongahela River. Letter dated August 20, 1803, place n.s., to the Reverend George Roberts of Philadelphia, Asbury MSS.

9. Entry of August 7, 1808, Asbury, *Journal,* III, 286.

10. Arminius, "Short Sketches," *op. cit.,* V (September, 1822), 352.

11. John G. Jones, *A Complete History of Methodism as Connected With the Mississippi Conference of the Methodist Episcopal Church, South* (Nashville, 1887-1908), I, 117-25.

12. Leaton, *op. cit.,* pp. 52-53.

13. Cartwright, *op. cit.,* p. 121.

14. Arminius, "Short Sketches," *op. cit.,* V (September, 1822), 352.

15. Wiley, "Methodism in Southeastern Indiana," *op. cit.* (March, 1927), p. 60.

16. Finley, *Autobiography,* p. 239.

17. Schermerhorn and Mills, *op. cit.,* pp. 16-17.

18. Wiley, "Methodism in Southeastern Indiana," *op. cit.* (June, 1927), p. 151.

19. The date of 1843 is given for an identical occurrence; see Gabriel, *op. cit.,* pp. 35-36. From Tennessee, circuiteer William Brownlow facetiously remarked that an opponent of his believed that the stars had been jarred loose from their moorings when Brownlow squeezed into Heaven, but was forcibly ejected because of his obnoxiousness. See E. Merton Coulter, *William G. Brownlow: Fighting Parson of the Southern Highlands* (Chapel Hill, 1937), p. 23.

20. Entry of October 1, 1807, Asbury, *Journal,* III, 268, and journal entry of September 8, 1810, Lakin MSS, No. 9.

21. *Ibid.*

22. Journal entry of July 24, 1812, *ibid.,* No. 11.

23. Journal entry of July 22, 1812, *ibid.,* and Jacob Young, *op. cit.,* pp. 300-301.

24. Entry of September 1, 1812, Asbury, *Journal,* III, 393.

25. See Boehm, *op. cit.,* p. 210. Henry Boehm was the son of John Phillip Boehm, one of the founders of the German Reformed Church in America.

26. For three August and September encampments see the *Western Christian Monitor* (Chillicothe), I (1816), 375-76, 424-25, 471-72.

27. The Western Conference comprised all the circuits west of the Alleghenies.

28. *Minutes of the Annual Conferences of the Methodist Episcopal Church,* I, 98, 209, and Beverly W. Bond, *The Civilization of the Old Northwest: A Study of Political, Social, and Economic Development, 1788-1812* (New York, 1934), pp. 313-14.

29. "Brother Lakin" led the meeting. *Western Christian Advocate* (Cincinnati), May 3, 1841.

30. Italics his. Boyd, *op. cit.,* pp. 94-96.

31. Consult William W. Sweet, *Circuit-Rider Days in Indiana. The Journals of the Indiana Conference, 1832-1842* (Indianapolis, 1916), pp. 23, 48.

32. Wiley, "Methodism in Southeastern Indiana," *op. cit.* (June, 1927), p. 208.

33. *Ibid.,* p. 247.

34. Leaton, *op. cit.,* p. 53.

35. By 1820 the line of settlement had reached the vicinity of Edwardsville and Vandalia. See Paul N. Angle and Richard L. Bayer, "A Handbook of Illinois History," *Papers in Illinois History and Transactions for the Year 1941,* pp. 87-88.

36. Bangs, *op. cit.,* II, 276-80.

37. On one of these hectic Illinois camp meetings of 1827 see Cartwright, *op. cit.,* pp. 270-72.

38. James Gilruth, "The Journal of James Gilruth" (MSS [typewritten], Divinity School, University of Chicago).

39. Avery Craven, *The Coming of the Civil War* (New York, 1942), pp. 114-15.

40. Boyd, *op. cit.,* p. 211. See also an Alabamian's denunciation as expressed to Tocqueville in 1832, "There is religion in the North, fanaticism here — the Methodist sect dominates." Quoted in Pierson, *op. cit.,* p. 642.

41. See journal entry of Lakin MSS, No. 11 (1815).

42. John D. Long, *Pictures of Slavery in Church and State* (Philadelphia, 1857), p. 159. Slaves were sometimes forced to attend; see West, *op. cit.,* pp. 606-7.

43. *Journals of the General Conference of the Methodist Episcopal Church, South* (Richmond, 1851), I (1846), 66.

44. See accounts of Reed and Matheson, *op. cit.,* I, 279, and Fredrika Bremer, *The Homes of the New World; Impressions of America* (New York, 1853), I, 314.

45. Ulrich B. Phillips, *Racial Problems, Adjustments and Disturbances in the Ante-Bellum South* (Richmond, 1909), p. 209.

46. William E. DuBois, *The Souls of Black Folk; Essays and Sketches* (Chicago, 1924), p. 190.

47. Phillips, *op. cit.,* pp. 207-8.

48. *Journal of the General Conference of the Methodist Episcopal Church* (New York, 1840-45), I, 44. The Cumberland Presbyterian Church also ordained colored preachers, who sometimes served at white camp meetings. McDonnald, *op. cit.,* p. 434.

49. This sermon was given at a Cincinnati encampment of 1839, but it is highly probable that similar messages were delivered at southern camp meetings. See the *Ladies' Repository,* VIII (1848), 341-42.

50. Howard W. Odum and Guy B. Johnson, *The Negro and His Songs, A Study of Typical Negro Songs in the South* (Chapel Hill, 1925), p. 19; Bremer, *op. cit.,* pp. 307-8; and Watson, *op. cit.,* pp. 30-31.

51. McDonnald, *op. cit.,* p. 434.

52. This is the view of a participant at a Virginia post-Civil War backwoods meeting. DuBois, *op. cit.,* p. 190.

53. Frederick L. Olmsted, *The Cotton Kingdom* (New York, 1861), II, 214-15.

54. Bremer, *op. cit.*, pp. 315-16. Negro membership in the Methodist Episcopal Church increased rapidly between 1800 and 1844. In 1821 there were around 40,000 colored members, and in 1844, 150,000. See *Minutes of the Annual Conferences of the Methodist Episcopal Church*, I, 28, and III, 476. In 1860 10 per cent of the total Negro population were Methodist. Consult Luther Jackson, "Religious Instruction of Negroes, 1830-1860, with Special Reference to South Carolina," *Journal of Negro History*, XV (January, 1930), 106.

55. For a recapitulation of Indian missions throughout the nation see Sweet, *The Methodists*, pp. 499-501.

56. J. G. Jones, *op. cit.*, II, 174-81.

57. W. Darrell Overdyke (ed.), "A Southern Family on the Missouri Frontier: Letters from Independence, 1843-1855," *Journal of Southern History*, XVII (May, 1951), 220-21.

58. Quoted in "Camp Meetings" by George C. Griffith, *Ladies' Repository* (Cincinnati), XXXV (1876), 115.

59. Nottingham, *op. cit.*, p. 142. Hugh Bourne compiled songbooks for their use, utilizing original camp meeting hymns from America. Many of the songs in Peggy Dow's compilation of *A Collection of Camp-Meeting Hymns* (2nd ed.; Philadelphia, 1816) were copied for an 1808 publication by Bourne, *General Collections of Hymns and Spiritual Songs for Camp Meetings*. The musical tone is indicated by the common saying of the times: "You sing like a Primitive." Loud, *op. cit.*, pp. 119-20.

60. Jackson, *White and Negro Spirituals*, pp. 93-94.

7. *A Camp Meeting Day*

1. Frances Trollope, *Domestic Manners of the Americans* (London, 1832), I, 233.

2. A. P. Mead, *Manna in the Wilderness* (Philadelphia, 1859), p. 59.

3. See Robert Carlton, *The New Purchase: or Seven and a Half Years in the Far West* (New York, 1843), II, 137-38. This chapter is based, in so far as possible, upon firsthand accounts of the services occurring during the respective hours mentioned.

4. While the service plan remained fairly constant, the exact hours of worship varied. A New Albany, Indiana, encampment of 1839 adhered to a meeting schedule of 8 A.M., 10 A.M., 12 N., 4 P.M., and 8 P.M. Consult *Western Christian Advocate* (Cincinnati), July 26, 1839.

5. Entry of Thursday, September 1, 1831, James Gilruth, Journal MSS.

6. Giles, *op. cit.*, pp. 238-39. On temperance activities at encampments see *Alton Observer*, October 16, 1836; *Western Christian Advocate*, August 7, 1835, and September 16, 1839; Milburn, *The Pioneers, Preachers and People of the Mississippi Valley*, p. 371; and Herbert Asbury, "The Father of Prohibitionism," *American Mercury*, IX (November, 1926), 344-48. This theme was more energetically advanced in the 1830's than the 1820's.

7. Italics his. R. H. Rivers, *The Life of Robert Paine, D.D., Bishop of the Methodist Episcopal Church, South* (Nashville, 1916), pp. 47-48.

8. Entry of Friday, September 2, 1831, James Gilruth, Journal MSS.

9. On love feasts see *Western Christian Advocate* (Cincinnati), May 9, 1834; *Journals of the General Conference of the Methodist Episcopal Church, South,* III (1858), 563; and Sweet, *The Methodists,* p. 209, n. 14. On Holy Communion see Mead, *op. cit.,* p. 235.

10. Described in Leaton, *op. cit.,* p. 53.

11. From "Sermon Notes" (unsorted), included in Lakin MSS.

12. William H. Milburn, *Ten Years of Preacher Life: Chapters from an Autobiography* (New York, 1859), p. 369.

13. Cartwright, *op. cit.,* pp. 226-28.

14. Wiley, "Methodism in Southeastern Indiana," *op. cit.* (March, 1927), p. 54, and Journal entry of August 8, 1810, Lakin MSS.

15. Although this exhortation was delivered in a backwoods church it could well have been given at a camp meeting. See William H. Milburn, *The Pioneer Preacher: or, Rifle, Axe, and Saddle-Bags, and Other Lectures* (New York, 1857), pp. 72-75.

16. Turpie, *op. cit.,* pp. 104-5. See also Nottingham, *op. cit.,* p. 62. The handshaking ceremony was also a feature of other Methodist gatherings. Novelist Eggleston tells of "Brother Magruder" arriving in a southern Ohio community for the first time and urging the holding of a Bible meeting, a "good, old-fashioned Methodist shake-hands." See Eggleston, *op. cit.,* pp. 86-92.

17. See Cartwright, *op. cit.,* pp. 228-29.

18. *Ibid.,* p. 218. For the social side of a camp meeting day see Chapter XII below.

19. The two preachers were Peter Cartwright and James Lotta, quoted in Leaton, *op. cit.,* p. 387.

20. Trollope, *op. cit.,* p. 246.

21. At a large encampment in Alabama in 1827 $100.00 was raised, but this was very uncommon. Three camp meetings in August and September, 1811, on the Scioto Circuit in Ohio produced collections of only $3.33, $8.87, and $2.45. See "Stewards Book of the Scioto Circuit, 1811-1812," quoted in Maxwell P. Gaddis, *Footprints of an Itinerant* (Cincinnati and Chicago, 1874), p. 231.

22. James B. Finley's "Manuscript History of the Wyandot Indians," printed in *Western Christian Advocate,* February 23, 1838.

23. At Deyamperts Camp Ground in Greene County, Alabama, 1843. West, *op. cit.,* pp. 560-65.

24. At an Indiana encampment of 1811 it was decided by vote to admonish a class leader "for failure to close the door" when he met his class. He was warned "if he did not amend, the preacher was requested to remove him." Wiley, "Methodism in Southeastern Indiana," *op. cit.* (March, 1927), p. 54.

25. See Finley, *Autobiography,* pp. 289-90.

26. *Circa* 1814. Wright, *op. cit.,* pp. 178-81.

27. Adam Wallace, *The Parson of the Islands. Biography of the Reverend Joshua Thomas* (Philadelphia, 1861), p. 222, quoted in Wroten, *op. cit.,* pp. 143-44. See also Brunson, *op. cit.,* I, 226. Bishop Asbury placed more faith in exhortation than in formal preaching, and advised that "we ought to communicate all we can, one with another." Letter to Daniel Hitt, undated, printed in the *Quarterly Review of the Methodist Episcopal Church, South,* XV (January, 1861), 630.

28. While it appears certain the altar was not a part of the Great Revival camp meetings, it is more difficult to state the exact time and place of its introduction. The years 1799, 1801, and 1803 are advanced as the times of the first indoor "altar service" in America. Since most of its claimants are eastern ministers, possibly the technique was originated in the East and later introduced in the West. Writing from the frontier town of Pittsburgh in 1810, Bishop Asbury discussed proper encampment procedures, specifically talking of a "mourner's bench" as standard camp meeting equipment. Thus the altar was certainly in general use by 1810. See letter, Francis Asbury, August 25, 1810, Asbury MSS. On the conflicting claims consult Samuel W. Williams, *Pictures of Early Methodism in Ohio* (Cincinnati and New York, 1909), ch. iv, "The Mourner's Bench"; and Bangs, *op. cit.*, III, 375.

29. Finley, *Sketches*, p. 328. Also see William Strickland, *Genius and Mission of Methodism*, p. 91.

30. R. Weiser, *The Mourner's Bench, or An Humble Attempt to Vindicate New Measures* (Bedford [*ca.* 1844]), pp. 1-4. The biblical sanction was that "he hath sent me to comfort those who mourn."

31. Trollope, *op. cit.*, I, 236.

32. *Camp-Meetings Described and Exposed*, pp. 3-4.

33. Theophilus Arminius, "An Appendix to Short Sketches of Revivals of Religion in the Western Country," printed in the *Methodist Magazine* (New York), XI (May, 1828), 189, and Bangs, *op. cit.*, II, 105.

34. Quoted in Benjamin St. James Fry, "The Early Methodist Song Writer," *Methodist Quarterly Review*, XLI (1859), 413.

35. Found in Orange Scott (compiler), *The New and Improved Camp Meeting Hymn Book. Being a Choice Selection of Hymns From the West* (3rd ed.; Brookfield, Mass., 1832), pp. 24, 142-43.

36. Song text printed in Mead, *op. cit.*, p. 41.

37. Entitled "Come and Taste Along With Me," found in Joseph Merriam (compiler), *The Wesleyan Camp Meeting Hymn-Book* (Wendell, Massachusetts, 1829), pp. 29-32.

38. Related by circuit rider Stephen R. Beggs, and printed in Leaton, *op. cit.*, pp. 144-45. The text was probably inspired by Charles Wesley's hymn in which the first two lines are identical. See George P. Jackson, *Down-East Spirituals and Others* (New York, 1939), pp. 130-31.

39. Flint, *op. cit.*, pp. 258-61.

40. Letter, John Collins, Chillicothe, Ohio, April 22, 1819, printed in the *Methodist Magazine* (New York), II (1819), 234-35.

41. Cartwright, *op. cit.*, pp. 233-34.

42. Reed and Matheson, *op. cit.*, I, 276, and Finley, *Autobiography*, p. 345.

43. Merriam, *op. cit.*, pp. 51-52.

44. Finley, *Autobiography*, pp. 322-25.

45. An 1816 camp meeting. See *ibid.*, p. 291.

46. A Georgia sermon at an 1850 encampment reported in Bremer, *op. cit.*, I, 314-15.

47. Entry of Thursday, September 1, 1831, James Gilruth, Journal MSS.

48. Quoted in Flint, *op. cit.*, p. 262.

49. See Turpie, *op. cit.*, pp. 311-13.

50. Finley, *Sketches*, pp. 324-25.

51. Trollope, *op. cit.*, I, 241, and "Now the Truth is Gaining Ground" (8 verses), printed in Merriam, *op. cit.*, pp. 74-76.

52. See Sweet, *Revivalism in America*, pp. 143-44.

53. Hall, *op. cit.*, II, 137-38.

54. Erasmus Manford, *Twenty-Five Years in the West* (Chicago, 1867), p. 130. Indicative of his subjectivity, which was typical of many, was his evaluation of the Episcopalian church as "conceived in sin and brought forth in iniquity," and his dismissal of the Catholic church as "the mother of harlots."

55. At a Northern Neck, Virginia, campground of 1834. Reed and Matheson, *op. cit.*, I, 281-83.

56. Jesse Lee, *op. cit.*, pp. 311-12.

57. For the routine at a Tennessee encampment of 1820 see letter, T. L. Douglass, Nashville District, October 15, 1820, *op. cit.*, p. 194; at an Indiana encampment of 1818, see Wiley, "Methodism in Southeastern Indiana," *op cit.* (June, 1927), p. 213. At the latter meeting the preacher in charge wrote the names of the converts "on notes of admission which he had prepared, directing the holders to present them to the several class leaders when they went home, which nearly all did." Excitement throughout the congregation was so strong that occasionally camp leaders did not get all the names of those eager to join the church. This occurred at a Booneville Circuit forest revival in the Indiana Conference of September, 1834. See *Western Christian Advocate* (Cincinnati), October 3, 1834.

58. *Camp-Meetings Described and Exposed*, pp. 4-5.

8. *Evangels of the Backwoods*

1. Italics his. Entry of September, 1840, "Journal of James Quinn," quoted in Wright, *op. cit.*, pp. 190-91.

2. Letter, Mr. C. Washburn, Benton County, Arkansas, September 8, 1846, printed in Sweet, *The Presbyterians*, p. 697. For similar comments see Eaton, *op. cit.*, p. 282; Ralph Rush, *The Literature of the Middle Western Frontier* (New York, 1925), I, 150-51; and Walter P. Posey, *The Development of Methodism in the Old Southwest* (Tuscaloosa, 1933), p. 99.

3. Brooks, *op. cit.*, p. 99.

4. Quoted from a Great Revival contemporary in Posey, *op. cit.*, p. 23. The itinerant's costume was not purposely awesome, but was in many cases outlandish because of financial poverty and the dictates of the Methodist *Discipline*. For example, the custom of wearing the hair clipped short in front and long in back was adopted for reasons of economy, and also because of the dictates of frontier fashion.

5. Leyburn, *op. cit.*, p. 199.

6. William P. Strickland (ed.), *The Life of Jacob Gruber* (New York, 1860), pp. iii, 18; and Elijah H. Pilcher, *Protestantism in Michigan* (Detroit, 1878), p. 117.

7. Cartwright, *op. cit.*, pp. 93-94.

8. An English traveler of the early 1830's observed that the Methodist preachers "perfectly understood the habits, beliefs, and prejudices of those

whom they address." Captain Thomas Hamilton, *Men and Manners in America* (Edinburgh, 1834), II, 393-94.

9. Cartwright, *op. cit.*, p. 208.

10. Journal entry of July 7, 1812, Lakin MSS, No. 10.

11. Letter to Bishop Asbury, Baltimore, July 4, 1806, printed in Henry Smith, *op. cit.*, p. 114; and Journal entry of November 19, 1809, Lakin MSS, No. 7.

12. Cartwright, *op. cit.*, pp. 270-72.

13. At Winchester, Virginia; see entry of August 23, 1802, "Journal of James Quinn," cited in Wright, *op. cit.*, pp. 69-70.

14. *Ibid.*, p. 104. In his long tours across the young nation Bishop Asbury, the English-born leader of American Methodism, set an example of selflessness and zealousness in the missionary cause that the itinerants followed. Approximately five feet, nine inches tall, and weighing but one hundred and fifty-seven pounds, the sickly Asbury labored ceaselessly until he died in 1816 at seventy-one years of age, worn out in the service of God. See Boehm, *op. cit.*, pp. 438-39.

15. Luther A. Weigle, *American Idealism. The Pageant of America: A Pictorial History of the United States,* ed. Ralph H. Gabriel, X (New Haven, 1928), 150.

16. The Baptist farmer-preacher, like the Methodist circuit rider, considered himself "called" to labor in the religious field. He, too, did not believe that the individual chose the preaching profession. It followed, therefore, that the Baptists viewed it as an impertinence to attempt to train a man "subsequent to such a call." The Baptists followed the Methodist pattern of laying less stress on a learned clergy than did the Presbyterians, and some of the most influential Baptist preachers were uneducated men. Piety and the demonstrated ability to preach, not formal learning, were the essential qualifications for both those democratic denominations. One of the corollaries to this belief was a strong prejudice against the theologically educated clergy. See John F. Cady, *The Origin and Development of the Missionary Baptist Church in Indiana* (Berne, Indiana, 1942), pp. 25-26, and William W. Sweet, *Religion on the American Frontier: The Baptists 1783-1850. A Collection of Source Materials.* I (New York, 1931), 75 and *passim.*

17. Practically the only source of information about Asbury's early life and family is contained in the charming but brief account in his *Journal,* entries of July 16, 1792, and February 22, 1795, II, 156-60, 257. See also Wright, *op. cit.*, p. 167.

18. Schermerhorn and Mills, *op. cit.*, p. 41.

19. Samuel K. Jennings, "Defense of Camp Meetings," quoted in Lorenzo Dow, *op. cit.*, pp. 586-88.

20. Journal entry of November 19, 1809, Lakin MSS No. 7.

21. Sarah C. Bowerman, "William H. Milburn," *D.A.B.,* XIII, 610-11.

22. He wrote in the *Methodist Magazine* (New York) and *Christian Advocate* under the pseudonym "Theophilus Arminius." See Boehm, *op. cit.*, pp. 405-6, and *Methodist Magazine and Quarterly Review,* XII (1830), 121-28.

23. Coulter, *op. cit.*, p. 262, and *passim.*

24. Bangs, *op. cit.*, II, 416.

25. Related to the writer by Professor William W. Sweet.

26. Francis Asbury to the Reverend John Wesley, August 15, 1788, quoted in John Telford, *The Letters of the Rev. John Wesley, A.M.* (London, 1931), VIII, 90-91.

27. William H. Milburn, *The Lance, Cross, and Canoe: The Flatboat, Rifle, and Plough in the Valley of the Mississippi* (New York, 1860), p. 350.

28. Entry of October 14, 1803, Asbury, *Journal*, III, 132.

29. Cartwright, *op. cit.*, pp. 216-17, and entry of August 6, 1802, William Colbert, Journal MSS, IV, 107-8.

30. Cartwright, *op. cit.*, p. 243.

31. Brunson, *op. cit.*, I, 246, and Journal entry of July 1, 1809, Lakin MSS, No. 7.

32. Journal entry of September 1, 1809, Lakin MSS, No. 7, and entry of September 3, 1809, *ibid*.

33. Entry of September 13, 1802, William Colbert, Journal MSS, IV, 114. Bishop Asbury voiced similar sentiments a decade later: "I want sleep, sleep, sleep. . . . I have a considerable fever; but we must move." Entry of October 27, 1812, Asbury, *Journal*, III, 396.

34. See Wright, *op. cit.*, p. 109.

35. Frederick B. Marryat, *A Diary in America with Remarks on its Institutions* (London, 1839), III, 116, 122.

36. Wiley, "Methodism in Southeastern Indiana," *op. cit.* (June, 1927), p. 153.

37. "Autobiography of Rev. William Burke," cited in Finley, *Sketches*, p. 87.

38. See "First Discipline, 1784," Robert Emory, *History of the Discipline of the Methodist Episcopal Church* (New York, 1844), pp. 40-41.

39. See Questions 49, 51, in *ibid.*, pp. 48-49, 133-35. Baptist ministers were subject to the same tight control, although theirs was exerted through the local church.

40. Cartwright commenced keeping a journal early in his ministry, and continued it for several years. He threw his "manuscript journals to the moles and bats" when he found many others keeping similar records. See Cartwright, *op. cit.*, p. vii.

41. Journal entry of April, 1811, Lakin MSS, No. 10.

42. Brunson, *op cit.*, I, 201, and Finley, *Sketches*, pp. 322-24.

43. Emory, *op. cit.*, p. 36. Consult also amendments to that rule in the Disciplines of 1792, 1803, and 1836.

44. Wightman, *op. cit.*, pp. 75-76, and entry on April 6, 1847, "Diary of Clara Frederick, 1845-47." Original in possession of Mrs. J. E. Hays, Director, Department of Archives and History, State of Georgia.

45. Boehm, *op. cit.*, p. 186.

46. "Discipline of 1816," Question 1. See Emory, *op. cit.*, p. 133, and Leaton, *op. cit.*, pp. 259-60.

47. While many church leaders feared formal training would dampen the enthusiasm of the frontier evangelists, they never opposed educational development. After 1820 the Methodists shared with the Baptists, Congregationalists, and the pace-setting Presbyterians in the founding of denominational colleges in the West. This issue was explored at length by William W. Sweet, who concluded that there was a close relationship between revivalism and the democratization and decentralization of higher learning

in ante-bellum America. See Sweet, *The American Churches,* pp. 59-60, and *The Methodists,* pp. 65-68. Allen Wiley was representative of other circuit riders in his interest in higher education. He was a founder and trustee of Indiana Asbury University.

48. Cartwright, *op. cit.,* p. 74.

49. Leaton, *op. cit.,* p. 266.

50. Wiley, "Methodism in Southeastern Indiana," *op. cit.* (June, 1927), p. 142. Cartwright speaks of this traveling library, saying that when an early Methodist preacher felt God's call, he hunted up not a college or a Biblical Institute, but "a hardy pony of a horse and some travelling apparatus." Thus armed he began his labors "with a text that never wore out nor grew stale . . . . 'Behold the Lamb of God, that taketh away the sin of the world.'" Cartwright, *op. cit.,* p. 243.

51. Milburn, *Lance, Cross and Canoe,* p. 350.

52. Gilruth used every spare moment for reading, arising at 5 A.M. to continue this pursuit before breakfast. During the months between April and June, 1831, he read some eleven volumes, including Reid's *Philosophy, The Koran,* Watson's *Theological Institutes,* Clarkson's *History of the Abolition of the Slave Trade,* the *Journal of Health,* the *Book of Mormon,* and James Fenimore Cooper's *The Prairie.* James Gilruth, Journal MSS, entries from April 4, 1831, to July 5, 1831.

53. An indication of the volume of book sales is shown in two statistics of 1817. In that year 1,203 books were sent to James B. Finley, presiding elder of the Ohio District, of which 236 were sold by Benjamin Lakin of the Limestone Circuit. See Sweet, *The Methodists,* p. 70.

54. Cartwright, *op. cit.,* p. 522.

55. James Quinn's report to the *Western Christian Advocate,* April, 1840, quoted in Wright, *op. cit.,* pp. 118, 120.

56. Robert Boyd, *Personal Memoirs; Together With a Discussion Upon the Hardships and Suffering of Itinerant Life* (Cincinnati, 1866), p. 90.

9. *Frontier Evangelism*

1. Milburn, *The Pioneers, Preachers and People of the Mississippi Valley,* pp. 402-3.

2. Based on ideas expressed in Wesley M. Gewehr, "Some Factors in the Expansion of Frontier Methodism, 1800-1811," *op. cit.,* p. 117.

3. See entry of August 11, 1815, Asbury, *Journal,* pp. 460-61. Based on II Cor. 5:2.

4. Davenport, *op. cit.,* p. 67.

5. T. Walter Johnson, "Peter Akers: Methodist Circuit Rider and Educator (1790-1886)," *Journal of the Illinois State Historical Society,* XXXII (Dec., 1939), 431; and Cartwright, *op. cit.,* p. 145.

6. Wiley, "Methodism in Southeastern Indiana," *op. cit.* (March, 1927), p. 37.

7. Leyburn, *op. cit.,* p. 196.

8. Charles G. Finney, "Lectures on Revivals," pp. 10-11, quoted in Gilbert H. Barnes, *The Antislavery Impulse 1830-1844* (New York and London, 1933), p. 11.

9. Milburn, *The Lance, Cross, and Canoe,* pp. 350-51.

10. Quoted in Tyler, *op. cit.,* p. 11.

11. See Edward S. Ames, *The Psychology of Religious Experience* (Boston and New York, 1910), pp. 258-66, for a psychological explanation of the three general stages of conversion. And consult Davenport, *op cit.,* p. 92, who concludes that "in Kentucky the motor automatisms, the voluntary muscles in violent action were the prevailing type, although there were many of the sensory. On the other hand, in Ulster [Scotch-Irish Revival in 1859] the sensory automatisms, trance, vision, the physical disability and the sinking of muscular energy were the prevailing type although there were many of the motor."

12. A. P. Mead, *Manna in the Wilderness* (Philadelphia, 1859), pp. 17-19.

13. Purviance, *op. cit.,* pp. 302-3, and Stone, *op. cit.,* p. 369.

14. See Pratt, *op. cit.,* pp. 184-90, for discussion of the whole process of emotionalism finding expression in muscular activity.

15. "Methodist Preaching," by an unidentified preacher, printed in *Methodist Quarterly Review,* IV (1852), 70-72.

16. "Arminian View of the Fall and Redemption," *Methodist Quarterly Review,* XIII (October, 1861), 656. From 1810 to 1820 a great doctrinal controversy arose among Methodist preachers as to whether infant purity or innate depravity prevailed. The latter view won out. The Calvinistic doctrine that man is corrupting nature was also denied, but the belief was accepted that man can practice virtue by performing good works and so develop character.

17. William James has put forth the view that conversion is essentially a normal adolescent phenomenon, coinciding with the passage from the child's small world of himself to the larger world of which one is aware in maturity. William James, *The Varieties of Religious Experience* (New York, 1902), p. 199.

18. Weiser, *op. cit.,* pp. 3, 7.

19. Barnes, *op. cit.,* p. 16.

20. Charles G. Finney, "Systematic Theology," quoted in Cannon, *op. cit.,* pp. 42-44. Finney defined "regeneration" and "conversion" as synonymous terms. Man by virtue of his conscience and the various agencies such as "mercies, judgments, men, measures, and in short, all things that conduce to enlightening the mind chooses God's way and at that very moment (conversion) God accepts him and he is born into the Kingdom (regeneration)."

21. Barnes, *op. cit.,* p. 16.

22. Italics his. Arminius, "Short Sketches," *op cit.,* V (September, 1822), 351.

23. Quoted by his friend Peter Cartwright. See Leaton, *op. cit.,* p. 90.

24. "Papers," in Lakin MSS. Lakin made a listing of his preaching places and the sermon texts used at each. His sermon bookkeeping illustrates how painstakingly methodical many preachers were to prevent sermon duplication. For a copy of Lakin's list of preaching places and sermon texts on the Miami Circuit, Ohio, during 1805-6, see Sweet, *The Methodists,* pp. 713-18.

25. Italics his. From "The Autobiography of Samuel Williams Esquire," quoted in Finley, *Sketches,* pp. 241-42.

26. Journal entry of August, 1818, Lakin MSS, No. 13.

27. Cartwright, *op. cit.,* p. 75.

28. Printed in Finley, *Sketches,* pp. 237-38. "The only temperance society that then existed [about 1812] and consequently the only standard raised against the overflowing scourge of intemperance, was the Methodist Church." See Finley, *Autobiography,* p. 248.

29. William Colbert, Journal MSS, III, 131-32.

30. James Quinn's Ohio sermon quoted in Wright, *op. cit.,* p. 176.

31. E. Thompson, "Rev. Jacob Young," *Ladies' Repository. A Monthly Periodical Devoted to Literature and Religion,* XVII (January, 1857), 6-8.

32. On the Methodist Conference's changing stand on the slave property question see Paine, *op. cit.,* pp. 130-32.

33. Entry of September 10, 1815, Asbury, *Journal,* III, 464.

34. "Papers" in Lakin MSS.

35. See Gaddis, *op. cit.,* p. 88, and Wiley, "Methodism in Southeastern Indiana," *op. cit.* (September, 1927), p. 214.

36. Schermerhorn and Mills, *op. cit.,* p. 31.

37. Wiley, "Methodism in Southeastern Indiana," *op. cit.* (March, 1927), p. 62.

38. See Manford, *op. cit.,* pp. 29, 58-71; Coulter, *op. cit.,* pp. 13-16; and *Western Christian Advocate* (Cincinnati), August 2, 1839.

39. *Camp-Meetings Described and Exposed,* p. 6.

40. Theodore Dwight Weld to Charles G. Finney, February 26, 1832, quoted in Barnes, *op. cit.,* p. 10.

41. Timothy Flint, *Recollections of the Last Ten Years* (Boston, 1826), p. 64.

42. Julian M. Sturtevant, Jr. (ed.), *Julian M. Sturtevant: An Autobiography* (New York, Chicago, Toronto, 1896), pp. 158-59.

43. Recollection of Jacob Gruber. Strickland, *The Life of Jacob Gruber,* p. 44.

44. Cartwright, *Autobiography,* p. 80; and issue of October 13, 1839.

45. Dick, *op. cit.,* p. 192. When the preacher ran out of breath, and uttered an "ah," the Baptists called it a "holy tone."

46. *Ibid.,* p. 191.

47. Finley, *Sketches,* pp. 327-28.

48. Coulter, *op. cit.,* p. 20.

49. Thomas Ford, *A History of Illinois From Its Commencement as A State in 1818 to 1847,* ed. Milo M. Quaife (Chicago, 1945), I, 39. A friendly letter from one itinerant to another gave this criticism of a sermon: "You took a good text; you introduced it without an explanation, applied it without an application, and concluded by saying much more might be said, but you studied brevity, and did not wish to weary the congregation." Strickland, *The Life of Jacob Gruber,* p. 282.

50. William Logue to J. Chambers, Somerville, Ohio, January 28, 1845, in "Benjamin St. James Fry Papers (1850-1851), " (MSS [handwritten], Ohio Wesleyan University, Delaware, Ohio).

51. This story about circuit rider John P. Durbin is related in Wiley, "Methodism in Southeastern Indiana," *op. cit.* (September, 1927), pp. 240-41.

52. Cartwright, *Autobiography,* pp. vi-vii.

53. Flint, *Flint's Letters From America,* p. 196.

54. Leaton, *op. cit.,* p. 155.

55. Eaton, op cit., p. 281.

56. Marryat, op. cit., II, 188.

57. William C. Smith, op. cit., pp. 46-47.

58. The Reverend M. Emory Wright, "Is the Modern Camp Meeting a Failure?" op. cit., p. 591.

59. Quoted by Samuel E. Morison and Henry S. Commager, The Growth of the American Republic (3rd rev. ed.; New York, 1942), p. 574.

60. Paine, op. cit., pp. 266-68.

61. Finley, Sketches, pp. 321-22.

62. James B. Finley elaborated upon one such talk of Cartwright's: "There are different sorts of sermons — the argumentary, the dogmatic, the postulary, the persuasive, the punitive, the combative, 'in orthodox blows and knocks,' the logical, and the poetic; but this specimen belonged to none of these categories. It was sui generis, and of a new species. It might properly be termed the waggish." Italics his. Finley, Autobiography, p. 322.

63. Italics his. Baptist Banner and Pioneer (Louisville), August 20, 1840. This prescription for a successful "protracted meeting" was applicable to camp meetings as well.

64. Brunson, op. cit., I, 317-19; and Thrift, op. cit., p. 311.

65. Gaddis, op. cit., pp. 159-61.

66. Italics his. William C. Smith, op. cit., pp. 280-82.

67. Ladies' Repository. A Monthly Periodical Devoted to Literature and Religion, XXIII (1862), 646.

68. Journal entry of July 29, 1810, Lakin MSS, No. 9.

69. Eggleston, op. cit., p. 104.

10. Camp Meeting Hymns

1. This Bible quotation apparently was inscribed or paraphrased on the introductory pages of a number of Methodist Hymnals. See, for example, The Methodist Pocket Hymn Book, revised and improved (13th ed.; New York, 1803), p. 5.

2. Robert G. McCutchan, "A Singing Church," printed in William K. Anderson (ed.), Methodism (Cincinnati, 1947), p. 149. See also J. Ernest Rattenbury, Wesley's Legacy to the World (Nashville, 1928), pp. 256-58, 292-308.

3. By 1843 there had also been published one Primitive Methodist and one Adventist songbook. After that date at least three Methodist camp hymnals were added down to 1867. This is in no sense a complete study, but merely includes those books unearthed in the Library of Congress files and other repositories by the writer. See also George P. Jackson, White and Negro Spirituals, Appendix, pp. 296-99.

4. For example, Orange Scott's compilation, The New and Improved Camp Meeting Hymn Book: Being a Choice Selection of Hymns from the West, first published in 1829, ran through at least three editions, as did Thomas S. Hinde's The Pilgrim Songster and Joseph Merriam's The Wesleyan Camp Meeting Hymn-Book.

5. Scott, op. cit., pp. iii-iv; and Anonymous compiler, The Camp-Meeting Hymn Book: Containing the most Approved Hymns and Spiritual Songs

Used by the Methodist Connexion in the United States (6th ed.; Ithaca, 1836).

6. 13th ed., p. 5.

7. *Methodist Magazine and Quarterly Review*, XIII, New Series II (April, 1831), 351-52; the writer is indebted to Robert G. McCutchan, outstanding musical scholar and editor of the *Methodist Hymnal*, for information given on this subject in a letter to the writer dated April 3, 1948.

8. The last country-sing manual to contain outdoor revival tunes was *The Olive Leaf*, published in Georgia, 1878. See George P. Jackson, *Spiritual Folk-Songs of Early America* (New York, 1937), p. 10.

9. Cited by the Reverend B. St. James Fry, "The Early Camp Meeting Song Writers," *Methodist Quarterly Review*, XI (1859), 401.

10. Arminius, "An Appendix to Short Sketches" *op. cit.*, XI (May, 1828), 190.

11. Bangs, *op cit.*, II, 105. John Fanning Watson was of the opinion that the singing of songs composed by Isaac Watts contributed to excessive emotionalism. "Dedicated to divine love, they are too amorous; and fitter to be addrest by a lover to his fellow mortal than by a sinner to the most high God." Watson, *op. cit.*, p. 10.

12. Howells, "Camp Meetings in the West Fifty Years Ago," *op. cit.*, p. 209.

13. The Reverend B. St. James Fry, "The Early Camp Meeting Song Writers," *op. cit.*, p. 209.

14. George P. Jackson has made exhaustive studies of folk music according to the three stated classifications. According to Arthur Palmer Hudson, "Folk-Songs of the Whites," in W. T. Couch (ed.), *Culture in the South* (Chapel Hill, 1935), p. 522: "The folk-song, as it is conceived today, is of no known authorship, or of an authorship that has been forgotten, has been transmitted orally for a respectable period of time, and exists in numerous variants."

15. George P. Jackson has found this text in a number of American collections from 1784 onward. See *Down-East Spirituals and Others*, p. 42, for listing.

16. Merriam, *op. cit.*, pp. 96-97, and Luther Cox, *et al.* (compilers), *Revival Hymns Designed for Protracted, Camp, Prayer, and Social Meetings* (Baltimore, 1843), p. 10.

17. Scott, *op. cit.*, p. 24.

18. Merriam, *op. cit.*, pp. 142-44.

19. Arminius, "An Appendix to Short Sketches," *op. cit.*, XI (May, 1828), 189.

20. *The Camp-Meeting Hymn Book*. There are a variety of Farewell Songs, different versions appearing in different songbooks. See Jackson, *Down-East Spirituals*, pp. 31-32, for the "Parting Hand," composed by Jeremiah Ingalls (1764-1838), a singing schoolmaster who lived in Massachusetts and Vermont. It was still used in the 1930's by Primitive Baptists and southern choral groups devoted to the *Sacred Harp*.

21. In *Spiritual Folk-Songs*, p. 6, Jackson states that the Methodists brought these songs from England in the eighteenth century. In *Down-East Spirituals*, pp. 3-5, he revised his interpretationand concluded that the Baptists brought the "folk-hymn singing tradition" with them, first to the Northeast from whence it spread to the Southeast — the old "Western

Territory" — and thus furnished the "song tinder" for the Great Revival. His bases include examination of English and American songbooks, historical evidence, and Baptist primacy in time and popularity relative to the outbreak of the Great Revival.

22. Kate M. Rabb, *A Tour Through Indiana: The Diary of John Parsons of Petersburg, Virginia* (New York, 1920), p. 309.

23. George P. Jackson, *White Spirituals in the Southern Uplands* (Chapel Hill, 1933), p. 219. This famous hymn by Samuel Stennett (1727-95) was presented in at least three variations.

24. Jackson, *Down-East Spirituals*, pp. 232-65. There are fourteen or sixteen verses to the song, varying according to the compiler.

25. Merriam, *op. cit.*, pp. 34-35.

26. See Jackson, *White Spirituals in the Southern Uplands*, p. 232, for "Go Preachers, and Tell It to the World."

27. Howells, "Camp Meetings in the West Fifty Years Ago," *op. cit.*, p. 209. Jackson, *Spiritual Folk-Songs of Early America*, p. 201, lists verses which Peter Cartwright is supposed to have composed. See Jackson's *Down-East Spirituals*, pp. 235-36, for "I wisht I had a heard ye when ye called me," transmitted in family circles from an ancestor who had heard it at a pre-Civil War Tennessee camp meeting.

28. Jackson, *Spiritual Folk-Songs of Early America*, p. 174. Subsequent verses are built up on "He will save you; O' believe him; He is able; He is willing," etc.

29. From Scott, *op. cit.*, p. 23; Merriam, *op. cit.*, pp. 95-96; Jackson, *Down-East Spirituals*, pp. 262-63. The phrase "sin-sick soul" which appears in the last-named song is obviously taken from Charles Wesley's couplet, "Savior of the sin-sick soul, Give me faith to make me whole." The Negroes' variation was "Brudder George is a-gwine to glory, Take car' de sin-sick soul."

30. Found in Stith Mead, *Hymns and Spiritual Songs* (Richmond, 1807), p. 79. This popular song had many versions. A copy found recently in a cornerstone of the Foundry Methodist Church of Washington, D.C., had twelve verses.

31. John Hope Franklin, *From Slavery to Freedom: A History of American Negroes* (New York, 1948), p. 206; and Stowe, *op. cit.*, p. 36.

32. Odum and Johnson, *op. cit.*, pp. 301-2.

33. *Ibid.*, pp. 53-54.

34. Roland Hayes, *My Songs — Aframerican Religious Folk Songs Arranged and Interpreted* (Boston, 1948), p. 29; and Melville J. Herskovits, *Patterns of Negro Music* (n.p. *ca.* 1940), p. 3.

35. Jackson, *White Spirituals in the Southern Uplands*, p. 277. Twenty songs are traced in this volume, and sixty more are added in *Spiritual Folk-Songs of Early America*.

36. Jackson, *White and Negro Spirituals*, p. 267.

37. Watson, *op. cit.*, p. 21.

38. "Mr. Wesley's Rules for Congregational Singing," published in 1765, quoted in the *Methodist Magazine* (New York), VII (1824), 189-90.

39. For example, the use of the hymn "Foundation," in *The Harvard Hymnal*; "Pleading Savior," in *The Hymnal of the Protestant Episcopal Church*; "Camp Meeting," in *The Methodist Hymnal*, and many others.

40. Jackson, *Spiritual Folk-Songs of Early America*, pp. 21, 22.

11. *Sociability in the Tented Grove*

1. "Camp Meetings and Agricultural Fairs," *Wesleyan Repository, and Religious Intelligencer* (Trenton), II (August, 1822), 143.
2. Professor William W. Sweet agrees with the writer that the evidence points to the fact that John Fanning Watson, author of *The Methodist Error* (New Jersey, 1819), also wrote under the name of "Scrutator."
3. Morris Birkbeck, *Notes on a Journey in America from the Coast of Virginia to the Territory of Illinois* (Philadelphia, 1817), p. 145.
4. Jackson, *Spiritual Folk-Songs of Early America,* p. 7, n. 2.
5. Entry of October 11, 1846, "Diary of Clara Frederick 1845-47."
6. Letter, Elvira Frederick, dated Indian Creek, Alabama, September 29, 1849. Frederick Letters (MSS [handwritten], in possession of Mrs. J. E. Hays, Director Department of Archives and History, State of Georgia).
7. Trollope, *op. cit.,* I, 245-46.
8. Von Raumer, *op. cit.,* p. 343.
9. Quoted in Brooks, *op. cit.,* p. 91, n. Carlton, *op. cit.,* II, 134-35.
10. Carlton, *op. cit.,* II, 132.
11. West, *op. cit.,* pp. 563-64. In the East, "island camp meetings" on Maryland's eastern shores attracted many neighboring islanders who came by boat to reach the encampment.
12. Carlton, *op. cit.,* II, 130.
13. Finley, *Autobiography,* pp. 202, 204; "Extracts from the Memorabilia of the Wachovia Congregations for the Year 1815," from Adelaide L. Fries (ed.), *Records of the Moravians in North Carolina* (Raleigh, 1947), II (1809-22), 3260.
14. Finley, *Sketches,* pp. 209-10.
15. See notice in August 27, 1836, *Cambridge Chronicle,* quoted in Wroten, *op. cit.,* pp. 150-51.
16. "Is the Modern Camp Meeting a Failure?" *Methodist Quarterly Review,* XIII (1861), 600-601.
17. See *Commentator* (Frankfort, Kentucky), August 28, 1822, and *Western Christian Advocate* (Cincinnati), September 17, 1873.
18. Carlton, *op. cit.,* II, 135-36.
19. Italics his. Finley, *Autobiography,* p. 317.
20. Editorial, "Preparing Food for Camp-Meetings," *Western Christian Advocate,* July 26, 1839.
21. Carlton, *op. cit.,* II, 136, and *Northwestern Christian Advocate,* April 14, 1915. Also see Bremer, *op. cit.,* I, 307.
22. Wiley, "Methodism in Southeastern Indiana," *op. cit.* (December, 1927), pp. 408-9.
23. Letter, entitled "Camp Meetings," by "D.K." dated June 30, 1837, printed in *Western Christian Advocate* (Cincinnati), July 28, 1837.
24. Wiley, "Methodism in Southeastern Indiana," *op. cit.* (June, 1927), pp. 212-13.
25. See advertisement in the *Weekly Recorder* (Chillicothe), September 26, 1814, printed in Carter, *op. cit.,* p. 66; Letter, Robert W. Finley, London, Ohio, April 16, 1825, James B. Finley Papers (MSS [handwritten], at Ohio Wesleyan University, Delaware, Ohio); and *Western Christian Advocate* (Cincinnati), September 13, 1839.

26. Arminius, "Short Sketches" *op. cit.,* V (September, 1812), 351-52.

27. *Christian Advocate and Journal* (New York), November 29, 1833.

28. See H. Vincent, *History of the Camp-Meeting and Grounds at Wesleyan Grove, Martha's Vineyard* (Boston, 1870), pp. 256-57, and Bangs, *op. cit.,* II, 266-68 for a listing of camp meeting rules.

29. John Scripps, "Early Methodism in the Far West," *Western Christian Advocate* (Cincinnati), January 6, 1843, and Henry Smith, *op. cit.,* p. 168.

30. Letter, Elvira Frederick, dated Indian Creek, Alabama, September 21, 1849, Frederick Letters MSS.

31. Lorenzo Dow, *op. cit.,* p. 249, and William C. Howells, "Camp Meetings in the West Fifty Years Ago," *Lippincott's Magazine of Popular Literature and Science,* X (1872), 208.

32. Printed in Lorenzo Dow, *op. cit.,* p. 585.

33. Extract of Letter, Henry Smith, 1806, Lakin MSS.

34. Finley, *Autobiography,* pp. 366-67.

35. See, for example, A. D. Field, *Memorials of Methodism in the Bounds of the Rock River Conference* (Cincinnati, 1886), p. 410.

36. See editorial, *Western Christian Advocate* (Cincinnati), September 13, 1839.

37. Brown, *op. cit.,* p. 43.

38. Ohio *Monitor and Patron of Industry* (Columbus), July 20, 1822.

39. Cartwright, *Autobiography,* pp. 141-42.

40. Bangs, *op. cit.,* II, 268.

41. See *Western Christian Advocate* (Cincinnati), August 13, 1841, for an amendment to an Ohio Statute of 1831. This law provided a fine of not less than $5.00 nor more than $50.00 for its violation. Also see issue of August 15, 1834.

42. *Ohio Monitor and Patron of Industry* (Columbus), July 20, 1822.

43. *Western Christian Advocate* (Cincinnati), July 26, 1839. Robert Riegel, discussing the effects of liquor drinking in *op. cit.,* p. 114, makes no mention of the fact that the sale of liquor was prohibited and constituted an underhanded activity, opposed by the camp sponsors.

44. Wiley, "Methodism in Southeastern Indiana," *op. cit.* (June, 1927), pp. 179-81.

45. Finley, *Autobiography,* pp. 350-51.

46. Article by "Methodius," *Ohio Monitor and Patron of Industry* (Columbus), July 20, 1822.

47. "Perhaps there never was a greater collection of rabble and rowdies. They came drunk and armed with dirks, clubs, knives, and horse-whips, and swore they would break up the meeting." See Cartwright, *Autobiography,* pp. 90-92. James B. Finley tells of a Rushville, Ohio, meeting in 1812, at which Bishops Asbury and McKendree were present. A brawny church leader, Birkhammer by name, whipped the mob leaders who attempted to break up the meeting, and the sheriff arrived in time to make ten of the rowdies prisoners. Preacher Finley reports Asbury speaking after order was restored, admonishing the toughs to leave the churchmen alone: "All our brothers in the Church are not yet sanctified . . . and if you get them angry and the devil should get in them, they are the strongest and hardest men to fight and conquer in the world. I advise you, if you do not like them to go home and let them alone." Finley, *Autobiography,* pp. 252-53.

48. Jacob Young, *op. cit.*, pp. 290-92, and "Some of the Early Pioneer Business men," *Old Northwest Genealogical Quarterly*, XV (1912), 104-5. 104-5.
49. Cartwright, *Autobiography*, pp. 141, 270-72; Brunson, *op. cit.*, I, 250; and Jacob Young, *op. cit.*, pp. 233-34.
50. Logan Esarey, *A History of Indiana From Its Exploration to 1850* (Indianapolis, 1915), p. 117.
51. William C. Smith, *op. cit.*, pp. 279-80.
52. Brunson, *op. cit.*, I, 283-89, and Entry of August 7, 1808, Asbury, *Journal*, III, 285.
53. Letter, John Collins, dated Chillicothe, Ohio, April 22, 1819, printed in the *Methodist Magazine* (New York), II (May, 1819), 234-35.

12. *Contemporary Appraisals*

1. Finley, *Autobiography*, p. 315.
2. One Scotch traveler quoted approvingly the confession of another author that "a book of travels must always be more or less a volume of inaccuracies." See Duncan, *op. cit.*, I, ix.
3. Flint, *op. cit.*, pp. 358-61, and Trollope, *op. cit.*, I, 236-45. Practically all that the English people knew of the American camp meeting for some years was based upon the jaundiced views of Flint and Trollope. Eccentric Lorenzo Dow's activity in England certainly did not drastically alter their impressions. Not until the publication of the works of Andrew Reed and James Matheson (1835), and Frederick Marryat (1839), would an English publication contain a less harsh appraisal.
4. Duncan, *op. cit.*, II, 370-71.
5. Hamilton, *op. cit.*, pp. 392, 394.
6. Reed and Matheson, *op. cit.*, I, 295, 298, and Marryat, *op cit.*, II, 188-89.
7. From Tocqueville, "Quinze Jours au Desert," printed in Pierson, *op. cit.*, p. 249.
8. Italics his. Carlton, *op. cit.*, II, 134-35.
9. Italics his. In the order quoted, "A Camp Meeting," *Western Messenger* (Cincinnati), II (November, 1836), 233; Alexander Campbell, "Aspects of Methodism," *Millennial Harbinger* (Bethany, Virginia), VII (August, 1843), 365.
10. A century is certainly a sufficient lapse of time for a balance sheet to be struck on the frontier camp meeting. Those authors who have undertaken to evaluate the institution, and have found it lacking, agree in part or *in toto* with the statement of two Mississippi historians: "At this late date [1944] it is hard to realize that any substantial good was derived from the camp meetings." See Francis A. Cabaniss and James A. Cabaniss, "Religion in Ante-Bellum Mississippi," *Journal of Mississippi History*, V (June, 1944), 212. In this general category fall the conclusions of Rusk, *op. cit.*, pp. 46-51; Eaton, *op. cit.*, pp. 281-83; Leyburn, *op. cit.*, pp. 97-200; Posey, *op. cit.*, pp. 23-24; Tyler, *op. cit.*, p. 35. In contrast, another group concurs with Professor William W. Sweet in believing that "the camp meeting, one of the by-products of frontier revivalism, served a very large social and religious need." See Sweet, *The Story of Religion in America*, p. 8; Kenneth

S. Latourette, *The Great Century, 1800-1914: Europe and the United States. A History of the Expansion of Christianity* (New York, 1938-44), IV, 194; Gabriel, *op cit.*, p. 32; Ralph E. Riegel, *America Moves West* (New York, 1947 ed.), pp. 95-96; Mode, *op. cit.*, pp. 53-56; John D. Barnhart, Jr., "The Rise of the Methodist Episcopal Church in Illinois from the Beginning to the Year 1832," *Journal of the Illinois State Historical Society*, XII (July, 1919), 189-90; and Edwin Poteat, Jr., "Religion in the South," in Couch, *op. cit.*, pp. 257-58.

11. Letter extract, undated, Dr. Samuel Miller, printed in appendix of *Lectures in Revivals of Religion*, reprinted in Schenck, *op. cit.*, p. 78.

12. See Nevin, *op. cit.*, pp. 81-82; *Baptist Banner and Western Pioneer* (Louisville), July 16, 1840; and Wiley, "Methodism in Southeastern Indiana," *op. cit.* (September, 1927), p. 261.

13. Italics his. *Camp-Meetings Described and Exposed*, p. 10.

14. John Fanning Watson (Scrutator), "Camp-Meetings and Agricultural Fairs," *op. cit.*, pp. 138-43. Adam Clarke wrote to Watson on December 27, 1821: "I am quite of your mind — That when the population lies thinly scattered as must be the case in many parts of America; and the places for public worship, either very few or out of the convenient reach of many. There such meetings as you call camp-meetings may be of great and indeed of effectual service — but where these necessities do not exist I think no such meetings should be instituted." Letter, Adam Clarke, dated Millbrook, Prescot, Lancashire, England. Quoted in Watson MS (Huntington Library, San Marino, California).

15. Undated letter, M. Lindsey, printed in the *Western Christian Monitor* (Chillicothe), I (1816), 424-25, and Arminius, "Short Sketches," *op. cit.*, V (September, 1822), 351.

16. In the order quoted, Cartwright, *Autobiography*, p. 523; Journal entry of September 10, 1810, Lakin MSS, No. 9; and William C. Smith, *op. cit.*, pp. 74-75.

17. M. Emory Wright, "Is the Modern Camp-Meeting a Failure?" *op. cit.*, p. 593.

18. Italics his. Weiser, *op. cit.*, pp. 31-32.

19. *Zion's Herald* (Boston), August 4, 1824.

20. Weiser, *op. cit.*, p. 3.

21. William C. Smith, *op. cit.*, p. 75.

22. Wiley, "Methodism in Southeastern Indiana," *op. cit.* (June, 1927), p. 179. See also James Quinn's statement in Wright, *op. cit.*, p. 121. Two presidents were claimed as camp meeting converts, Franklin Pierce and William Henry Harrison. See Frank A. Harder, "The Camp-Meeting and Methodism," in *Northwestern Christian Advocate*, July 28, 1909.

23. All were circuit riders, with the exception of John Stewart, a freeborn Virginia mulatto who pioneered in Methodist Indian missions, and John Dempster, founder of the first Methodist Bible Institute (1845) and Garrett Biblical Institute (1854). See Field, *op. cit.*, pp. 410-15.

24. Joint letter, Francis Asbury and Henry Boehm, dated Camden, New Jersey, November 10, 1808, Asbury MSS. Maxwell Gaddis was converted at age 13, after six hours as a penitent in the "circle of brotherly love"; Stephen Bangs at age 19; and John Dempster was converted as a "wild" youth of 18. During the Great Revival, John Lyle noted that "almost all

who fell there [at Salem, 1801] were either religious people or children of religious parents." Lyle, Diary MSS, p. 48.

13. *Decline of the Backwoods Revival*

1. "Methodism in Southeastern Indiana," *op. cit.* (June, 1927), pp. 183-84.

2. *Western Christian Advocate* (Cincinnati), September 27, 1839.

3. *An Essay on Camp Meetings* ["By the Author of the True Evangelist"] (New York, 1849), p. 11. Another camp meeting manual writer, B. W. Gorham, lamented "the danger" of the "undue multiplicity of Camp Meetings" in the New York region during the 1840's. See Gorham, *op. cit.,* p. viii.

4. Bangs, *op. cit.,* II, 269-70, and Wiley, "Methodism in Southeastern Indiana," *op. cit.* (June, 1927), pp. 179-80.

5. Consult, for example, reports from Mt. Carmel, Illinois, encampment, and a Sangamon camp meeting in 1839, in *Western Christian Advocate* (Cincinnati), September 20, 1839.

6. In the order quoted, Mode, *op. cit.,* p. 56; Coulter, *op. cit.,* p. 12; and William W. Sweet, *Methodism in American History* (New York, Cincinnati, and Chicago, 1933), p. 159. For other historical views on the longevity of the camp meeting, consult William C. Howells, "Camp Meetings in the West Fifty Years Ago," *op. cit.,* p. 203; Cain, *op. cit.,* p. 26, and Nottingham, *op. cit.,* p. 209.

7. A. P. Mead, *op. cit.,* p. 25, and letter, Orceneth Fisher, dated Stockton, October 3, 1856. A year later, Fisher and two other Southern Methodists while on their way to the Oregon country stopped off at a "Debate Campmeeting" at Vacaville, California. The Campbellites were having a spirited theological discussion with the Methodists upon the issue of immersion. See a historical sketch by Fisher, in letter form, entitled "Introduction of Southern Methodism into Oregon," printed in Sweet, *The Methodists,* pp. 481, 492-93.

8. Marryat, *op. cit.,* II, 180-83. See also *Western Christian Advocate* (Cincinnati), September 17, 1873.

9. See *Western Christian Advocate* (Cincinnati), August 28, 1840, and illustration, *Gleason's Pictorial Drawing Room Companion,* II (July, 1852), 200. Bremer, *op. cit.,* p. 306.

10. Strickland, *The Life of Jacob Gruber,* pp. 39-40.

11. "Old-Fashioned Camp-Meetings versus New-Fashioned Camp-Meetings," by "An Old Preacher," *Western Christian Advocate* (Cincinnati), September 17, 1873. See also issue of July 28, 1909.

12. Italics his. Brunson, *op. cit.,* I, 417-18; Cady, *op. cit.,* pp. 140-41.

13. In the order cited, Gaddis, *op. cit.,* pp. 186-87; "Journal of James Quinn," Wright, *op. cit.,* p. 121; and *ibid.,* p. 106. Consult also Sweet, *Revivalism in America,* pp. 161-66, on the indoor protracted meeting.

14. Consult the index to Volume V (April 1838-April 1839) through XII (April 1845-April 1846), *Western Christian Advocate.*

15. See *Methodist Magazine* (New York), 1822-28; *Methodist Magazine and Quarterly Review,* 1830-40; and *Methodist Quarterly Review,* 1841-48.

16. Consult Bangs, *op. cit.*, III and IV, *passim;* Guion G. Johnson, "The Camp Meeting in Ante-Bellum North Carolina," *North Carolina Historical Review*, X (April, 1933), 95-110; and *New York Christian Advocate*, May 3, 1843, quoted in Wroten, *op. cit.*, p. 153.

17. See Sweet, *Revivalism in America*, pp. 131-32, and Nottingham, *op. cit.*, p. 206.

18. Mead, *op. cit.*, p. 66.

19. See Gorham, *op. cit.*, pp. 22, 24, 27, and *An Essay on Camp Meetings.*

20. In the order quoted, William C. Smith, *op. cit.*, p. 75; "Journal of James Quinn," Wright, *op cit.*, p. 121; and Cartwright, *Autobiography*, pp. 523-24.

21. Almer M. Pennewell, *The Methodist Movement in Illinois* (Sycamore, Illinois, 1942), pp. 273-300; Carter, *op. cit.*, pp. 95-96; and Sweet, *The American Churches*, p. 56 and *Revivalism in America*, p. 164.

22. The Reverend Arnold Weaver of the Church of the Brethren has related to the author tales of the Bryan camp meetings. A strange carry-over has been the use of the "tongue of the Lord." Having received the spirit, a worshiper "speaks gibberish" which is then translated by a devout interpreter.

23. *Washington Post* (D.C.), June 24, 1949.

24. Many political pundits described the Progessive Party Convention of 1912 and the New Party (Wallace-Progressive) Convention of 1948 as "camp meetings."

Bibliography

I. MANUSCRIPTS

"Account of an Extraordinary Revival of Religion in Kentucky." Pamphlet MS (handwritten), including a letter dated August 16, 1801, unsigned. Durrett Collection, University of Chicago.

Asbury, Bishop Francis. Letters. MSS (handwritten). Forty-one items including a few letters from others than Asbury. Methodist Historical Society of the Baltimore Conference, repository at the First Methodist Church, Baltimore.

Brunson, Alfred. Journals and Letter Books. MSS (handwritten). Wisconsin Historical Society, Madison.

Butler, Mann. "Manners and Habits of the Western Pioneers." MS (handwritten), 1836. Durrett Collection, University of Chicago.

Colbert, William. "A Journal of the Travels of William Colbert, Methodist Preacher Thro' Parts of Maryland, Pennsylvania, New York, Delaware and Virginia in 1790 to 1838." MSS (typewritten), Vols. III-X (1798-1838), 10 vols. Garrett Biblical Institute, Evanston.

Dromgoole, Edward. Letters. MSS (typewritten). Garrett Biblical Institute, Evanston.

Finley, James B. Papers. MSS (handwritten), 1,227 letters and documents (1794-1858) received by him relating to Ohio Methodism and the Wyandot Mission, indexed, and including drafts of articles for publication in magazines and newspapers. Ohio Wesleyan University, Delaware.

Frederick, Elvira and Olivia. Letters from Alabama and Mississippi, 1849, and Extract Diary of Clara Frederick, 1845-1847. MSS (handwritten). Originals in possession of Mrs. J. E. Hayes, Director, Department of Archives and History, State of Georgia, Atlanta.

Fry, Benjamin St. James. Papers (1850-1851). MSS (handwritten). Letters on frontier Methodism in Ohio, Indiana, and Kentucky. Ohio Wesleyan University, Delaware.

Gilruth, James. Journal (1793-1873). MSS (typewritten). Vols. I, II. Nineteen manuscript booklets. Durrett Collection, Chicago. Original in possession of W. A. Gilruth, Chicago.

Hickman, William. "Autobiography of Rev. William Hickman." MS (handwritten), 1838. Durrett Collection, Chicago.

Lakin, Benjamin. Journal (1794-1820). MSS (handwritten), 13 booklets. Durrett Collection, Chicago.

———. Papers. MSS (handwritten). Durrett Collection, Chicago.

Letters of Agents to the American Home Missionary Society. MSS

(handwritten). Hammond Library, Chicago Theological Seminary, Chicago.
Letters of the Shakers. MSS (handwritten). Western Reserve Historical Society Collection, Cleveland.
Lyle, John. Diary (1801-1803). MS (typewritten). Durrett Collection, Chicago.

II. Official Church Documents

Emory, Robert. *History of the Discipline of the Methodist Episcopal Church.* New York, 1844.
Fries, Adelaide L. (ed.). *Records of the Moravians in North Carolina.* Raleigh, 1947.
Journals of the General Conference of the Methodist Episcopal Church. Vol. I (1796-1836), Vol. II (1840-44). New York, 1855.
Journals of the General Conference of the Methodist Episcopal Church, South. Vol. I (1846-1850), Vol. III (1858). Richmond, 1851-59.
Minutes of the Annual Conferences of the Methodist Episcopal Church. Vol. I (1773-1828), Vol. II (1829-30), Vol. III (1839-45). New York, 1840-45.
Sweet, William W. *Circuit-Rider Days Along the Ohio. Being the Journals of the Ohio Conference from Its Organization in 1812 to 1828.* Edited with Introduction and Notes. New York and Cincinnati, 1923.
———. *Circuit-Rider Days in Indiana; The Journals of the Indiana Conference (1832-1842).* Indianapolis, 1916.
———. *The Rise of Methodism in the West. Being the Journal of the Western Conference 1800-1811.* New York and Cincinnati, 1919.

III. Printed Source Collections

Bushnell, Horace. *Barbarism the First Danger. A Discourse for Home Missions.* New York, 1847.
Mode, Peter G. (compiler). *Source Book and Bibliographical Guide for American Church History.* Menasha, Wisconsin, 1921.
Sweet, William W. *Religion on the American Frontier.* Vol. I. *The Baptists 1783-1830. A Collection of Source Materials.* New York, 1931.
———. *Religion on the American Frontier.* Vol. II. *The Presbyterians. 1783-1840. A Collection of Source Materials.* New York and London, 1936.
———. *Religion on the American Frontier. 1783-1840.* Vol. IV. *The Methodists. A Collection of Source Materials.* Chicago, 1946.

Telford, John. *The Letters of the Rev. John Wesley, A.M.* 8 vols. London, 1931.

IV. Diaries and Travel Accounts

Asbury, Francis. *Journal of Rev. Francis Asbury.* 3 vols. New York, 1852.

Birkbeck, Morris. *Notes on a Journey in America from the Coast of Virginia to the Territory of Illinois.* Philadelphia, 1817.

Bremer, Fredrika, *The Homes of the New World; Impressions of America.* 2 vols. Translated by Mary Howitt. Vol. I. New York, 1853.

Brown, William. *America: A Four Years Residence in the United States and Canada.* Leeds, 1849.

Carlton, Robert [Hall, Baynard Rush]. *The New Purchase: Or Seven and a Half Years in the Far West.* 2 vols. Vol. II. New York, 1843.

Cuming, Fortescue. *Sketches of a Tour to the Western Country Through the States of Ohio and Kentucky . . . . Winter of 1807 and Concluded in 1809.* Pittsburgh, 1810.

Curnock, Nehemiah (ed.). *The Journal of the Rev. John Wesley, A.M.* 8 vols. London, 1909-16.

Duncan, John M. *Travels Through Part of the United States and Canada in 1818 and 1819.* 2 vols. Glasgow, 1823.

Flint, James. *Flint's Letters from America, 1818-1820. (Early Western Travels, 1748-1846,* ed. Reuben G. Thwaites. Vol. IX) 32 vols. Cleveland, 1904-07.

Flint, Timothy. *Recollections of the Last Ten Years, Passed in Occasional Residences and Journeyings in the Valley of the Mississippi, from Pittsburgh and the Missouri to the Gulf of Mexico, and from Florida to the Spanish Frontier.* Boston, 1826.

Gallaher, James. *The Western Sketch Book.* (3rd ed.), Boston, 1852.

Hall, Lt. Francis. *Travels in Canada and the United States, in 1816 and 1817.* (2nd ed.), London, 1819.

Hall, James. *Legends of the West.* Philadephia, 1832.

————. *Letters from the West: Containing Sketches of Scenery, Manners, and Customs.* London, 1828.

Hamilton, Capt. Thomas. *Men and Manners in America.* 2 vols. Vol. II. Edinburgh, 1834.

Marryat, Frederick B. *A Diary in America with Remarks on Its Institutions.* 6 vols. Vols. II and III. London, 1839.

Martineau, Harriet. *Retrospect of Western Travel.* 3 vols. London, 1838.

Olmsted, Frederick L. *The Cotton Kingdom.* 2 vols. New York, 1861.

Pierson, George W. *Tocqueville and Beaumont in America.* New York, 1938. [Based on Tocqueville MSS.]

Raumer, Frederick von. *America and the American People.* Translated from the German. New York, 1846.

Reed, Andrew, and Matheson, James. *A Narrative of the Visit to the American Churches, by the Deputation from the Congregational Union of England and Wales.* 2 vols. New York, 1835.

Schermerhorn, John F., and Mills, Samuel J. *A Correct View of That Part of the United States Which Lies West of the Alleghany Mountains, with Regard to Religion and Morals.* Hartford, 1814. [Missionaries of the Massachusetts Baptist Missionary Society.]

Tocqueville, Alexis de. *Democracy in America.* Translated by Henry Reeve, revised by Francis Bowen, edited by Phillips Bradley. 2 vols. Vol. II. New York, 1945.

Trollope, Frances. *Domestic Manners of the Americans.* 2 vols. Vol. I. London, 1832.

V. RELIGIOUS NARRATIVES

Pre-Camp Meeting Literature

Edwards, Jonathan. *A Faithful Narrative of the Surprising Work of God in the Conversion of Many Hundred Souls in Northampton and the Neighbouring Towns . . . in a Letter to the Rev. Dr. Benjamin Colman of Boston.* London, 1737.

Tracy, Joseph. *The Great Awakening: A History of the Revival of Religion in the Time of Edwards and Whitefield.* Boston, 1842.

Comprehensive Works on the Camp Meeting

Boehm, Henry. *Reminiscences, Historical and Biographical of Sixty-four Years in the Ministry,* ed. Joseph B. Wakely. New York, 1865.

Cartwright, Peter. *Autobiography of Peter Cartwright, the Backwoods Preacher,* ed. W. P. Strickland. New York, 1857.

——. *Fifty Years As a Presiding Elder,* ed. W. S. Hooper. Cincinnati, 1871.

Finley, James B. *Autobiography of Rev. James B. Finley; or, Pioneer Life in the West,* ed. W. P. Strickland. Cincinnati, 1853.

——. *Life Among the Indians; or Personal Reminiscences and Historical Incidents Illustrative of Indian Life and Character,* ed. Rev. D. W. Clark. Cincinnati, 1857.

——. *Sketches of Western Methodism: Biographical, Historical, and Miscellaneous. Illustrative of Pioneer Life,* ed. W. P. Strickland. Cincinnati, 1854.

Milburn, William H. *The Lance, Cross, and Canoe: The Flatboat, Rifle, and Plough in the Valley of the Mississippi.* New York, 1892.

————. *The Pioneer Preacher: or, Rifle, Axe, and Saddlebags, and Other Lectures.* New York, 1857.

————. *The Pioneers, Preachers and People of the Mississippi Valley.* New York, 1859.

————. *Ten Years of Preacher Life: Chapters from an Autobiography.* New York, 1859.

Paine, Robert. *Life and Times of William McKendree.* Nashville, 1922. [Includes much material from McKendree's Diary, Journals, and other MSS.]

Stevens, Abel. *Life and Times of Nathan Bangs, D.D.* New York, 1863.

Strickland, W. P. *The Pioneer Bishop: or, the Life and Times of Francis Asbury.* New York, 1858.

Camp Meetings of the Great Revival

Cossitt, Franceway R. *The Life and Times of Rev. Finis Ewing, One of the Fathers and Founders of the Cumberland Presbyterian Church. To Which Is Added Remarks on Davidson's History, or, A Review of His Chapters on the Revival of 1800 and His History of the Cumberland Presbyterians.* Louisville, 1853.

McGready, James. *The Posthumous Works of James McGready.* 2 vols., ed. James Smith. Louisville, 1831. [Presbyterian]

McNemar, Richard. *The Kentucky Revival; or, A Short History of the Late Extraordinary Outpouring of the Spirit of God in the Western States of America.* New York, 1846. [1st ed. 1807.] [Shaker]

Purviance, Levi. *The Biography of Elder David Purviance, With His Memoirs . . . Written by Himself . . . Together With a Historical Sketch of the Great Kentucky Revival.* Dayton, Ohio, 1848. [Shaker]

Smith, Henry. *Recollections and Reflections of an Old Itinerant. A Series of Letters Originally Published in the Christian Advocate and Journal and the Western Christian Advocate,* ed. George Peck. New York, 1848.

Stone, Barton W. *The Biography of Eld. Barton Warren Stone, Written by Himself: With Additions and Reflections by Elder John Rogers Written in Part by John Rogers.* Cincinnati, 1847. [Presbyterian]

Thrift, Minton. *Memoir of the Rev. Jesse Lee With Extracts From His Journals.* New York, 1823. [Lee's MS Journals since destroyed.]

Ware, Thomas. *Sketches of the Life and Travels of Rev. Thomas Ware.* New York, 1842.

Later Camp Meetings

A Sketch of the Life of Rev. John Collins, Late of the Ohio Conference. Cincinnati, 1849.

Beggs, Stephen R. *Pages From the Early History of the West and Northwest.* Cincinnati, 1868.

Boyd, Robert. *Personal Memoirs; Together With a Discussion Upon the Hardships and Sufferings of Itinerant Life.* Cincinnati, 1886.

Brunson, Alfred. *A Western Pioneer: or, Incidents of the Life and Times of Rev. Alfred Brunson.* 2 vols. Cincinnati, 1872-79.

Camp-Meetings Described and Exposed and "Strange Things" Stated. n.p., n.d. [ca. 1826] [Main Reading Room, Library of Congress.]

Coulter, E. Merton. *William G. Brownlow, Fighting Parson of the Southern Highlands.* Chapel Hill, 1937.

Dow, Lorenzo. *History of Cosmopolite; or the Writings of Rev. Lorenzo Dow; Containing His Experience and Travels, in Europe and America, Up to Near His Fiftieth Year. Also, His Polemic Writings. To Which Is Added, "The Journey of Life" by Peggy Dow. Revised and Corrected With Notes.* Cincinnati, 1858.

————. *The Chain of Lorenzo; by the Request of His Friends, as a Farewell to Georgia.* Augusta, 1803.

Eggleston, George C. *The First of the Hoosiers. Reminiscences of Edward Eggleston.* Philadephia, 1903.

Gaddis, Maxwell P. *Brief Recollections of the Late Rev. George W. Walker.* Cincinnati, 1857.

————. *Footprints of an Itinerant.* Cincinnati and Chicago, 1874.

Gavitt, Elnathan C. *Crumbs from My Saddle Bags; or Reminiscences of Pioneer Life and Biographical Sketches.* Toledo, 1884.

Giles, Charles. *Pioneer: A Narrative of the Nativity, Experience, Travels, and Ministerial Labours of Rev. Charles Giles.* New York, 1844.

Jones, Charles C. *The Religious Instruction of the Negroes.* Savannah, 1842.

Long, John D. *Pictures of Slavery in Church and State.* Philadelphia, 1857.

Manford, Erasmus. *Twenty-five Years in the West.* Chicago, 1867. [Universalist]

Nevin, John W. *The Anxious Bench.* Chambersburg, Pennsylvania, 1844.

Pilcher, James E. *Life and Labors of Elijah H. Pilcher.* New York, 1892.

Richardson, Robert. *Memoirs of Alexander Campbell.* 2 vols. Philadelphia, 1870. [Based on personal papers of the Disciples or Christian Church founder.]

Rivers, R. H. *The Life of Robert Paine, D.D., Bishop of the Methodist Episcopal Church, South.* Nashville, 1916.

Smith, John C. *Reminiscences of Early Methodism in Indiana.* Indianapolis, 1879.

Smith, William C. *Indiana Miscellany.* Cincinnati, 1867.

Strickland, William P. (ed.). *The Life of Jacob Gruber.* New York, 1860.

———. *The Pioneers of the West, or Life in the Woods.* New York, 1856.

Sturtevant, Julian M., Jr. (ed.). *Julian M. Sturtevant. An Autobiography.* New York, Chicago, Toronto, 1896. [Congregational]

Turpie, David. *Sketches of My Own Times.* Indianapolis, 1903.

Vincent, H. *History of the Camp-meeting and Grounds at Wesleyan Grove, Martha's Vineyard.* Boston, 1870.

[Watson, John Fanning] "By a Wesleyan Methodist." *Methodist Error; or Friendly, Christian Advice, to Those Methodists Who Indulge in Extravagant Emotions and Bodily Exercises.* Trenton, New Jersey, 1819, improved edition. [MS on file at the Huntington Library, San Marino, California. Bound with it are letters and copies of several reviews which identify the work as the writing of John Fanning Watson, a Methodist layman of Germantown, Pennsylvania.]

Weiser, R. *The Mourner's Bench, or An Humble Attempt to Vindicate New Measures.* Bedford, Pennsylvania, [ca. 1844]. [Main Reading Room, Library of Congress.]

Wightman, William M. *Life of William Capers, D.D., One of the Bishops of the Methodist Episcopal Church, South; Including an Autobiography.* Nashville, 1902.

Wright, John F. *Sketches of the Life and Labors of James Quinn.* Cincinnati, 1851. [Includes partial "Journal of James Quinn" and other MSS.]

Young, Jacob. *Autobiography of a Pioneer.* Cincinnati, 1857.

VI. Camp Meeting Manuals

An Essay on Camp Meetings. "By the Author of the True Evangelist." New York, 1849.

Gorham, B. W. *Camp Meeting Manual, A Practical Book for the Camp Ground.* Boston, 1854.

Mead, A. P. *Manna in the Wilderness; or the Grove and Its Altar,, Offerings, and Thrilling Incidents. Containing a History of the Origin and Rise of Camp Meetings . . . also an Account of a Wyoming Camp Meeting.* Philadelphia, 1859.

VII. REVIVAL HYMNOLOGY AND FOLK MUSIC

Methodist Camp Meeting Hymnals

Bourne, Hugh (compiler). *A Collection of Hymns, for Camp Meetings, Revivals, etc., for the Use of the Primitive Methodists.* Bemersley, England, 1829. [Primitive Methodist]

————. *General Collection of Hymns and Spiritual Songs for Camp Meetings.* London, 1808. [Primitive Methodist]

Camp Meeting Chorister. Philadephia, 1830.

Camp Meeting Harp: Selections of Stirring Hymns. Wilmington, Delaware, 1854.

The Camp-Meeting Hymn Book: Containing the Most Approved Hymns and Spiritual Songs by the Methodist Connexion in the United States. (6th ed.) Ithaca, 1836.

A Choice Selection of Hymns and Spiritual Songs Designed for Camp Meetings. (3rd ed.) Montpelier, 1827.

Cox, Luther, *et al.* (compilers). *Revival Hymns, Designed for Protracted, Camp, Prayer, and Social Meetings.* Baltimore, 1843.

Dow, Peggy (compiler). *A Collection of Camp-Meeting Hymns.* (2nd ed.) Philadelphia, 1816.

Harrod, John (compiler). *Social and Camp-Meeting Songs.* Baltimore, 1817.

Henry, George W. (compiler). *The Golden Harp or Camp-Meeting Hymns.* Auburn, New York, 1855.

Hinde, Thomas S. (compiler). *The Pilgrim Songster: Or a Choice Collection of Spiritual Songs from the Best Authors.* Cincinnati, 1810.

Mason, Thomas (compiler). *Zion's Songster or a Collection of Hymns and Spiritual Songs Usually Sung at Camp Meetings.* (10th ed.) Cincinnati, 1843.

Mead, Stith. *Hymns and Spiritual Songs.* Richmond, 1807.

Merriam, Joseph (compiler). *The Wesleyan Camp Meeting Hymn-Book.* (4th ed.) Wendell, Massachusetts, 1829.

Meyers, Peter D. (compiler). *The Zion Songster.* (10th ed.) New York, 1832.

Mintz, David B. (compiler). *Spiritual Song Book.* Halifax, North Carolina, 1805.

A New Collection of Choice Hymns Written for Camp Meetings and Social Worship. Brooklyn, 1808.

A New Selection of Hymns and Spiritual Songs . . . for . . . Camp Meetings. Woodstock, 1832.

Scott, Orange (compiler). *The New and Improved Camp Meeting Hymn Book: a Choice Selection of Hymns from the West.* (3rd ed.) Brookfield, Massachusetts, 1832.

Second Advent Hymns: Designed to Be Used in Prayer and Camp Meetings. (3rd ed.) Concord, 1843. [Adventist]

Totten, John C. (compiler). *A Collection of the Most Admired Hymns and Spiritual Songs, With the Choruses Affixed as Usually Sung at Camp Meetings.* New York, 1809.

Wiatt, Solomon (compiler). *Impartial Selection of Hymns and Spiritual Songs.* Philadelphia, 1809.

Methodist Hymnology

The Methodist Hymnal. New York, Cincinnati, and Chicago, 1935.

The Methodist Pocket Hymn Book, Revised and Improved. (13th ed.) New York, 1803.

Rattenbury, J. Ernest. *Wesley's Legacy to the World.* Nashville, 1928.

Folk Music Studies

Hayes, Roland. *My Songs — Aframerican Religious Folk Songs Arranged and Interpreted.* Boston, 1948.

Herskovits, Melville J. *Patterns of Negro Music.* n.p., n.d. [*ca.* 1940.]

Jackson, George P. (coll. and ed.). *Down-East Spirituals and Others.* New York, 1939.

————. *Spiritual Folk-Songs of Early America.* New York, 1937.

————. *White and Negro Spirituals. Their Life Span and Kinship.* New York, 1943.

————. *White Spirituals in the Southern Uplands.* Chapel Hill, 1933.

Johnson, Guy B. "Negro Folk Songs in the South." *Culture in the South,* W. T. Couch (ed.). Chapel Hill, 1934, pp. 547-69.

Odum, Howard W., and Johnson, Guy B. *Negro Workaday Songs.* Chapel Hill, 1926.

————. *The Negro and His Songs. A Study of Typical Negro Songs in the South.* Chapel Hill, 1925.

VIII. Nineteenth-Century Denominational Periodicals

Methodist Newspapers (Weekly)

Christian Advocate and Journal. New York, 1826-28. Issues of April 28, 1827; May 9, 1828; August 30, 1833-August 6, 1845. Became the *Christian Advocate* (1826 —). [The first official weekly publication of American Methodism.]

Christian Advocate and Journal, and Zion's Herald. New York, 1828-33.

Northwestern Christian Advocate. Chicago, 1852-1929. Issues of January 5, 12, 19, 1853; April 30, June 11, 15, July 16, 23, August 13, 1862; July 28, 1900; April 14, 1915.
Western Christian Advocate. Cincinnati, 1834-1929. Issues of May 2, 1834-April 12, 1844; July 27-October 26, 1859; September 17, 24, 1873; April 16, 1902.
Zion's Herald. Boston, 1823-28. Issues of January 1, 1824-August 27, 1828. Merged with the *Christian Advocate and Journal* (1828-33).

Methodist Magazines and Reviews

Ladies' Repository. A Monthly Periodical Devoted to Literature and Religion. Cincinnati, 1841-76. Issues of Vol. VIII (1848), Vol. XIII (1853), Vol. XVII (1857), Vol. XVIII (1858), Vol. XXIII (1863), Vol. XXIV (1864), and Vol. XXXVI (1876).
Methodist Magazine. London, 1792-1821. Vol. XXI (1798), Vol. XXVI (1803), Vol. XXXV (1812). A continuation of the *Arminian Magazine*, London, 1789-90.
Methodist Magazine. New York, 1818-28. Issues of First Series, Vols. II-XI (1819-28). Became the *Methodist Magazine and Quarterly Review* (1830-40). New Series, Vol. VII (1836). Became the *Methodist Quarterly Review* (1841-84). Issues of Fourth Series, Vol. I (1849), Vol. IV (1852), Vol. VI (1854), Vol. XIII (1861), Vol. XIV (1862), and Vol. XVII (1865). Became the *Methodist Review* (1885-1931); and *Religion in Life* (1932 —).
Methodist Quarterly Review. Louisville, Nashville, 1847-1930. Methodist Episcopal Church, South. Issues of Vol. XV (1861).
Wesleyan Repository, and Religious Intelligencer. Trenton and Philadelphia, 1821-24. Issues of Vol. I (April, 1821-March, 1822), and Vol. II (April, 1822-March, 1823).
Western Christian Monitor. Chillicothe, Ohio, 1816.

Other Denominational Periodicals (Weekly)

Alton Observer. Alton, Illinois, 1836-38. [Presbyterian]
Baptist Banner and Western Pioneer. Louisville, 1839-40. [Baptist]
Christian Messenger. Georgetown, Kentucky, and Jacksonville, Florida, 1826-44. Scattered issues. [Christian]
Herald of Gospel Liberty. Portsmouth, Portland, and Philadelphia, 1808-10, 1814-15. [Purportedly the first religious newspaper published in America.]
National Banner. Nashville (? - ?). Issue of December 7, 1830. [Cumberland Presbyterian]
Nashville Banner and Nashville Whig. Nashville, 1822-37. Issues of March 7, 1831, and March 11, 1831. [Cumberland Presbyterian]
New York Baptist Register. Utica, New York, 1824-31. [Baptist]

New York Observer. New York, 1823 —. Issues of May 17, 1823, to December 25, 1824. [Presbyterian]
Revivalist. Nashville, 1832-34. Issue of September 18, 1833. [Cumberland Presbyterian]

Other Denominational Magazines and Reviews

Christian Baptist. Bethany, Virginia, 1823-30. Vol. II (1824-25). Superseded by the *Millennial Harbinger.* [Christian or Disciples]
Millennial Harbinger. Bethany, Virginia, 1831-43. [Christian or Disciples]
New York Missionary Magazine, and Repository of Religious Intelligence. New York, 1800-1803. Issues of Vol. III (1802), and Vol. IV (1803). [Presbyterian]
Western Messenger Devoted to Religion and Literature. Cincinnati and Louisville, 1835-41. [Unitarian]

IX. NINETEENTH-CENTURY NONDENOMINATIONAL PERIODICALS

Newspapers

Clinton Gazette. Clinton, Mississippi, 1833-40. Scattered Issues.
Delaware Patron. Delaware, Ohio, 1823-30. Scattered issues from April 16, 1823 to June 12, 1828.
Mirror. Russellville, Kentucky, 1806-12. Issues of May 8, 1807; June 30, 1808; July 7, 1808.
Mississippian. Jackson, Mississippi, 1832-65. Scattered issues.
Ohio Monitor. Columbus, Ohio, 1816-36. Issues of June 26, 1817, and September 23, 1819. Known as *Ohio Monitor and Patron of Industry* (1821-25). Issues of August 10, 1822, and November 16, 1822.
Ohio State Journal. Columbus, Ohio, 1811-1904. Issues of October 6, 1837-October 24, 1838.
Southern Sun. Jackson, Mississippi, 1838 —. Scattered issues of March 17, 1838-June 12, 1840.
Spectator. Edwardsville, Illinois, 1819-26.
Weekly Recorder. Chillicothe, Ohio, 1814-18.

Magazines

Gleason's Pictorial Drawing-Room Companion. Boston, 1851-54. III (1852), 120-22. Became *Balleau's Pictorial Drawing-Room Companion* (1854-59).

Lippincott's Magazine of Popular Literature and Science. Philadelphia, 1871-85. X (1872), 202-12.

Southern Bivouac: A Monthly Literary and Historical Magazine. Louisville, 1882-87. V (1886), 49-52.

X. TWENTIETH-CENTURY PERIODICAL ARTICLES

Frontier Religious Conditions

Asbury, Herbert. "The Father of Prohibitionism," *American Mercury,* IX (1926), 344-48.

――――. "The Palmy Days of Methodism," *American Mercury,* IX (1926), 435-44.

Gewehr, Wesley M. "Some Factors in the Expansion of Frontier Methodism, 1800-1811," *Journal of Religion,* VIII (1928), 98-120.

Kofoid, C. P. "Puritan Influences in the Formative Years of Illinois History," *Publication of the Illinois State Historical Society,* No. 10 (1905).

Sweet, William W. "The Churches as Moral Courts of the Frontier," *Church History,* II (1933), 3-21.

――――. "The First Circuit Riders in the West," *Methodist Review Quarterly,* LXVI (1917), 563-75.

――――. "Religion and Culture in the Middle West," *Journal of Bible and Religion,* XIV (1946), 191-97.

Camp Meetings in the Old Southwest

Cabaniss, Frances A., and Cabaniss, James A. "Religion in Ante-Bellum Mississippi," *Journal of Mississippi History,* V (1944), 191-224.

Galloway, Charles B. "Lorenzo Dow in Mississippi," *Publications of the Mississippi Historical Society,* IV (1901), 233-44.

Jackson, Luther P. "Religious Instruction of Negroes, 1830 to 1860, With Special Reference to South Carolina," *Journal of Negro History,* XV (1930), 72-114.

Johnson, Guion G. "The Camp Meeting in Ante-Bellum North Carolina," *North Carolina Historical Review,* X (1933), 95-110.

――――. "Revival Movements in Ante-Bellum North Carolina," *North Carolina Historical Review,* X (1933), 21-43.

Lewis, Virgil A. "Methodism in West Virginia in the Year 1800 to the Organization of the Pittsburgh Conference in 1825," *West Virginia History. A Quarterly Magazine,* III (1941), 18-58.

Posey, Walter B. "Influence of Slavery Upon the Methodist Church in the Early South and Southwest," *Mississippi Valley Historical Review,* XVII (1931), 530-42.

Puckett, Newbell N. "Religious Folk-Beliefs of Whites and Negroes," *Journal of Negro History,* XVI (1931), 9-35.

Windell, Marie G. "The Camp Meeting in Missouri," *Missouri Historical Review,* XXXVII (1943), 253-70.

Camp Meetings in the Old Northwest

Angle, Paul N., and Beyer, Richard L. "A Handbook of Illinois History," *Papers in Illinois History and Transactions for the Year, 1941,* pp. 72-168.

Barnhart, John D., Jr. "The Rise of the Methodist Episcopal Church in Illinois from the Beginning to the Year 1832," *Journal of the Illinois State Historical Society,* XII (1919), 149-217.

Griffith, S. M. "Sketch of the Early History of Methodism in the Southwest Part of the State of Michigan," *Report of the Pioneer Society of the State of Michigan,* II (1930), 152-71.

Iglehart, John E. "The Life and Times of John Shrader. Including the Introduction and Progress of Methodism in Southwestern Indiana," *Indiana Magazine of History,* XVII (1921), 3-49, 117-49.

Johnson, T. Walter. "Peter Akers: Methodist Circuit Rider and Educator (1790-1886)," *Journal of the Illinois State Historical Society,* XXXII (1939), 417-41.

Love, N. C. "An Indiana Camp Meeting," *Ohio Archaeological and Historical Publications,* XV (1906), 39-43.

MacLean, John P. "The Kentucky Revival and Its Influence on the Miami Valley," *Ohio Archaeological and Historical Quarterly,* XII (1903), 242-86. [Contains source materials on camp meetings at the turn of the nineteenth century.]

Ryan, John H. "Old Time Camp Meetings in Central Illinois," *Transactions of the Illinois State Historical Society for the Year 1924,* pp. 64-69.

Sweet, William W. "Peter Cartwright in Illinois History," *Transactions of the Illinois State Historical Society for the Year 1921,* pp. 116-27.

"Some of the Early Pioneer Business Men," *Old Northwest Genealogical Quarterly,* XV (1912), 104-5.

Wiley, Allen. "Methodism in Southeastern Indiana," *Western Christian Advocate,* 1845-46. Reprinted in *Indiana Magazine of History,* XXIII (1927), 3-64, 130-216, 239-332, 393-466.

Moody, V. Alton. "Early Religious Efforts in the Lower Mississippi Valley," *Mississippi Valley Historical Review,* XXII (1935), 61-76.

XI. Denominational National Histories

Methodist

Atkinson, John. *Centennial History of American Methodism.* New York, 1884.

Bangs, Nathan. *A History of the Methodist Episcopal Church.* (3rd ed.) 4 vols. New York, 1845.

Barclay, Wade C. *Missionary Motivation and Expansion. History of Methodist Missions.* 6 vols. Vol. I. New York, 1949.

Lee, James. *A Short History of the Methodists in the United States of America; Beginning in 1766, and Continued till 1809.* Baltimore, 1810.

Strickland, William P. *Genius and Mission of Methodism.* Boston, 1851.

———. *History of the Missions of the Methodist Episcopal Church From the Organization of the Missionary Society to the Present Time.* Cincinnati, 1850.

Sweet, William W. *Methodism in American History.* New York, Cincinnati, and Chicago, 1933.

Baptist

Benedict, David. *A General History of the Baptist Denomination in America, and Other Parts of the World.* 2 vols. Boston, 1813.

Fisher, Miles M. *Short History of the Baptists.* Nashville, 1933.

Cumberland Presbyterian

Beard, Richard. *Brief Biographical Sketches of Some of the Early Ministers of the Cumberland Presbyterian Church.* Nashville, 1867.

McDonnald, B. W. *History of the Cumberland Presbyterian Church.* Nashville, 1888.

Smith, James. *History of the Christian Church, From Its Origins to the Present Time; Compiled from Various Authors. Including a History of the Cumberland Presbyterian Church, Drawn from Authentic Documents.* Nashville, 1835.

"New Light" Presbyterian or Christian

Garrison, Winfred E. *Religion Follows the Frontier. A History of the Disciples of Christ.* New York and London, 1931.

Tyler, B. B., Thomas, A. C., *et al. A History of the Disciples of Christ, the Society of Friends, the United Brethren in Christ and the*

Evangelical Association. (The American Church History Series, ed. Philip Schaff, *et al.* 13 vols. Vol. XII.) New York, 1893-1927.

Shaker

Green, Calvin, and Wells, Seth. *A Summary View of the Millennial Church, or United Society of Believers, Commonly Called Shakers.* (2nd ed.) Albany, 1848.

MacLean, John P. *Shakers of Ohio. Fugitive Papers Concerning the Shakers of Ohio, With Unpublished Manuscripts.* Columbus, 1907.

McNemar, Richard. *Investigator, or a Defence of the Order, Government, and Economy of the United Society Called Shakers.* Lexington, 1828.

XII. STATE HISTORIES

Denominational

Bennett, William W. *Memorials of Methodism in Virginia, From Its Introduction Into the State, in the Year 1772, to the Year 1829.* Richmond, 1871.

Burkitt, Lemuel B., and Read, Jesse. *A Concise History of the Kehukee Baptist Association From Its Original Rise Down to 1803.* Philadelphia, 1850.

Cady, John F. *The Origin and Development of the Missionary Baptist Church in Indiana.* Berne, Indiana, 1942.

Cain, John B. *Methodism in the Mississippi Conference, 1846-1870.* Jackson, 1939.

Davidson, Robert. *History of the Presbyterian Church in the State of Kentucky.* New York, 1847.

Field, A. D. *Memorials of Methodism in the Bounds of the Rock River Conference.* Cincinnati, 1896.

Jones, John G. *A Complete History of Methodism as Connected with the Mississippi Conference of the Methodist Episcopal Church, South.* 2 vols. Nashville, 1887-1908.

Leaton, James. *History of Methodism in Illinois, From 1793 to 1832.* Cincinnati, 1883.

McFerrin, John B. *History of Methodism in Tennessee.* 3 vols. Nashville, 1869-73.

Nottingham, Elizabeth K. *Methodism and the Frontier. Indiana Proving Ground.* New York, 1941.

Pennewell, Almer M. (ed.). *The Methodist Movement in Northern Illinois.* Sycamore, Illinois, 1942.

Pilcher, Elijah H. *Protestantism in Michigan.* Detroit, 1878.

Redford, Albert H. *The History of Methodism in Kentucky.* 4 vols. Nashville, 1868-76.

Riley, Benjamin. *A History of the Baptists in the Southern States East of the Mississippi.* Philadelphia, 1898.

Semple, Robert B. *A History of the Rise and Progress of the Baptists in Virginia,* ed. G. B. Beale. Richmond, 1810.

Shipp, Albert M. *The History of Methodism in South Carolina.* Nashville, 1884.

Smith, George G. *The History of Georgia Methodism from 1786 to 1866.* Atlanta, 1913.

Smith, John L. *Indiana Methodism.* Valparaiso, Indiana, 1892.

West, Anson. *A History of Methodism in Alabama.* Nashville, 1893.

Williams, Samuel W. *Pictures of Early Methodism in Ohio.* Cincinnati and New York, 1909.

Wilson, Elizabeth. *Methodism in Eastern Wisconsin, Section One. From The Arrival of the First Missionary in 1832 to the First Publication of the Wisconsin Conference Minutes in 1850.* Milwaukee, 1938.

Nondenominational

Ford, Thomas. *A History of Illinois From Its Commencement As a State in 1818 to 1847,* ed. Milo M. Quaife. 2 vols. Vol. I. Chicago, 1945-46.

Ramsey, David. *The History of South Carolina, 1670-1808.* 2 vols. Charleston, 1809.

XIII. UNPUBLISHED THESES AND DISSERTATIONS

Barnhart, John D., Jr. "The Rise of the Methodist Episcopal Church in Illinois from the Beginning to the year 1832." Master's thesis, Northwestern University, 1919.

Cannon, Ross. "The American Revival 1800-1840." Ph.D. dissertation, Department of Theology, Chicago Theological Seminary, 1937.

Carter, Ernest L. "The Early Camp-Meeting Movement in the Ohio Valley." Master's thesis, Ohio Wesleyan University, 1922.

Cutshall, Elmer G. "The Doctrinal Training of the Traveling Ministry of the Methodist Episcopal Church." Ph.D. dissertation, Divinity School, University of Chicago, 1922.

Eller, Paul H. "Revivalism and the German Churches in Pennsylvania, 1783-1816." Ph.D. dissertation, Divinity School, University of Chicago, 1933.

Merrill, Horace S. "An Early History of the Black River Falls Region." Master's thesis, University of Wisconsin, 1933.

Parkinson, Ralph T. "The Religious Instruction of Slaves. 1820-1860." Master's thesis, University of North Carolina, 1948.

Wroten, William H., Jr. "A Chronicle of the Religious Beginning of Dorchester County, Maryland." Master's thesis, University of Maryland, 1948. [Contains much material on island camp meetings and Delaware encampments of the early nineteenth century. Based on "The Duncan Noble Collection," Taylor's Island, Dorchester County, Maryland.]

Index